PENGUIN BOOKS
LISTENING TO GRASSHOPPERS

Arundhati Roy is the author of *The God of Small Things*, which won the Booker Prize in 1997. Two volumes of her non-fiction writing, *The Algebra of Infinite Justice* and *An Ordinary Person's Guide to Empire*, were published in 2001 and 2005 respectively. *The Shape of the Beast*, a collection of her interviews, was published in 2008.

Arundhati Roy lives in New Delhi.

LISTENING TO GRASS-HOPPERS

FIELD NOTES ON DEMOCRACY

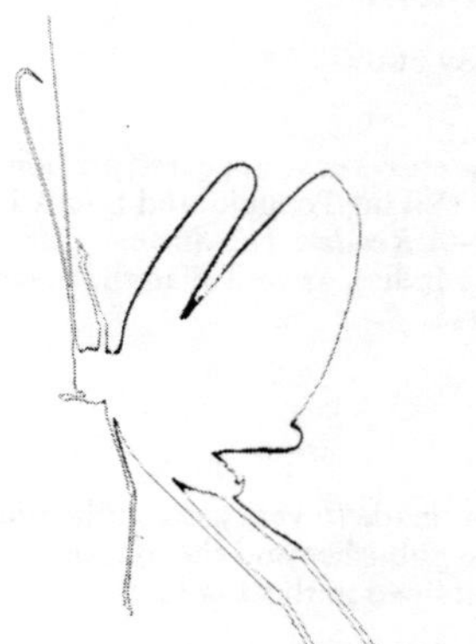

ARUNDHATI ROY

PENGUIN BOOKS

PENGUIN BOOKS
Published by the Penguin Group
Penguin Books India Pvt. Ltd, 11 Community Centre, Panchsheel Park, New Delhi 110 017, India
Penguin Group (USA) Inc., 375 Hudson Street, New York, New York 10014, USA
Penguin Group (Canada), 90 Eglinton Avenue East, Suite 700, Toronto, Ontario, M4P 2Y3, Canada (a division of Pearson Penguin Canada Inc.)
Penguin Books Ltd, 80 Strand, London WC2R 0RL, England
Penguin Ireland, 25 St Stephen's Green, Dublin 2, Ireland (a division of Penguin Books Ltd)
Penguin Group (Australia), 250 Camberwell Road, Camberwell, Victoria 3124, Australia (a division of Pearson Australia Group Pty Ltd)
Penguin Group (NZ), 67 Apollo Drive, Rosedale, North Shore 0632, New Zealand (a division of Pearson New Zealand Ltd)
Penguin Group (South Africa) (Pty) Ltd, 24 Sturdee Avenue, Rosebank, Johannesburg 2196, South Africa

Penguin Books Ltd, Registered Offices: 80 Strand, London WC2R 0RL, England

First published in Hamish Hamilton by Penguin Books India 2009
Published in Penguin Books 2010

Book design by Bena Sareen

Author's note: Some of these essays have appeared previously in the books *An Ordinary Person's Guide to Empire* (Viking/Penguin and South End Press), *War Talk* (South End Press), *13 December—A Reader: The Strange Case of the Attack on the Indian Parliament* (Penguin Books India), as well as in the magazines and newspapers cited at the beginning of each essay.

10 9 8 7 6 5 4 3 2 1

ISBN 9780143415213

For sale in India and Nepal only

Typeset in Bembo 10.5/13.5 by Eleven Arts, New Delhi
Printed at Gopsons Papers Ltd, Noida

To those who have learned to divorce hope from reason

Where should we go after the last frontiers?
Where should the birds fly after the last sky?
Where should the plants sleep after the last breath of air?

—'The Earth is Closing on Us'
Mahmoud Darwish

CONTENTS

The international boundaries on the map of India are neither purported to be correct nor authentic by Survey of India directives.

Map not to scale

INTRODUCTION
DEMOCRACY'S FAILING LIGHT

WHILE WE'RE still arguing about whether there's life after death, can we add another question to the cart? Is there life after democracy? What sort of life will it be? By *democracy* I don't mean democracy as an ideal or an aspiration. I mean the working model: Western liberal democracy, and its variants, such as they are.

So, is there life after democracy?

Attempts to answer this question often turn into a comparison of different systems of governance, and end with a somewhat prickly, combative defence of democracy. It's flawed, we say. It isn't perfect, but it's better than everything else that's on offer. Inevitably, someone in the room will say: 'Afghanistan, Pakistan, Saudi Arabia, Somalia . . . is that what you would prefer?'

Whether democracy should be the utopia that all 'developing' societies aspire to is a separate question altogether. (I think it should. The early, idealistic phase can be quite heady.) The question about life after democracy is addressed to those of us who already live in democracies, or in countries that pretend to be democracies. It isn't meant to suggest that we lapse into older, discredited models of totalitarian or authoritarian governance. It's meant to suggest that the system of representative democracy—too much representation, too little democracy—needs some structural adjustment.

The question here, really, is what have we done to democracy? What have we turned it into? What happens once democracy has been used up? When it has been hollowed out and emptied of meaning? What happens when each of its institutions has metastasized into something dangerous? What happens now that democracy and the Free Market have fused into a single predatory organism with a thin, constricted imagination that revolves almost entirely around the idea of maximizing profit? Is it possible to reverse this process? Can something that has mutated go back to being what it used to be?

What we need today, for the sake of the survival of this planet, is long-term vision. Can governments whose very survival depends on immediate, extractive, short-term gain provide this? Could it be that democracy, the sacred answer to our short-term hopes and prayers, the protector of our individual freedoms and nurturer of our avaricious dreams, will turn out to be the endgame for the human race? Could it be that democracy is such a hit with modern humans precisely because it mirrors our greatest folly—our nearsightedness? Our inability to live entirely in the present (like most animals do) combined with our inability to see very far into the future makes us strange in-between creatures, neither beast nor prophet. Our amazing intelligence seems to have outstripped our instinct for survival. We plunder the earth hoping that accumulating material surplus will make up for the profound, unfathomable thing that we have lost.

It would be conceit to pretend that the essays in this book provide answers to any of these questions. They only demonstrate, in some detail, the fact that it looks as though the beacon could be failing and that democracy can perhaps no longer be relied upon to deliver the justice and stability we once dreamed it would. All the essays were written as urgent, public interventions at critical moments in India—during the state-backed genocide of Muslims in Gujarat; just before the date set for the hanging of Mohammad Afzal, the accused in the 13 December 2001 Parliament Attack; during US President George Bush's visit to India; during the mass uprising in Kashmir in the summer of 2008; after the 26 November 2008 Mumbai attacks. Often they were not just responses to events, they were responses to the responses.

Though many of them were written in anger, at moments when keeping quiet became harder than saying something, the essays do have a common thread. They're not about unfortunate anomalies or aberrations in the democratic process. They're about the *consequences of* and the *corollaries to* democracy; they're about the fire in the ducts. I should also say that they do not provide a panoramic overview. They're a detailed *under*view of specific events that I hoped would reveal some of the ways in which democracy is practised in the world's largest democracy. (Or the world's largest 'demon-crazy', as a Kashmiri protestor on the streets of Srinagar once put it. His placard said: 'Democracy without Justice=Demon Crazy.')

As a writer, a fiction writer, I have often wondered whether the attempt to always be precise, to try and get it all factually right somehow *reduces* the epic scale of what is really going on. Does it eventually mask a larger truth? I worry that I am allowing myself to be railroaded into offering prosaic, factual precision when maybe what we need is a feral howl, or the transformative power and real precision of poetry. Something about the cunning, Brahmanical, intricate, bureaucratic, file-bound, 'apply-through-proper-channels' nature of governance and subjugation in India seems to have made a clerk out of me. My only excuse is to say that it takes odd tools to uncover the maze of subterfuge and hypocrisy that cloaks the callousness and the cold, calculated violence of the world's favourite new Superpower. Repression 'through proper channels' sometimes engenders resistance 'through proper channels'. As resistance goes this isn't enough, I know. But for now, it's all I have. Perhaps someday it will become the underpinning for poetry and for the feral howl.

~

'Listening to Grasshoppers', the essay from which this collection draws its title, was a lecture I gave in Istanbul in January 2008 on the first anniversary of the assassination of the Armenian journalist Hrant Dink. He was shot down on the street outside his office for daring to raise a subject that is forbidden in Turkey—the 1915 genocide of Armenians in which more than one million people were killed. My lecture was about the history of genocide and genocide denial, and the old, almost organic relationship between 'progress' and genocide.

I have always been struck by the fact that the political party in Turkey that carried out the Armenian genocide was called the Committee for Union and Progress. Most of the essays in this collection are, in fact, about the contemporary correlation between Union and Progress, or, in today's idiom, between Nationalism and Development—those unimpeachable twin towers of modern, Free Market Democracy. Both of these in their extreme form are, as we now know, encrypted with the potential of bringing about ultimate, apocalyptic destruction (nuclear war, climate change).

Though these essays were written between 2002 and 2008, the invisible marker, the starting gun, is the year 1989, when in the rugged mountains of Afghanistan capitalism won its long jihad against Soviet Communism. (Of course, the wheel's in spin again. Could it be that those same mountains are now in the process of burying capitalism? It's too early to tell.) Within months of the collapse of the Soviet Union and the fall of the Berlin Wall, the Indian government, once a leader of the Non-Aligned Movement, performed a high-speed somersault and aligned itself completely with the United States, monarch of the new unipolar world.

The rules of the game changed suddenly and completely. Millions of people who lived in remote villages and deep in the heart of untouched forests, some of whom had never heard of Berlin or the Soviet Union, could not have imagined how events that occurred in those faraway places would affect their lives. The process of their dispossession and displacement had already begun in the early 1950s, when India opted for the Soviet-style development model in which huge steel plants (Bhilai, Bokaro) and large dams (thousands of them) would occupy the 'commanding heights' of the economy. The era of Privatization and Structural Adjustment accelerated that process at a mind-numbing speed.

Today, words like 'Progress' and 'Development' have become interchangeable with economic 'Reforms', Deregulation and Privatization. 'Freedom' has come to mean 'choice'. It has less to do with the human spirit than with different brands of deodorant. 'Market' no longer means a place where you go to buy provisions. The 'Market' is a de-territorialized space where faceless corporations do business, including buying and selling 'futures'. 'Justice' has come to mean 'human rights' (and of those, as they say, 'a few will do'). This theft of language, this technique of usurping words and deploying them like weapons, of using them to mask intent and to mean exactly the opposite of what they have traditionally meant, has been one of the most brilliant strategic victories of the Tsars of the new dispensation. It has allowed them to marginalize their detractors, deprive them of a language in which to voice their critique and dismiss them as being 'anti-progress', 'anti-development', 'anti-reform' and of course 'anti-national'—negativists of the worst sort. Talk about saving a river or protecting a forest and they say, 'Don't you believe in Progress?' To people whose land is being submerged by dam reservoirs and whose homes are being bulldozed they say, 'Do you have an alternative development model?' To those who believe that a government is duty bound to provide people with basic education, healthcare and social security, they say, 'You're against the Market.' And who except a cretin could be against the Market?

To reclaim these stolen words requires explanations that are too tedious for a world with a short attention span, and too expensive in an era when Free Speech has become unaffordable for the poor. This language heist may prove to be the keystone of our undoing.

Two decades of this kind of 'Progress' in India has created a vast middle class punch drunk on sudden wealth and the sudden respect that comes with it—and a much, much vaster, desperate underclass. Tens of millions of people have been dispossessed and displaced from their land by floods, droughts and desertification caused by indiscriminate environmental engineering and massive infrastructural projects, dams, mines and Special Economic Zones. All of them developed in the name of the poor, but really meant to service the rising demands of the new aristocracy.

The battle for land lies at the heart of the 'Development' debate. Before he became India's finance minister, P. Chidambaram was Enron's lawyer and member of the Board of Directors of Vedanta, a multinational mining corporation that is currently devastating the Niyamgiri hills in Orissa. Perhaps his career graph informed his world view. Or maybe it's the other way around. In an interview a year ago, he said that his vision was to get 85 per cent of India's population to live in cities.[1] Realizing this 'vision' would require social engineering on an unimaginable scale. It would mean inducing, or forcing, about *five hundred million* people to migrate from the countryside into cities. That process is well under way and is quickly turning India into a police state in which people who refuse to surrender their land are being made to do so at gunpoint. Perhaps this is what makes it so easy for P. Chidambaram to move so seamlessly from being finance minister to being home minister. The portfolios are separated only by an osmotic membrane. Underlying this nightmare masquerading as 'vision' is the plan to free up vast tracts of land and all of India's natural resources, leaving them ripe for corporate plunder. In effect, to reverse the post-Independence policy of Land Reforms.

Already forests, mountains and water systems are being ravaged by marauding multinational corporations, backed by a State that has lost its moorings and is committing what can only be called 'ecocide'. In eastern India bauxite and iron ore mining is destroying whole ecosystems, turning fertile land into desert. In the Himalayas hundreds of high dams are being planned, the consequences of which can only be catastrophic. In the plains, embankments built along rivers, ostensibly to control floods, have led to rising river beds, causing even more flooding, more waterlogging, more salinization of agricultural land and the destruction of livelihoods of millions of people. Most of India's holy rivers, including the Ganga, have been turned into unholy drains that carry more sewage and industrial effluent than water. Hardly a single river runs its course and meets the ocean.

Based on the absurd notion that a river flowing into the sea is a waste of water, the Supreme Court, in an act of unbelievable hubris, has arbitrarily ordered that India's rivers be interlinked, like a mechanical water-supply system. Implementing this would mean tunnelling through mountains and forests, altering natural contours and drainage systems of river basins and destroying deltas and estuaries. In other words, wrecking the ecology of the entire subcontinent. (B.N. Kirpal, the judge who passed this order, joined the Environmental Board of Coca-Cola after he retired. Nice touch!)

The regime of Free Market economic policies, administered by people who are blissfully ignorant of the fate of civilizations that grew too dependent on artificial irrigation, has led to a worrying shift in cropping patterns. Sustainable food crops, suitable to local soil conditions and micro-climates, have been replaced by water-guzzling, hybrid and genetically modified 'cash' crops which, apart from being wholly dependent on the market, are also heavily dependent on chemical fertilizers, pesticides, canal irrigation and the indiscriminate mining of ground water. As abused farmland, saturated with chemicals, gradually becomes exhausted and infertile, agricultural input costs rise, ensnaring small farmers in a debt trap. Over the last few years, more than 180,000 Indian farmers have committed suicide.[2] While state granaries are bursting with food, that eventually rots, starvation and malnutrition approaching the same levels as in sub-Saharan Africa stalk the land.[3] Truly the 9 per cent growth rate is beginning to look like a downward spiral. The higher the rate of this kind of growth, the worse the prognosis. Any oncologist will tell you that.

It's as though an ancient society, decaying under the weight of feudalism and caste, was churned in a great machine. The churning has ripped through the mesh of old inequalities, recalibrating some of them but reinforcing most. Now the old society has curdled and separated into a thin layer of thick cream—and a lot of water. The cream is India's 'market' of many million consumers (of cars, cell phones, computers, Valentine's Day greeting cards), the envy of international business. The water is of little consequence. It can be sloshed around, stored in holding ponds, and eventually drained away.

Or so they think, the men in suits. They didn't bargain for the violent civil war that has broken out in India's heartland: Chhattisgarh, Jharkhand, Orissa, West Bengal.

~

Coming back to 1989. As if to illustrate the connection between 'Union' and 'Progress', at exactly the same time that the Congress government was opening up India's markets to international finance, the right-wing Bharatiya Janata Party (BJP), then in the opposition, began its virulent campaign of Hindu nationalism (popularly known as 'Hindutva'). In 1990, its leader, L.K. Advani, travelled across the country whipping up hatred against Muslims and demanding that the Babri Masjid, an old sixteenth-century mosque that stood on a disputed site in Ayodhya, be demolished and a Ram Temple built in its place. In 1992, a mob, egged on by Advani, demolished the mosque. In early 1993, a mob rampaged through Mumbai attacking Muslims, killing almost one thousand people. As revenge, a series of bomb blasts ripped through the city, killing about two hundred and fifty people.[4] Feeding off the communal frenzy it had generated, the BJP, which had only two seats in Parliament in 1984, defeated the Congress in 1998 and came to power at the Centre.

It's not a coincidence that the rise of Hindutva corresponded with the historical moment when America substituted Communism with Islam as it's great enemy. The radical Islamist Mujahideen—

whom President Reagan once entertained in the White House and compared to America's Founding Fathers—suddenly began to be called terrorists. CNN's live broadcast of the 1990–91 Gulf War—Operation Desert Storm—made it to elite drawing rooms in Indian cities, bringing with it the early thrills of satellite TV. Almost simultaneously, the Indian Government, once a staunch friend of the Palestinians, turned into Israel's 'natural ally'. Now India and Israel do joint military exercises, share intelligence and probably exchange notes on how best to administer occupied territories.

By 1998, when the BJP took office, the 'Progress' project of Privatization and Liberalization was about eight years old. Though it had campaigned vigorously against the economic reforms, saying they were a process of 'looting through liberalization', once it came to power the BJP embraced the Free Market enthusiastically and threw its weight behind huge corporations like Enron. (In representative democracies, once they're elected, the peoples' representatives are free to break their promises and change their minds.)

Within weeks of taking office, the BJP conducted a series of thermonuclear tests. Though India had thrown its hat into the nuclear ring in 1975, politically, the 1998 nuclear tests were of a different order altogether. The orgy of triumphant nationalism with which the tests were greeted introduced a chilling new language of aggression and hatred into mainstream public discourse. None of what was being said was new, only that what was once considered unacceptable was suddenly being celebrated. Since then, Hindu communalism and nuclear nationalism, like corporate globalization, have vaulted over the stated ideologies of political parties. The venom has been injected straight into our bloodstream. It's there now—in all its violence and banality—for us to deal with in our daily lives, regardless of whether the government at the centre calls itself 'secular' or not. The Muslim community has seen a sharp decline in its fortunes and is now at the bottom of the social pyramid, along with Dalits and Adivasis.[5]

Certain events that occur in the life of a nation have the effect of parting the curtains and giving ordinary people a glimpse into the future. The 1998 nuclear tests were one such. You didn't need the gift of prophecy to tell in which direction India was heading. This is an excerpt from 'The End of Imagination', an essay (not in this collection) that I wrote after the nuclear tests:

> 'Explosion of Self-esteem', 'Road to Resurgence', 'A Moment of Pride', these were headlines in the papers in the days following the nuclear tests . . . .
>
> 'These are not just nuclear tests, they are nationalism tests,' we were repeatedly told.
>
> This has been hammered home, over and over again. The bomb is India, India is the bomb. Not just India, Hindu India. Therefore, be warned, any criticism of it is not just anti-national, but anti-Hindu . . . . This is one of the unexpected perks of having a nuclear bomb. Not only can the government use it to threaten the enemy, it can use it to declare war on its own people. Us . . . .
>
> Why does it all seem so familiar? Is it because, even as you watch, reality dissolves and seamlessly rushes forward into the silent, black-and-white images from old films—scenes of people being hounded out of their lives, rounded up and herded into camps? Of massacre, of mayhem, of endless columns of broken people making their way to nowhere? Why is there no soundtrack? Why is the hall so quiet? Have I been seeing too many films? Am I mad? Or am I right?

> Could those images be the inescapable culmination of what we have set into motion? Could our future be rushing forward into our past?[6]

The *Us* I referred to were those of us who do not belong to—or identify ourselves with—the 'Hindu' majority. By *past*, I was referring to the Partition of India in 1947, when more than one million Hindus and Muslims killed each other, and eight million became refugees.

~

In February 2002, following the burning of a train coach in which fifty-eight Hindu pilgrims returning from Ayodhya were burned alive, the BJP government in Gujarat, led by Chief Minister Narendra Modi, presided over a carefully planned genocide of Muslims in the state. The Islamophobia generated all over the world by the 11 September 2001 attacks put the wind in their sails. The machinery of the state of Gujarat stood by and watched while more than two thousand people[7] were massacred. Women were gang-raped and burned alive. One hundred and fifty thousand Muslims were driven from their homes. The community was, and continues to be, ghettoized, socially and economically ostracized. Gujarat has always been a communally tense state. There had been riots before. But this was not a riot. It was a genocidal massacre, and though the number of victims was insignificant compared to the horror of say Rwanda, Sudan or the Congo, the Gujarat carnage was designed as a public spectacle whose aims were unmistakable. It was a public warning to Muslim citizens from the government of the world's favourite democracy.

After the carnage, Narendra Modi pressed for early elections. He was returned to power with a mandate from the people of Gujarat.

Five years later he repeated his success: he is now serving a third term as chief minister, widely appreciated by business houses for his faith in the Free Market. To be fair to the people of Gujarat, the only alternative they had to Narendra Modi's brand of Hindutva (Nuclear), was the Congress Party's candidate, Shankarsinh Vaghela, a disgruntled former BJP chief minister. All he had to offer was his own brand of Hindutva (Lite & Muddled). Not surprisingly, it didn't make the cut.

The Gujarat genocide is the subject of the first essay in this collection, 'Democracy: Who's She When She's at Home?', written in May 2002 when murderous mobs *still* roamed the streets, killing and intimidating Muslims. I have deliberately not updated the text of any of the essays, because I thought it would be interesting to see how a hard look at the *systemic* nature of what is going on often contains within it a forecast of events that are still to come. So instead of updating the essays, I've added new endnotes. For example, a paragraph in the essay on the Gujarat genocide says:

> Can we expect an anniversary celebration next year? Or will there be someone else to hate by then? Alphabetically: Adivasis, Buddhists, Christians, Dalits, Parsis, Sikhs? Those who wear jeans or speak English or those who have thick lips or curly hair? We won't have to wait long.

Mobs led by Congress Party leaders had already slaughtered thousands of Sikhs on the streets of Delhi in 1984, as revenge for the assassination of Indira Gandhi by her Sikh bodyguards. Goons belonging to the Bajrang Dal, a Hindu militia, had attacked an Australian missionary, Graham Staines, and his two young sons, and burned them alive in January 1999.[8] By December 2007, attacks on Christians by Hindu militias moved beyond stray incidents. In several states—Gujarat, Karnataka, Orissa—Christians were attacked, churches gutted. In Kandhamal, Orissa, at least sixteen Dalit and Adivasi Christians were killed by 'Hindu' Dalits and Adivasis.[9] Tens of thousands of Christians now live in refugee camps or hide in the surrounding forests, afraid to venture out to tend their fields and crops. Right now, 'Hinduizing' Dalits and Adivasis, pitting them against each other, as well as against Muslims and Maoists, is *the* most important part of the Hindutva project. (Once again, it's not a coincidence that these communities live in forests and on mineral rich lands which corporations have their eyes on and governments want vacated. So the Hindutva 'shivirs' [camps], under the pretext of bringing them into the 'Hindu fold', are a means of controlling people.)

In December 2008, protected by the first-ever BJP government to come to power in a southern state, Hindu vigilante mobs in Bangalore and Mangalore—the hub of India's IT industry—began to attack women who wear jeans and Western clothes.[10] The threat is ongoing. Hindu militias have vowed to turn Karnataka into another Gujarat. That the BJP has struck roots in states like Karnataka and Gujarat, both frontrunners in the globalization project, once again illustrates the organic relationship between 'Union' and 'Progress'. Or, if you like, between Fascism and the Free Market.

In January 2009 that relationship was sealed with a kiss at a public function. The CEOs of two of India's biggest corporations, Ratan Tata (of the Tata Group) and Mukesh Ambani (of Reliance Industries), while accepting the Gujarat Garima—Pride of Gujarat—award, celebrated the development policies of Narendra Modi, architect of the Gujarat genocide, and warmly endorsed him as a future candidate for prime minister.

~

As this book goes to press, the nearly two billion dollar 2009 General Election has just been concluded.[11] That's a lot more than the budget of the US elections. According to some media reports the actual amount that was spent is closer to *ten* billion dollars.[12] Where, might one ask, does that kind of money come from?

The Congress and its Allies, the United Progressive Alliance (UPA), have won a comfortable majority. Interestingly, more than 90 per cent of the independent candidates who stood for elections lost. Clearly, without sponsorship it's hard to win an election. And independent candidates cannot promise subsidized rice, free TVs and cash-for-votes, those demeaning acts of vulgar charity that elections have been reduced to.[13]

When you take a closer look at the calculus that underlies election results, words like 'comfortable' and 'majority' turn out to be deceptive, if not outright inaccurate. For instance, the actual share of votes polled by the UPA in these elections works out to only 10.3 per cent of the country's population! It's interesting how the cleverly layered mathematics of electoral democracy can turn a tiny minority into a thumping mandate.[14] Anyway, be that as it may, the point is that it will not be L.K. Advani, hate-monger incarnate, but secular Dr Manmohan Singh, gentle architect of the market reforms, a man who has never won an election in his life, who will be prime minister of the world's largest democracy for a second term.

In the run-up to the polls, there was absolute consensus across party lines about the economic 'reforms'. Govindacharya, formerly the chief ideologue of the BJP, progenitor of the Ram Janamabhoomi movement, sarcastically suggested that the Congress and BJP form a coalition.[15] In some states they already have. In Chhattisgarh, for example, the BJP runs the government and Congress politicians run the Salwa Judum, a vicious government-backed 'people's' militia. The

Judum and the government have formed a joint front against the Maoists in the forests who are engaged in a deadly and often brutal armed struggle against displacement and against land acquisition by corporations waiting to set up steel factories and to begin mining iron ore, tin and all the other wealth stashed below the forest floor. So, in Chhattisgarh, we have the remarkable spectacle of the two biggest political parties of India in an alliance against the Adivasis of Dantewara, India's poorest, most vulnerable people. Already 644 villages have been emptied. Fifty thousand people have moved into Salwa Judum camps. Three hundred thousand are hiding in the forests and are being called Maoist terrorists or sympathizers. The battle is raging, and the corporations are waiting.

It is significant that India is one of the countries that blocked a European move in the UN asking for an international probe into war crimes that may have been committed by the government of Sri Lanka in its recent offensive against the Tamil Tigers.[16] Governments in this part of the world have taken note of Israel's Gaza blueprint as a good way of dealing with 'terrorism': keep the media out and close in for the kill. That way they don't have to worry too much about who's a 'terrorist' and who isn't. There may be a little flurry of international outrage, but it goes away pretty quickly.

Things do not augur well for the forest-dwelling people of Chhattisgarh.

Reassured by the sort of 'constructive' collaboration, the consensus between political parties, few were more enthusiastic about the recent general elections than some major corporate houses. They seem to have realized that a democratic mandate can legitimize their pillaging in a way that nothing else can. Several corporations ran extravagant advertising campaigns on TV, some featuring Bollywood film stars urging people, young and old, rich and poor, to go out and vote. Shops and restaurants in Khan market, Delhi's most tony market, offered discounts to those whose index (voting) fingers were marked with indelible ink. Democracy suddenly became the cool new way to be. You know how it is: the Chinese do Sport, so they had the Olympics; India does Democracy, so we had an election. Both are heavily sponsored, TV friendly spectator sports.

The BBC commissioned a coach on a train—the India Election Special—that took journalists from all over the world on a sightseeing tour to witness the miracle of Indian elections. The train coach had a slogan painted on it: Will India's voters revive the World's Fortunes?[17] BBC (Hindi) had a poster up in a café near my home. It featured a hundred dollar bill (with Ben Franklin) morphing into a 500 rupee note (with Gandhi). It said: *Kya India ka vote bachayega duniya ka note?* (Will India's votes rescue the world's currency notes?) In these flagrant and unabashed ways an electorate has been turned into a market, voters are seen as consumers, and democracy is being welded to the Free Market. Ergo: those who cannot consume do not matter.

What does the victory of the UPA mean in this election? Obviously a myriad things. The debate is wide open. Interpreting an Indian election is about as exact a science as sorcery. Voting patterns are intricately connected with local issues and caste and community equations that vary, quite literally, from polling booth to polling booth. There can be no reliable Big Conclusion. But here's something to think about.

In its time in office, in order to mitigate the devastation caused by its economic policies the former Congress regime passed three progressive (critics call them populist and controversial) Parliamentary Acts. The Forest Rights Act (which gave forest dwellers legal right to land and the traditional use of forest produce), the Right to Information Act and, most important of all, the National Rural Employment Guarantee Act (NREGA). The NREGA guarantees every rural family a hundred days of work (hard, manual labour) a year at minimum wages. It amounts to an average of Rs 8000 (about $170) per *family* per *year*. Enough for a good meal in a restaurant, including wine and dessert. Imagine how hellish times must be for even that tiny amount of money to come as a relief to millions of people who are reeling under the impact of the precipitous loss of their lands and their livelihoods. (Talk about crumbs from the high table. But then, which one of us has the heart, or the right, to argue that no crumbs are better than crumbs? Or, indeed, that no elections are better than meaningless elections?) Implementing the NREGA, seeing that the crumbs actually reach the people they're meant for, has occupied all the time and energy of some of India's finest and most committed social activists for the last several years. They have had to battle cartels of corrupt government officers, power-brokers and middlemen. They have faced threats and a fair amount of violence. One rural activist in Jharkhand immolated himself in anger and frustration at the injustice of it all.

Ironically, the NREGA only made it through Parliament because of pressure brought to bear on the UPA government by the Left Front and, it must be said, by Sonia Gandhi. It was passed *despite* tremendous resistance from the mandarins of the Free Market within the Congress Party. The Corporate Media was more or less unanimously hostile to the Act. Needless to say, come election-time and the NREGA became one of the main planks of the Congress Party's election campaign. There's little doubt that the goodwill it generated amongst the very poor translated into votes for the Congress. But now that the elections are over, victory is being attributed to the very policies that the NREGA was passed to mitigate! The Captains of Industry have lost no time in claiming the 'Peoples' Mandate' as their own. 'It's fast-forward for markets', the business papers crowed the morning after, 'Vote [was] for reforms, says India Inc'.[18]

There is an even greater irony: the Left Front, acting with the duplicity that has become second nature to all parliamentary political parties, took a sharp turn to the right. Even while it criticized the government's economic policies at the Centre, it tried to enforce similar ones on its home turf in West Bengal. It announced that it was going to build a chemical hub in the district of Nandigram, a manufacturing unit for the Tata Nano in Singur, and a Jindal Steel plant in the forests of Lalgarh in Purulia. It began to acquire land, most of it fertile farmland, virtually at gunpoint. The massive, militant uprisings that followed were put down with bullets and lathi charges. Lumpen 'Party' militias ran amok among the protestors, raping women and killing people. But eventually the combination of genuine mass mobilization and militancy worked. The people prevailed. They won all three battles, and forced the government to back off. The Tatas had to move the Nano project to Gujarat, that laboratory of fascism, which offered a 'good investment climate'. The Left Front was decimated in the elections in West Bengal, something that had not happened in thirty years.

The irony doesn't end there. In a fiendishly clever sleight of hand, the defeat of the Left is being attributed to its obstructionism and anti-Development policies! 'Corporate captains feel easy without Left', the papers said.[19] The stock market surged, looking forward to 'a summer of joy'. CEOs on TV channels celebrated the new government's 'liberation' from the Left. Hectoring news anchors have announced that the UPA no longer has any excuse to prevaricate on implementing Reforms, unless of course it has 'closet Socialists' hiding in its midst.

This is the wonderful thing about democracy. It can mean anything you want it to mean.

The absence of a genuinely left-wing party in mainstream politics is not something to celebrate. But the parliamentary Left has only itself to blame for its humiliation. It's not a tragedy that it has been cut to size. Perhaps this will create the space for some truly progressive politics.

For the sake of argument, let's for a moment contemplate the absurd and accept that India Inc and the Captains of Industry are right and that India's millions *did* in fact vote for the speeding up of market 'reforms'. Is that good news or bad news? Should we be celebrating the fact that millions of people who have something to teach the world, who have another imagination, another world view and a more sustainable way of life, have decided to embrace a discredited ideology, one that has pushed this planet into a crisis from which it may never recover?

What good will forest rights be when there are no forests? What good will the Right to Information do if there is no redress for our grievances? What good are rivers without water? What good are plains without mountains to water and sustain them? It's as though we're hurtling down a cliff in a bus without brakes and fighting over what songs to sing.

'Jai Ho!' perhaps?[20]

~

For better or for worse, the 2009 elections seem to have ensured that the 'Progress' project is up and running. However it would be a serious mistake to believe that the 'Union' project has fallen by the wayside.

As the 2009 election campaign unrolled, two things got saturation coverage in the media. One was the 100,000 rupee (two thousand dollar) 'people's car', the Tata Nano—the wagon for the *volks*—rolling out of Modi's Gujarat. (The sops and subsidies Modi gave the Tatas had a lot to do with Ratan Tata's warm endorsement of him.[21]) The other is the hate speech of the BJP's monstrous new debutant, Varun Gandhi (another descendent of the Nehru dynasty), who makes even Narendra Modi sound moderate and retiring. In a public speech Varun Gandhi called for Muslims to be forcibly sterilized. 'This will be known as a Hindu bastion, no ★★★★★ Muslim dare raise his head here,' he said, using a derogatory word for someone who has been circumcised. 'I don't want a single Muslim vote.'[22]

Varun Gandhi is a modern politician, working the democratic system, doing everything he can to *create* a majority and consolidate his vote bank. A politician needs a vote bank, like a corporation needs a mass market. Both need help from the mass media. Corporations buy that help. Politicians must earn it. Some earn it by dint of hard work, others with dangerous circus stunts. Varun Gandhi's hate speech bought him national headlines. His brief stint in prison (for violating the Election Commission's Code of Conduct), cut short by a court order, made him an instant martyr. He was gently chastised for his impetuousness by his party elders (on TV, for public consumption). But then, in order to export his coarse appeal, he, like Narendra Modi, was flown around in a chopper as a star campaigner for the BJP in other constituencies.

Varun Gandhi won his election with a colossal margin. It makes you wonder—are 'the people' always right? It is worrying to think what lessons the BJP will draw from its few decisive victories and its many decisive losses in this election. In several of the constituencies where it has won, hate speech (and deed) have served it well. It still remains by far the second largest political party, with a powerful national presence, the only real challenge to the Congress. It will certainly live to fight another day. The question is, will it turn the burners up or down?

This said, it would be a travesty to lay all the blame for divisive politics at the door of the BJP. Whether it's nuclear tests, the unsealing of the locks of the Babri Masjid, the culture of creating fissures and pitting castes and communities against each other, or passing retrograde laws, the Congress got there first and has never been shy of keeping the ball in play. In the past, both parties have used massacres to gain political mileage. Sometimes they feast off them obliquely, sometimes they accuse each other of committing mass murder. In this election, both the Congress and the BJP brazenly fielded candidates believed to be involved in public lynching and mass murder. At no point has either seen to it that the guilty are punished or that justice is delivered. Despite their vicious public exchange of accusations, so far they have colluded to protect one another from real consequences.

Eventually the massacres get absorbed into the labyrinth of India's judicial system where they are left to bubble and ferment before being trundled out as campaign material for the next election. You could say it's all a part of the fabric of Indian democracy. Hard to see from a train window. Whether the new infusion of young blood into the Congress will change the old Party's methods of doing business remains to be seen.

As will be obvious from the essays in this book, the hoary institutions of Indian democracy—the judiciary, the police, the 'free' press and, of course, elections—far from working as a system of checks and balances, quite often do the opposite. They provide each other cover to promote the larger interests of Union and Progress.

In the process, they generate such confusion, such a cacophony, that voices raised in warning just become part of the noise. And that only helps to enhance the image of the tolerant, lumbering, colourful, somewhat chaotic democracy. The chaos is real. But so is the consensus.

~

Speaking of consensus, there's the small and ever-present matter of Kashmir. When it comes to Kashmir the consensus in India is hard-core. It cuts across every section of the establishment—including the media, the bureaucracy, the intelligentsia and even Bollywood.

The war in the Kashmir valley is almost twenty years old now, and has claimed about seventy thousand lives. Tens of thousands have been tortured, several thousand have 'disappeared', women have been raped and many thousands widowed. Half a million Indian troops patrol the Kashmir valley, making it the most militarized zone in the world. (The United States had about one hundred and sixty-five thousand active-duty troops in Iraq at the height of its occupation.) The Indian army now claims that it has, for the most part, crushed militancy in Kashmir. Perhaps that's true. But does military domination mean victory?

How does a government that claims to be a democracy justify a military occupation? By holding regular elections, of course. Elections in Kashmir have had a long and fascinating past. The blatantly rigged state election of 1987 was the immediate provocation for the armed uprising that began in 1990. Since then elections have become a finely honed instrument of the military occupation, a sinister playground for India's Deep State. Intelligence Agencies have created political parties and decoy politicians, they have constructed and destroyed political careers at will. It is they more than anyone else who decide what the outcome of each election will be. After every election, the Indian establishment declares that India has won a popular mandate from the people of Kashmir.

In the summer of 2008, a dispute over land being allotted to the Amarnath Shrine Board coalesced into a massive, nonviolent uprising. Day after day, hundreds of thousands of people defied soldiers and policemen—who fired straight into the crowds, killing scores of people—and thronged the streets. From early morning to late in the night, the city reverberated to chants of 'Azadi! Azadi!' ('Freedom! Freedom!'). Fruit sellers weighed fruit chanting, 'Azadi! Azadi!' Shopkeepers, doctors, houseboat owners, guides, weavers, carpet sellers—everybody was out with placards, everybody shouted 'Azadi! Azadi!' The protests went on for several days.

The protests were massive. They were democratic, and they were nonviolent. For the first time in decades fissures appeared in mainstream public opinion in India.[23] The Indian state panicked. Unsure of how to deal with this mass civil disobedience, it ordered a crackdown. It enforced the harshest curfew in recent memory with shoot-at-sight orders. In effect, for days on end, it virtually caged millions of people. The major pro-freedom leaders were placed under house arrest, several others were jailed. House to house searches culminated in the arrest of hundreds of people. The Jama Masjid was closed for Friday prayers for an unprecedented seven weeks at a stretch.

Once the rebellion was brought under control, the government did something extraordinary—it announced elections in the state. Pro-independence leaders called for a boycott. They were re-arrested. Almost everybody believed the elections would become a huge embarrassment for the Indian government. The security establishment was convulsed with paranoia. Its elaborate network of spies, renegades and embedded journalists began to buzz with renewed energy. No chances were taken. (Even I, who had nothing to do with any of what was going on, was put under house arrest in Srinagar for two days.)

Calling for elections was a huge risk. But the gamble paid off. People turned out to vote in droves. It was the biggest voter turnout since the armed struggle began. It helped that the polls were scheduled so that the first districts to vote were the most militarized even within the Kashmir valley.

None of India's analysts, journalists and psephologists cared to ask why people who had only weeks ago risked everything, including bullets and shoot-at-sight orders, should have suddenly changed their minds. None of the high-profile scholars of the great festival of democracy—who practically live in TV studios when there are elections in mainland India, picking apart every forecast, exit poll and minor percentile swing in the vote share—talked about what elections mean in the presence of such a massive, year-round troop deployment. (An armed soldier for every twenty civilians.) No one speculated about the mystery of hundreds of unknown candidates who materialized out of nowhere to represent political parties that had no previous presence in the Kashmir valley. Where had they come from? Who was financing them? No one was curious.

No one spoke about the curfew, the mass arrests, the lockdown of constituencies that were going to poll. Not many talked about the fact that campaigning politicians went out of their way to de-link 'Azadi' and the Kashmir dispute from elections, which they insisted were only about municipal issues—roads, water, electricity. No one talked about why people who have lived under a military occupation for decades—where soldiers could barge into homes and whisk away people at any time of the day or night—might need *someone* to listen to them, to take up their cases, to represent them.[24]

The minute elections were over, the establishment and the mainstream press declared victory (for India) once again. The most worrying fallout was that in Kashmir, people began to parrot their colonizers' view of themselves as a somewhat pathetic people who deserved what they got. 'Never trust a Kashmiri,' several Kashmiris said to me. 'We're fickle and unreliable.' Psychological warfare has been an instrument of official policy in Kashmir. Its depredations over decades—its attempt to destroy people's self-esteem—are arguably the worst aspect of the occupation.

But only weeks after the elections it was back to business as usual. The protests and demands for Azadi and the summary killings by security forces have begun again. Newspapers report that militancy is on the rise. Unsurprisingly, the poor turnout in the subsequent general elections did not elicit much comment.

It's enough to make you wonder whether there is any connection at all between elections and democracy.

The trouble is that Kashmir sits on the fault lines of a region that is awash in weapons and sliding into chaos. The Kashmiri freedom struggle, with its crystal clear sentiment but fuzzy outlines, is caught in the vortex of several dangerous and conflicting ideologies—Indian Nationalism (corporate as well as 'Hindu', shading into imperialism), Pakistani Nationalism (breaking down under the burden of its own contradictions), US Imperialism (made impatient by a tanking economy), and a resurgent medieval-Islamist Taliban (fast gaining legitimacy, despite its insane brutality, because it is seen to be resisting an occupation). Each of these ideologies is capable of a ruthlessness that can range from genocide to nuclear war. Add Chinese imperial ambitions, an aggressive, re-incarnated Russia, the huge reserves of natural gas in the Caspian region and persistent whispers about natural gas, oil and uranium reserves in Kashmir and Ladakh, and you have the recipe for a new Cold War (which, like the last one, is cold for some and hot for others).

In the midst of all this, Kashmir is set to become the conduit through which the mayhem unfolding in Afghanistan and Pakistan spills into India, where it will find purchase in the anger of the young among India's one hundred and fifty million Muslims who have been brutalized, humiliated and marginalized. Notice has been given by the series of terrorist strikes that culminated in the Mumbai attacks of 2008.

There is no doubt that the Kashmir dispute ranks right up there, along with Palestine, as one of the oldest, most intractable disputes in the world. That does not mean that it cannot be resolved. Only that the solution will not be completely to the satisfaction of any one party, one country or one ideology. Negotiators will have to be prepared to deviate from the 'party line'. Of course, we haven't yet reached the stage where the Government of India is even prepared to admit that there's a problem, let alone negotiate a solution. Right now it has no reason to. Internationally, its stocks are soaring. Its economy is still ticking over, and while its neighbours deal with bloodshed, civil war, concentration camps, refugees and army mutinies, India has just concluded a beautiful election.

However, Demon-crazy can't fool all the people all the time. India's temporary, shotgun solutions to the unrest in Kashmir (pardon the pun) have magnified the problem and driven it deep into a place where it is poisoning the aquifers.

~

Perhaps the story of the Siachen Glacier, the highest battlefield in the world, is the most appropriate metaphor for the insanity of our times. Thousands of Indian and Pakistani soldiers have been deployed there, enduring chill winds and temperatures that dip to minus 40 Celsius. Of the hundreds who have died there, many have died just from the cold—from frostbite and sunburn. The glacier has become a garbage dump now, littered with the detritus of war, thousands of empty artillery shells, empty fuel drums, ice-axes, old boots, tents and every other kind of waste that thousands of warring human beings generate. The garbage remains intact, perfectly preserved at those icy temperatures, a pristine monument to human folly. While the Indian and Pakistani governments spend billions of dollars on weapons and the logistics of high altitude warfare, the battlefield has begun to melt. Right now, it has shrunk to about half its size. The melting has less to do with the military standoff than with people far away, on the other side of the world, living the good life. They're good people who believe in peace, free speech and human rights. They live in thriving democracies whose governments sit on the UN Security Council and whose economies depend heavily on the export of war and the sale of weapons to countries like India and Pakistan. (And Rwanda, Sudan, Somalia, the Republic of Congo, Iraq, Afghanistan . . . it's a long list.) The glacial melt will cause severe floods in the subcontinent, and eventually severe drought that will affect the lives of millions of people.[25] That will give us even more reasons to fight. We'll need more weapons. Who knows, that sort of consumer confidence may be just what the world needs to get over the current recession. Then everyone in the thriving democracies will have an even better life—and the glaciers will melt even faster.

~

While I read 'Listening to Grasshoppers' to a tense audience packed into a university auditorium in Istanbul (tense because words like *unity, progress, genocide* and *Armenian* tend to anger the Turkish authorities when they are uttered close together), I could see Rakel Dink, Hrant Dink's widow, sitting in the front row, crying the whole way through. When I finished, she hugged me and said, 'We keep hoping. Why do we keep hoping?'

We, she said. Not you.

The words of Faiz Ahmed Faiz, sung so hauntingly by Abida Parveen, came to me:

> *nahin nigah main manzil to justaju hi sahi*
> *nahin wisaal mayassar to arzu hi sahi*

I tried to translate them for her (sort of):

> If dreams are thwarted, then yearning must take their place
> If reunion is impossible, then longing must take its place

You see what I meant about poetry?

DEMOCRACY WHO'S SHE WHEN SHE'S AT HOME?

This essay first appeared in Outlook *magazine (India) on 6 May 2002.*

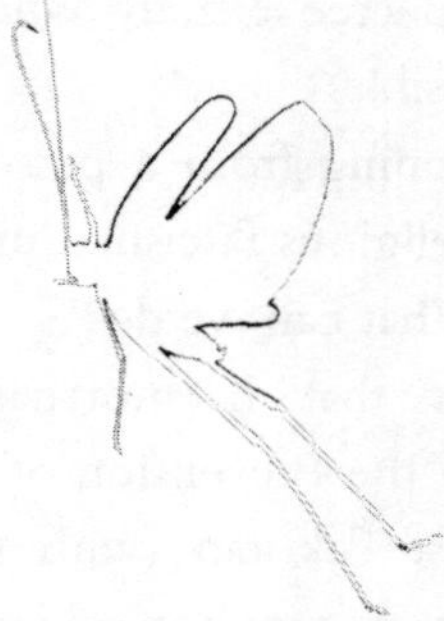

LAST NIGHT a friend from Vadodara called. Weeping. It took her fifteen minutes to tell me what the matter was. It wasn't very complicated. Only that a friend of hers, Sayeeda, had been caught by a mob. Only that her stomach had been ripped open and stuffed with burning rags. Only that after she died, someone carved 'OM' on her forehead.[1]

Precisely which Hindu scripture preaches this?

Prime Minister A.B. Vajpayee justified the savagery in Gujarat as part of the retaliation by outraged Hindus against Muslim 'terrorists' who burned alive fifty-eight Hindu passengers on the Sabarmati Express in Godhra.[2] Each of those who died that hideous death was someone's brother, someone's mother, someone's child. Of course they were. Which particular verse in the Koran required that they be roasted alive?

The more the two sides try and call attention to their religious differences by slaughtering each other, the less there is to distinguish them from one another. They worship at the same altar. They're both apostles of the same murderous god, whoever he is. In an atmosphere so vitiated, for anybody, and in particular the prime minister, to arbitrarily decree exactly where the cycle started is malevolent and irresponsible.

Right now we're sipping from a poisoned chalice—a flawed democracy laced with religious fascism. Pure arsenic.

What shall we do? What can we do?

We have a ruling party that's haemorrhaging. Its rhetoric against terrorism, the passing of the Prevention of Terrorism Act (POTA), the sabre-rattling against Pakistan (with the underlying nuclear threat), the massing of almost a million soldiers on the India–Pakistan border on hair-trigger alert and, most dangerous of all, the attempt to communalize and falsify school history textbooks—none of this has prevented it from being humiliated in election after election.[3] Even its old party trick—the revival of the plans to replace the destroyed mosque in Ayodhya with the Ram Mandir—didn't quite work out. Desperate, it has now turned for succour to the state of Gujarat.

Gujarat, the only major state in India to have a Bharatiya Janata Party (BJP) government, has for some years been the petri dish in which Hindu fascism has been fomenting an elaborate political experiment. In March 2002, the initial results were put on public display.

Within hours of the Godhra outrage, a meticulously planned pogrom was unleashed against the Muslim community. It was led from the front by the Hindu nationalist Vishwa Hindu Parishad (VHP) and the Bajrang Dal. Officially the number of dead is eight hundred. Independent reports put the figure as high as two thousand.[4]

More than one hundred and fifty thousand people, driven from their homes, now live in refugee camps. Women were stripped, gang-raped; parents were bludgeoned to death in front of their children. Two hundred and forty shrines and one hundred and eighty mosques were destroyed. In Ahmedabad, the tomb of Wali Gujarati, the founder of the modern Urdu poem, was demolished and paved over in the course of a night. The tomb of the musician Ustad Faiyaz Ali Khan was desecrated and wreathed in burning tyres. Arsonists burned and looted shops, homes, hotels, textile mills, buses and private cars belonging to Muslims. Tens of thousands of Muslims have lost their jobs.[5]

A mob surrounded the house of former Congress Member of Parliament Ehsan Jaffri. His phone calls to the director general of police, the police commissioner, the chief secretary, the additional chief secretary (home) were ignored. The mobile police vans around his house did not intervene. The mob dragged Ehsan Jaffri out of his house and dismembered him.[6]

Of course, it's only a coincidence that Jaffri was a trenchant critic of Gujarat's chief minister, Narendra Modi, during his campaign for the Rajkot Assembly by-election in February.

Across Gujarat, thousands of people made up the mobs. They were armed with petrol bombs, guns, knives, swords and tridents.[7] Apart from the VHP and Bajrang Dal's usual lumpen constituency, there were Dalits and Adivasis who were brought in buses and trucks.[8] Middle-class people participated in the looting. (On one memorable occasion a family arrived in a Mitsubishi Lancer.[9]) There was a deliberate, systematic attempt to destroy the economic base of the Muslim community. The leaders of the mob had computer-generated cadastral lists marking out Muslim homes, shops, businesses and even partnerships. They had mobile phones to coordinate the action. They had trucks loaded with thousands of gas cylinders, hoarded weeks in advance, which they used to blow up Muslim commercial establishments. They had not just police protection and police connivance but also covering fire.[10]

While Gujarat burned, our prime minister was on MTV promoting his new poems.[11] (Reports say cassettes have sold a hundred thousand copies.) It took him more than a month—and two vacations in the hills—to make it to Gujarat.[12] When he did, shadowed by the chilling Modi, he gave a speech at the Shah Alam refugee camp.[13] His mouth moved, he tried to express concern, but no real sound emerged except the mocking of the wind whistling through a burned, bloodied, broken world. Next we knew, he was bobbing around in a golf cart, striking business deals in Singapore.[14]

The killers still stalk Gujarat's streets. For weeks the lynch mob was the arbiter of the routine affairs of daily life: who can live where, who can say what, who can meet whom, and where and when. Its mandate expanded from religious affairs to property disputes, family altercations and the planning and allocation of water resources. (Which is why Medha Patkar of the Narmada Bachao Andolan was assaulted).[15] Muslim businesses have been shut down. Muslim people are not served in restaurants. Muslim children are not welcome in schools. Muslim students are too terrified to sit for their exams.[16] Muslim parents live in dread that their infants might forget what they've been told and give themselves away by saying 'Ammi!' or 'Abba!' in public and invite sudden and violent death.

Notice has been given: this is just the beginning.

Is this the Hindu Rashtra, the Nation that we've all been asked to look forward to? Once the Muslims have been 'shown their place', will milk and Coca-Cola flow across the land? Once the Ram Mandir is built, will there be a shirt on every back and a roti in every belly?[17] Will every tear be wiped from every eye? Can we expect an anniversary celebration next year? Or will there be someone else to hate by then? Alphabetically: Adivasis, Buddhists, Christians, Dalits, Parsis, Sikhs? Those who wear jeans or speak English or those who have thick lips or curly hair? We won't have to wait long. It's started already. Will the established rituals continue? Will people be beheaded, dismembered and urinated on? Will foetuses be ripped from their mothers' wombs?[18]

What kind of depraved vision can even imagine India without the range and beauty and spectacular anarchy of all these cultures? India would become a tomb and smell like a crematorium.

No matter who they were, or how they were killed, each person who died in Gujarat in the weeks gone by deserves to be mourned. There have been hundreds of outraged letters to journals and newspapers asking why the 'pseudo-secularists' do not condemn the burning of the Sabarmati Express in Godhra with the same degree of outrage with which they condemn the killings in the rest of Gujarat. What they don't seem to understand is that there is a fundamental difference between a pogrom such as the one taking place in Gujarat now and the burning of the Sabarmati Express in Godhra. We still don't know who exactly was responsible for the carnage in Godhra. Home Minister Lal Krishna Advani made a public statement claiming that the burning of the train was a plot by Pakistan's Inter-Services Intelligence (ISI).[19] Months later, the police have not found a shred of evidence to support that claim. The Gujarat government's forensic report says that sixty litres of petrol was poured on to the floor by someone who was inside the carriage. The doors were locked, possibly from the inside. The burned bodies of the passengers were found in a heap in the middle of the carriage. So far, nobody really knows who started the fire.

There are theories to suit every political position: it was a Pakistani plot; it was Muslim extremists who managed to get into the train; it was the angry mob; it was a VHP/Bajrang Dal plot staged to set off the horror that followed. No one really knows.[20]

Whoever did it—whatever their political or religious persuasion—committed a terrible crime. But every independent report says the pogrom against the Muslim community in Gujarat—billed by the government as a spontaneous 'reaction'—has at best been conducted under the benign gaze of the state and, at worst, with active state collusion.[21] Either way, the state is criminally culpable. And the state acts in the name of its citizens. So, as citizens we have to acknowledge that we are somehow made complicit in the Gujarat pogrom. It is this that puts a completely different complexion on the two massacres.

After the Gujarat massacres, at its convention in Bangalore, the Rashtriya Swayamsevak Sangh (RSS), the moral and cultural guild of the BJP, of which the prime minister, the home minister and Chief Minister Modi himself are all members, called on Muslims to earn the 'goodwill' of the majority community.[22]

At the meeting of the national executive of the BJP in Goa, Narendra Modi was greeted as a hero. His smirking offer to resign from the chief minister's post was unanimously turned down.[23] In a recent public speech he compared the events of the last few weeks in Gujarat to Gandhi's Dandi March—both, according to him, significant moments in the Struggle for Freedom.

While the parallels between contemporary India and pre-war Germany are chilling, they're not surprising. (The founders of the RSS have, in their writings, been frank in their admiration for Hitler and his methods.[24]) One difference is that here in India we don't have a Hitler. We have, instead, a travelling extravaganza, a mobile symphonic orchestra. The hydra-headed, many-armed Sangh Parivar—the 'joint family' of Hindu political and cultural organizations—with the BJP, the RSS, the VHP and the Bajrang Dal, each playing a different instrument. Its utter genius lies in its apparent ability to be all things to all people at all times.

The Parivar has an appropriate head for every occasion. Atal Bihari Vajpayee, an old versifier with rhetoric for every season. A rabble-rousing hardliner, L.K. Advani, for Home Affairs; a suave one, Jaswant Singh, for Foreign Affairs; a smooth, English-speaking lawyer, Arun Jaitley, to handle TV debates; a cold-blooded creature, Narendra Modi, for a chief minister; and the Bajrang Dal and the VHP, grassroots workers in charge of the physical labour that goes into the business of genocide. Finally, this many-headed extravaganza has a lizard's tail which drops off when it's in trouble and grows back again: George Fernandes, a specious socialist dressed up as defence minister, who it sends on its damage-limitation missions—wars, cyclones, genocides. They trust him to press the right buttons, hit the right notes.

The Sangh Parivar speaks in as many tongues as a whole corsage of tridents. It can say several contradictory things simultaneously. While one of its heads (the VHP) exhorts millions of its cadres to prepare for the Final Solution, its titular head (the prime minister) assures the nation that all citizens, regardless of their religion, will be treated equally. It can ban books and films and burn paintings for 'insulting Indian culture'. Simultaneously, it can mortgage the equivalent of 60 per cent of the entire country's rural development budget as profit to Enron.[25] It contains within itself the full spectrum of political opinion so what would normally be a public fight between two adversarial political parties is now just a family matter. However acrimonious the quarrel, it's always conducted in public, always resolved amicably, and the audience always goes away satisfied it's got value for its money—anger, action, revenge, intrigue, remorse, poetry and plenty of gore. It's our own vernacular version of Full Spectrum Dominance.

But when the chips are down, really down, the squabbling heads quiet, and it becomes chillingly apparent that underneath all the clamour and the noise, a single heart beats. And an unforgiving mind with saffron-saturated tunnel vision works overtime.

There have been pogroms in India before, every kind of pogrom—directed at particular castes, tribes, religious faiths. In 1984, following the assassination of Indira Gandhi, the Congress Party presided over the massacre of three thousand Sikhs in Delhi, every bit as macabre as the one in Gujarat.[26] At the time, Rajiv Gandhi, never known for an elegant turn of phrase, said, 'When a large tree falls, the earth shakes.' In 1985, the Congress swept the polls. On a sympathy wave. Eighteen years have gone by and almost no one has been punished.

Take any politically volatile issue—the nuclear tests, the Babri Masjid, the *Tehelka* scam, the stirring of the communal cauldron for electoral advantage—and you'll see the Congress Party has been there before. In every case, the Congress sowed the seed and the BJP has swept in to reap the hideous harvest. So in the event that we're called on to vote, is there a difference between the two? The answer is a faltering but distinct 'yes'. Here's why: It's true that the Congress Party has sinned, and grievously, and for decades together. But it has done by night what the BJP does by day. It has done covertly, stealthily, hypocritically, shamefacedly what the BJP does with pride. And this is an important difference.

Whipping up communal hatred is part of the mandate of the Sangh Parivar. It has been planned for years. It has been injecting a slow-release poison directly into civil society's bloodstream. Hundreds of RSS shakhas and Saraswati Shishu Mandir schools across the country have been indoctrinating thousands of children and young people, stunting their minds with religious hatred and falsified history, including wildly exaggerated accounts of the rape and pillaging of Hindu women and Hindu temples by Muslim rulers in the pre-colonial period. They're no different from, and no less dangerous than, the madrassas all over Pakistan and Afghanistan which spawned the Taliban. In states like Gujarat, the police, the administration and the political cadres at every level have been systematically penetrated.[27]

The whole enterprise has huge popular appeal, which it would be foolish to underestimate or misunderstand. It has a formidable religious, ideological, political and administrative underpinning. This kind of power, this kind of reach, can only be achieved with state backing.

Some madrassas, the Muslim equivalent of hothouses cultivating religious hatred, try and make up in frenzy and foreign funding what they lack in state support. They provide the perfect foil for Hindu communalists to dance their dance of mass paranoia and hatred. (In fact, they serve that purpose so perfectly they might just as well be working as a team.)

Under this relentless pressure, what will most likely happen is that the majority of the Muslim community will resign itself to living in ghettos as second-class citizens, in constant fear, with no civil rights and no recourse to justice. What will daily life be like for them? Any little thing, an altercation in a cinema queue or a fracas at a traffic light, could turn lethal. So they will learn to keep very quiet, to accept their lot, to creep around the edges of the society in which they live. Their fear will transmit itself to other minorities. Many, particularly the young, will probably turn to militancy. They will do terrible things. Civil society will be called on to condemn them. Then President Bush's canon will come back to us: 'Either you are with us or you are with the terrorists.'

Those words hang frozen in time like icicles. For years to come, butchers and genocidists will fit their grisly mouths around them (film-makers call it 'lip synch') in order to justify their butchery.

Bal Thackeray of the Shiv Sena, who has lately been feeling a little upstaged by Modi, has the lasting solution. He's called for civil war. Isn't that just perfect? Then Pakistan won't need to bomb us, we can bomb ourselves. Let's turn all of India into Kashmir. Or Bosnia. Or Palestine. Or Rwanda. Let's all suffer forever. Let's buy expensive guns and explosives to kill each other with. Let the British arms dealers and the American weapons manufacturers grow fat on our spilled blood.[28] We could ask the Carlyle group—of which the Bush and bin Laden families were both shareholders—for a bulk discount.[29]

Maybe if things go really well, we'll become like Afghanistan. (And look at the publicity they've gone and got themselves.) When all our farmlands are mined, our buildings destroyed, our infrastructure reduced to rubble, our children physically maimed and mentally wrecked, when we've nearly wiped ourselves out with self-manufactured hatred, maybe we can appeal to the Americans to help us out. Airdropped airline meals, anyone?[30]

How close we have come to self-destruction! Another step and we'll be in free fall. And yet the government presses on. At the Goa meeting of the BJP's national executive, the prime minister of secular, democratic India, A.B. Vajpayee, made history. He became the first Indian prime minister to cross the threshold and publicly unveil an unconscionable bigotry against Muslims, which even George Bush and Donald Rumsfeld would be embarrassed to own up to. 'Wherever Muslims are,' he said, 'they do not want to live peacefully.'[31]

In the immediate aftermath of the Gujarat holocaust, confident of the success of its 'experiment', the BJP wants a snap poll. 'The gentlest of people,' my friend from Vadodara said to me, 'the gentlest of people, in the gentlest of voices, say "Modi is our hero."'

Some of us nurtured the naive hope that the magnitude of the horror of the last few weeks would make the secular parties, however self-serving, unite in sheer outrage. On its own, the BJP does not have the mandate of the people of India. It does not have the mandate to push through the Hindutva project. We hoped that the twenty-two allies that make up the BJP-led coalition would withdraw their support. We thought, quite stupidly, that they would see that there could be no bigger test of their moral fibre, of their commitment to their avowed principles of secularism.

It's a sign of the times that not a single one of the BJP's allies has withdrawn support. In every shifty eye you see that faraway look of someone doing mental math to calculate which constituencies and portfolios they'll retain and which ones they'll lose if they pull out. Deepak Parekh is the only CEO of India's corporate community to condemn what happened.[32] Farooq Abdullah, chief minister of Jammu and Kashmir and the only prominent Muslim politician left in India, is currying favour with the government by supporting Modi because he nurses the dim hope that he might become vice president of India very soon.[33] And worst of all, Mayawati, leader of the Bahujan Samaj Party (BSP), the great hope of the lower castes, has forged an alliance with the BJP in Uttar Pradesh.[34] The Congress and the Left parties have launched a public agitation asking for Modi's resignation.[35]

Resignation? Have we lost all sense of proportion? Criminals are not meant to resign. They're meant to be charged, tried and convicted. As those who burned the train in Godhra should be. As the mobs and those members of the police force and the administration who planned and participated in the pogrom in the rest of Gujarat should be. As those responsible for raising the pitch of the frenzy to boiling point must be. The Supreme Court has the option of acting against Modi and the Bajrang Dal and the VHP.[36] There are hundreds of testimonies. There is masses of evidence.

But in India if you are a butcher or a genocidist who happens to be a politician, you have every reason to be optimistic. No one even expects politicians to be prosecuted. To demand that Modi and his henchmen be arraigned and put away would make other politicians vulnerable to their own unsavoury pasts. So instead they disrupt Parliament, shout a lot. Eventually those in power set up commissions of inquiry, ignore the findings, and between themselves makes sure the juggernaut chugs on.

Already the issue has begun to morph. Should elections be allowed or not? Should the Election Commission decide that or the Supreme Court? Either way, whether elections are held or deferred, by allowing Modi to walk free, by allowing him to continue with his career as a politician, the fundamental, governing principles of democracy are not just being subverted but deliberately sabotaged. This kind of democracy is the problem, not the solution. Our society's greatest strength is being turned into her deadliest enemy. What's the point of us all going on about 'deepening democracy', when it's being bent and twisted into something unrecognizable?

What if the BJP does win the elections? After all, George Bush had a sixty per cent rating in his War Against Terror, and Ariel Sharon has an even stronger mandate for his bestial invasion of Palestine.[37] Does that make everything all right? Why not dispense with the legal system, the constitution, the press, the whole shebang, why not chuck morality itself, and put everything up for a vote? Genocides can become the subject of opinion polls, and massacres can have marketing campaigns.

Fascism's firm footprint has appeared in India. Let's mark the date: Spring 2002. While we can thank the US president and the Coalition Against Terror for creating a congenial international atmosphere for fascism's ghastly debut, we cannot credit them for the years it has been brewing in our public and private lives.

~

It breezed in after the Pokaran nuclear tests in 1998.[38] From then onwards, the massed energy of bloodthirsty patriotism became openly acceptable political currency. The 'weapons of peace' trapped India and Pakistan in a spiral of brinkmanship—threat and counter-threat, taunt and counter-taunt.[39] And now, one war and hundreds of dead later, more than a million soldiers from both armies are massed at the border, eyeball to eyeball, locked in a pointless nuclear standoff.[40]

The escalating belligerence against Pakistan has ricocheted off the border and entered our own body politic, like a sharp blade slicing through the vestiges of communal harmony and tolerance between the Hindu and Muslim communities. In no time at all, the godsquadders from hell have colonized the public imagination. And we allowed them in. Each time the hostility between India and Pakistan is cranked up, within India there's a corresponding increase in the hostility toward the Muslims. With each battle cry against Pakistan, we inflict a wound on ourselves, on our way of life, on our spectacularly diverse and ancient civilization, on everything that makes India different from Pakistan.

Increasingly, Indian nationalism has come to mean Hindu nationalism, which defines itself not through a respect or regard for itself, but through a hatred of the Other. And the Other, for the moment, is not just Pakistan, it's Muslims. It's disturbing to see how neatly nationalism dovetails into fascism. While we must not allow the fascists to define what the nation is, or who it belongs to, it's worth keeping in mind that nationalism—in all its many avatars, communist, capitalist, fascist—has been at the root of almost all the genocide of the twentieth century. On the issue of nationalism, it's wise to proceed with caution.

Can we not find it in ourselves to belong to an ancient civilization instead of to just a recent nation? To love a land instead of just patrolling a territory? The Sangh Parivar understands nothing of what civilization means. It seeks to limit, reduce, define, dismember and desecrate the memory of what we were, our understanding of what we are and our dreams of who we want to be. What kind of India do they want? A limbless, headless, soulless torso, left bleeding under the butcher's cleaver with a flag driven deep into her mutilated heart? Can we let that happen? Have we let it happen?

The incipient, creeping fascism of the past few years has been groomed by many of our 'democratic' institutions. Everyone has flirted with it—Parliament, the press, the police, the administration, the public. Even 'secularists' have been guilty of helping to create the right climate. Each time you defend the right of an institution, any institution (including the Supreme Court), to exercise unfettered, unaccountable powers that must never be challenged, you move toward fascism.

The national press has been startlingly courageous in its denunciation of the events of the last few weeks. Many of the BJP's fellow travellers, who have journeyed with it to the brink, are now looking down the abyss into the hell that was once Gujarat and turning away in genuine dismay. But how hard and for how long will they fight? This is not going to be like a publicity campaign for an upcoming cricket season. And there will not always be spectacular carnage to report on. Fascism is also about the slow, steady infiltration of all the instruments of state power. It's about the slow erosion of civil liberties, about unspectacular day-to-day injustices. Fighting it means fighting to win back the minds and hearts of people. Fighting it does not mean asking for RSS shakhas and the madrassas that are overtly communal to be banned. It means working towards the day when they're voluntarily abandoned as bad ideas. It means keeping an eagle eye on public institutions and demanding accountability. It means putting your ear to the ground and listening to the whispering of the truly powerless. It means giving a forum to myriad voices from the hundreds of resistance movements across the country which are speaking about real things—about bonded labour, marital rape, sexual preferences, women's wages, uranium dumping, unsustainable mining, weavers' woes, farmers' suicides. It means fighting displacement and dispossession and the relentless, everyday violence of abject poverty.

Fighting it also means not allowing your newspaper columns and prime-time TV spots to be hijacked by their spurious passions and their staged theatrics, which are designed to divert attention from everything else.

While most people in India have been horrified by what happened in Gujarat, many thousands of the indoctrinated are preparing to journey deeper into the heart of the horror. Look around you and you'll see in little parks, in empty lots, in village commons, the RSS is marching, hoisting its saffron flag. Suddenly they're everywhere, grown men in khaki shorts marching, marching, marching. To where? For what?

Their disregard for history shields them from the knowledge that fascism will thrive for a short while and then self-annihilate because of its inherent stupidity. But unfortunately, like the radioactive fallout of a nuclear strike, it has a half-life that will cripple generations to come. These levels of rage and hatred cannot be contained, cannot be expected to subside with public censure and denunciation. Hymns of brotherhood and love are great, but not enough.

Historically, fascist movements have been fuelled by feelings of national disillusionment. Fascism has come to India after the dreams that fuelled the Freedom Struggle have been frittered away, like so much loose change.

Independence itself came to us as what Gandhi famously called a 'wooden loaf'—a notional freedom tainted by the blood of the thousands who died during Partition.[41]

For more than half a century now, the hatred and mutual distrust has been exacerbated, toyed with, and never allowed to heal by politicians, led from the front by Indira Gandhi. Every political party has mined the marrow of our secular parliamentary democracy for electoral advantage. Like termites excavating a mound, they've made tunnels and underground passages, undermining the meaning of 'secular', until it has become just an empty shell that's about to implode. Their tilling has weakened the foundations of the structure that connects the Constitution, Parliament and the courts of law—the configuration of checks and balances that forms the backbone of a parliamentary democracy. Under the circumstances, it's futile to go on blaming politicians and demanding from them a morality of which they're incapable. There's something pitiable about a people that constantly bemoans its leaders. If they've let us down, it's only because we've allowed them to. It could be argued that civil society has failed its leaders as much as leaders have failed civil society. We have to accept that there is a dangerous, systemic flaw in our parliamentary democracy that politicians will exploit. And that's what results in the kind of conflagration that we have witnessed in Gujarat. There's fire in the ducts. We have to address this issue and come up with a systemic solution.

But politicians' exploitation of communal divides is by no means the only reason that fascism has arrived on our shores. Over the past fifty years, ordinary citizens' modest hopes for lives of dignity, security and relief from abject poverty have been systematically snuffed out. Every 'democratic' institution in this country has shown itself to be unaccountable, inaccessible to the ordinary citizen and either unwilling or incapable of acting in the interests of genuine social justice. Every strategy for real social change—land reform, education, public health, the equitable distribution of natural resources, the implementation of positive discrimination—has been cleverly, cunningly and consistently scuttled and rendered ineffectual by those castes and that class of people which have a stranglehold on the political process. And now corporate globalization is being relentlessly and arbitrarily imposed on an essentially feudal society, tearing through its complex, tiered social fabric, ripping it apart culturally and economically.

There is very real grievance here. And the fascists didn't create it. But they have seized on it, upturned it and forged from it a hideous, bogus sense of pride. They have mobilized human beings using the lowest common denominator—religion. People who have lost control over their lives, people who have been uprooted from their homes and communities, who have lost their culture and their language, are being made to feel proud of something. Not something they have striven for and achieved, not something they can count as a personal accomplishment, but something they just happen to be. Or, more accurately, something they happen not to be. And the falseness, the emptiness, of that pride is fuelling a gladiatorial anger that is then directed toward a simulated target that has been wheeled into the amphitheatre.

How else can you explain the project of trying to disenfranchise, drive out, or exterminate the second-poorest community in this country, using as your foot soldiers the very poorest? How else can you explain why Dalits and Adivasis in Gujarat, who have been despised, oppressed and treated worse than refuse by the upper castes for thousands of years, have joined hands with their oppressors to turn on those who are only marginally less unfortunate than they themselves? Are they just wage slaves, mercenaries for hire? Is it all right to patronize them and absolve them of responsibility for their own actions? Or am I being obtuse?

Perhaps it's common practice for the unfortunate to vent their rage and hatred on the next most unfortunate, because their real adversaries are inaccessible, seemingly invincible and completely out of range. Because their own leaders have cut loose and are feasting at the high table, leaving them to wander rudderless in the wilderness, spouting nonsense about returning to the Hindu fold. (The first step, presumably, toward founding a global Hindu empire, as realistic a goal as fascism's previously failed projects—the restoration of Roman glory, the purification of the German race, or the establishment of an Islamic sultanate.)

One hundred and fifty million Muslims live in India. Hindu fascists regard them as legitimate prey. Do people like Modi and Bal Thackeray think that the world will stand by and watch while they're liquidated in a 'civil war'? Press reports say that the European Union and several other countries have condemned what happened in Gujarat and likened it to Nazi rule.[42] The Indian government's portentous response is that foreigners should not use the Indian media to comment on what is an 'internal matter'[43] (Like the chilling goings-on in Kashmir?).

What next? Censorship? Closing down the Internet? Blocking international calls? Killing the wrong 'terrorists' and fudging the DNA samples?[44] There is no terrorism like state terrorism.

But who will take them on? Their fascist cant can perhaps be dented by some blood and thunder from the opposition. So far only

Laloo Yadav, head of the Rashtriya Janata Dal (RJD), the National People's Party, in Bihar, has shown himself to be truly passionate: 'Kaun mai ka lal kehtha hai ki yeh Hindu Rashtra hai? Usko yahan bhej do, chhaahti phad doonga!' (Which mother's son says this is a Hindu Nation? Send him here, I'll tear his chest open.)[45]

Unfortunately, there's no quick fix. Fascism itself can only be turned away if all those who are outraged by it show a commitment to social justice that equals the intensity of their indignation.

Are we ready to get off our starting blocks? Are we ready, many millions of us, to rally, not just on the streets, but at work and in schools and in our homes, in every decision we take, and every choice we make?

Or not just yet . . .?

If not, then years from now, when the rest of the world has shunned us (as it should), we too will learn, like the ordinary citizens of Hitler's Germany, to recognize revulsion in the gaze of our fellow human beings. We too will find ourselves unable to look our own children in the eye, for the shame of what we did and didn't do. For the shame of what we allowed to happen.

This is us. In India. Heaven help us make it through the night.

HOW DEEP SHALL WE DIG?

This is the full text of the first I.G. Khan Memorial Lecture, delivered at Aligarh Muslim University in Aligarh, India, on 6 April 2004.[1] *It was first published in Hindi in* Hindustan *on 23–24 April 2004, and in English in* The Hindu *on 25 April 2004.*

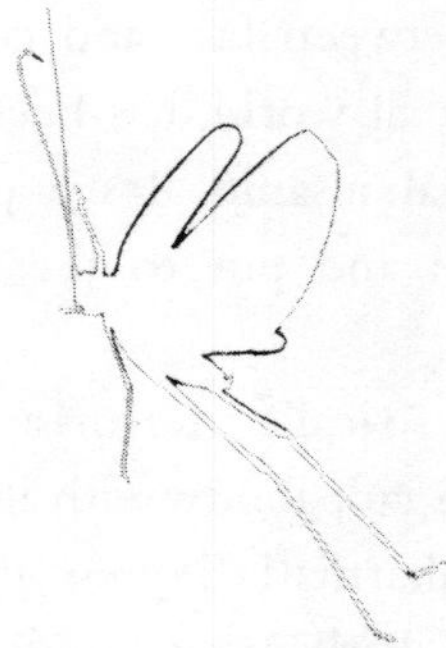

RECENTLY, A YOUNG Kashmiri friend was talking to me about life in Kashmir. Of the morass of political venality and opportunism, the callous brutality of the security forces, of the osmotic, inchoate edges of a society saturated in violence, where militants, police, intelligence officers, government servants, businessmen and even journalists encounter each other, and gradually, over time, become each other. He spoke of having to live with the endless killing, the mounting 'disappearances', the whispering, the fear, the unresolved rumours, the insane disconnection between what is actually happening, what Kashmiris know is happening, and what the rest of us are told is happening in Kashmir. He said, 'Kashmir used to be a business. Now it's a mental asylum.'

The more I think about that remark, the more apposite a description it seems for all of India. Admittedly, Kashmir—and the northeastern states of Manipur, Nagaland and Mizoram—are separate wings that house the more perilous wards in the asylum. But in the heartland, too, the schism between knowledge and information, between what we know and what we're told, between what is unknown and what is asserted, between what is concealed and what is revealed, between fact and conjecture, between the 'real' world and the virtual world, has become a place of endless speculation and potential insanity. It's a poisonous brew which is stirred and simmered and put to the most ugly, destructive, political purpose.

Each time there is a so-called terrorist strike, the government rushes in, eager to assign culpability with little or no investigation. The burning of the Sabarmati Express in Godhra in February 2002, the attack on the Parliament building in December 2001, or the massacre of Sikhs by so-called terrorists in Chattisinghpora, Kashmir, in March 2000 are only a few high-profile examples. (The 'terrorists' who were later killed by security forces turned out to be innocent villagers. The state government subsequently admitted that fake blood samples were submitted for DNA testing.[2]) In each of these cases, the evidence that eventually surfaced raised very disturbing questions and so was immediately put into cold storage. Take the case of Godhra: As soon as it happened, the home minister announced it was an ISI plot. The VHP says it was the work of a Muslim mob throwing petrol bombs.[3] Serious questions remain unanswered. There is endless conjecture. Everybody believes what they want to believe, but the incident is used to cynically and systematically whip up communal frenzy.

The US government used the lies and disinformation generated around the September 11 attacks to invade not just one country, but two—and heaven knows what else is in store. The Indian government uses the same strategy, not with other countries, but against its own people.

Over the last decade, the number of people who have been killed by the police and security forces runs into the thousands. Recently several Mumbai policemen spoke openly to the press about how many 'gangsters' they had eliminated on 'orders' from their senior officers.[4] Andhra Pradesh chalks up an average of about two hundred 'extremists' in 'encounter' deaths a year.[5] In Kashmir, in a situation that almost amounts to war, an estimated seventy thousand people have been killed since 1989. Thousands have simply 'disappeared'.[6] According to the records of the Association of Parents of Disappeared People (APDP), more than three thousand people were killed in 2003, of which four hundred and sixty-three were soldiers.[7] Since the Mufti Mohammed Sayeed government came to power in October 2002 on the promise of bringing a 'healing touch', the APDP says, there have been fifty-four custodial deaths.[8] In this age of hyper-nationalism, as long as the people who are killed are labelled gangsters, terrorists, insurgents or extremists, their killers can strut around as crusaders in the national interest and are answerable to no one. Even if it were true (which it most certainly isn't) that every person who has been killed was in fact a gangster, terrorist, insurgent or extremist—it only tells us there is something terribly wrong with a society that drives so many people to take such desperate measures.

The Indian state's proclivity to harass and terrorize people has been institutionalized, consecrated by the enactment of the Prevention of Terrorism Act (POTA), which has been promulgated in ten states. A cursory reading of POTA will tell you that it is draconian and ubiquitous. It's a versatile, hold-all law that could apply to anyone—from an Al-Qaeda operative caught with a cache of explosives, to an Adivasi playing his flute under a neem tree, to you or me. The genius of POTA is that it can be anything the government wants it to be. We live on the sufferance of those who govern us. In Tamil Nadu, it has been used to stifle criticism of the state government.[9] In Jharkhand thirty-two hundred people, mostly poor Adivasis accused of being Maoists, have been indicted under POTA.[10] In eastern Uttar Pradesh, the act is used to clamp down on those who dare to protest about the alienation of their land and livelihood rights.[11] In Gujarat and Mumbai, it is used almost exclusively against Muslims.[12] In Gujarat after the 2002 state-assisted pogrom in which an estimated two thousand Muslims were killed and one hundred and fifty thousand driven from their homes, two hundred and eighty-seven people have been accused under POTA. Of these, two hundred and eighty-six are Muslim and one is a Sikh.[13] POTA allows confessions extracted in police custody to be admitted as judicial evidence. In effect, under the POTA regime, police torture tends to replace police investigation. It's quicker, cheaper and ensures results. Talk of cutting back on public spending.

In March 2004, I was a member of a peoples' tribunal on POTA.[14] Over a period of two days we listened to harrowing testimonies of what goes on in our wonderful democracy. Let me assure you that in our police stations it's everything: from people being forced to drink urine to being stripped, humiliated, given electric shocks, burned with cigarette butts, having iron rods put up their anuses to being beaten and kicked to death.

Across the country hundreds of people, including some very young children charged under POTA, have been imprisoned and are being held without bail, awaiting trial in special POTA courts that are not open to public scrutiny. A majority of those booked under POTA are guilty of one of two crimes. Either they're poor—for the most part Dalit and Adivasi. Or they're Muslim. POTA inverts the accepted dictum of criminal law: that a person is innocent until proven guilty. Under POTA you cannot get bail unless you can prove you are innocent—of a crime that you have not been formally charged with. Essentially, you have to prove you're innocent even if you're unaware of the crime you are supposed to have committed. And that applies to all of us. Technically, we are a nation waiting to be accused.

It would be naïve to imagine that POTA is being 'misused'. On the contrary. It is being used for precisely the reasons it was enacted. Of course, if the recommendations of the Malimath Committee are implemented, POTA will soon become redundant. The Malimath Committee recommends that in certain respects normal criminal law should be brought in line with the provisions of POTA.[15] There'll be no more criminals then. Only terrorists. It's kind of neat.

Today in Jammu and Kashmir and many northeastern states of India, the Armed Forces Special Powers Act allows not just officers but even junior commissioned officers and non-commissioned officers of the army to use force (and even kill) any person on suspicion of disturbing public order or carrying a weapon.[16] On *suspicion* of! Nobody who lives in India can harbour any illusions about what that leads to. The documentation of instances of torture, disappearances, custodial deaths, rape and gang rape (by security forces) is enough to make your blood run cold. The fact that despite all this, India retains its reputation as a legitimate democracy—in the international community and among its own middle class—is a triumph.

The Armed Forces Special Powers Act is a harsher version of the ordinance that Lord Linlithgow passed in 15 August 1942, to handle the Quit India Movement. In 1958, it was clamped on parts of Manipur, which were declared 'disturbed areas'. In 1965, the whole of Mizoram, then still part of Assam, was declared 'disturbed'. In 1972, the act was extended to Tripura. By 1980, the whole of Manipur had been declared 'disturbed'.[17] What more evidence does anybody need to realize that repressive measures are counter-productive and only exacerbate the problem?

Juxtaposed against this unseemly eagerness to repress and eliminate people is the Indian state's barely hidden reluctance to investigate and bring to trial cases in which there is plenty of evidence: the massacre of three thousand Sikhs in Delhi in 1984 and the massacres of Muslims in Mumbai in 1993 and in Gujarat in 2002 (not one conviction to date); the murder a few years ago of Chandrashekhar Prasad, former president of the Jawaharlal Nehru University student union; and the murder twelve years ago of Shankar Guha Niyogi of the Chhattisgarh Mukti Morcha are just a few examples.[18] Eyewitness accounts and masses of incriminating evidence are not enough when all of the state machinery is stacked against you.

Meanwhile, economists cheering from the pages of corporate newspapers inform us that the GDP growth rate is phenomenal, unprecedented. Shops are overflowing with consumer goods government storehouses are overflowing with foodgrain. Outside this circle of light, farmers steeped in debt are committing suicide in the hundreds.[19] Reports of starvation and malnutrition come in from across the country. Yet the government allowed sixty-three million tons of grain to rot in its granaries.[20] Twelve million tons were exported and sold at a subsidized price the Indian government was not willing to offer the Indian poor.[21] Utsa Patnaik, the well known agricultural economist, has calculated foodgrain availability and foodgrain absorption in India for nearly a century, based on official statistics. She calculates that in the period between the early 1990s and 2001, foodgrain absorption has dropped to levels lower than during the World War II years, including during the Bengal Famine, in which three million people died of starvation.[22] As we know from the work of Professor Amartya Sen, democracies don't take kindly to starvation deaths. They attract too much adverse publicity from the 'free press'.[23]

So, dangerous levels of malnutrition and permanent hunger are the preferred model these days. Forty-seven per cent of India's children below three suffer from malnutrition, 46 per cent are stunted.[24] Utsa Patnaik's study reveals that about 40 per cent of the rural population in India has the same food grain absorption level as sub-Saharan Africa.[25] Today, an average rural family eats about one hundred kilograms less food in a year than it did in the early 1990s.[26]

But in urban India, wherever you go—shops, restaurants, railway stations, airports, gymnasiums, hospitals—you have TV monitors in which election promises have already come true. India's Shining, Feeling Good. You only have to close your ears to the sickening crunch of the policeman's boot on someone's ribs, you only have to raise your eyes from the squalor, the slums, the ragged broken people on the streets and seek a friendly TV monitor and you will be in that other beautiful world. The singing-dancing world of Bollywood's permanent pelvic thrusts, of permanently privileged, permanently happy Indians waving the tricolour flag and Feeling Good. It's becoming harder and harder to tell which one's the real world and which one's virtual. Laws like POTA are like buttons on a TV. You can use it to switch off the poor, the troublesome, the unwanted.

~

There is a new kind of secessionist movement taking place in India. Shall we call it New Secessionism? It's an inversion of Old Secessionism. It's when people who are actually part of a whole different economy, a whole different country, a whole different *planet*, pretend they're part of this one. It is the kind of secession in which a relatively small section of people become immensely wealthy by appropriating everything—land, rivers, water, freedom, security, dignity, fundamental rights, including the right to protest—from a large group of people. It's a vertical secession, not a horizontal, territorial one. It's the real Structural Adjustment—the kind that separates India Shining from India. India Private Limited from India the Public Enterprise.

It's the kind of secession in which public infrastructure, productive public assets, water, electricity, transport, telecommunications, health services, education, natural resources, assets that the Indian state is supposed to hold in trust for the people it represents, assets that have been built and maintained with public money over decades—are sold by the state to private corporations. In India 70 per cent of the population—seven hundred million people—live in rural areas.[27] Their livelihoods depend on access to natural resources. To snatch these away and sell them as stock to private companies is beginning to result in dispossession and impoverishment on a barbaric scale.

India Private Limited is on its way to being owned by a few corporations and major multinationals. The CEOs of these companies will control this country, its infrastructure and its resources, its media and its journalists, but will owe nothing to its people. They are completely unaccountable—legally, socially, morally, politically. Those who say that in India a few of these CEOs are more powerful than the prime minister know exactly what they're talking about.

Quite apart from the economic implications of all this, even if it were all that it is cracked up to be (which it isn't)—miraculous, efficient, amazing—is the *politics* of it acceptable to us? If the Indian state chooses to mortgage its responsibilities to a handful of corporations, does it mean that the theatre of electoral democracy is entirely meaningless? Or does it still have a role to play?

The 'free market' (which is actually far from free) needs the state, and needs it badly. As the disparity between the rich and poor grows in poor countries, states have their work cut out for them. Corporations on the prowl for 'sweetheart deals' that yield enormous profits cannot push through those deals and administer those projects in developing countries without the active connivance of state machinery. Today corporate globalization needs an international confederation of loyal, corrupt, preferably authoritarian governments in poorer countries to push through unpopular reforms and quell the mutinies. It's called 'Creating a Good Investment Climate'.

When we vote, we choose which political party we would like to invest the coercive, repressive powers of the state in.

Right now in India we have to negotiate the dangerous cross-currents of neo-liberal capitalism and communal neo-fascism. While the word capitalism hasn't completely lost its sheen yet, using the word fascism often causes offence. So we must ask ourselves, are we using the word loosely? Are we exaggerating our situation, does what we are experiencing on a daily basis qualify as fascism?

When a government more or less openly supports a pogrom against members of a minority community in which more than two thousand people are brutally killed, is it fascism? When women of that community are publicly raped and burned alive, is it fascism? When authorities collude to see to it that nobody is punished for these crimes, is it fascism? When one hundred and fifty thousand people are driven from their homes, ghettoized, and economically and socially boycotted, is it fascism? When the cultural guild that runs hate camps across the country commands the respect and admiration of the prime minister, the home minister, the law minister, the disinvestment minister, is it fascism? When painters, writers, scholars and film-makers who protest are abused, threatened and have their work burned, banned and destroyed, is it fascism?[28] When a government issues an edict requiring the arbitrary alteration of school history textbooks, is it fascism? When mobs attack and burn archives of ancient historical documents, when every minor politician masquerades as a professional medieval historian and archaeologist, when painstaking scholarship is rubbished using baseless populist assertion, is it fascism?[29] When murder, rape, arson and mob justice are condoned by the party in power and its stable of stock intellectuals as an appropriate response to a real or perceived historical wrong—committed centuries ago—is it fascism? When the middle class and the well heeled pause a moment, tut tut, and then go on with their lives, is it fascism? When the prime minister who presides over all of this is hailed as a statesman and visionary, are we not laying the foundations for full-blown fascism?

That the history of oppressed and vanquished people remains for the large part unchronicled is a truism that does not apply only to Savarna Hindus. If the politics of avenging historical wrongs is our chosen path, then surely the Dalits and Adivasis of India have the right to murder, arson and wanton destruction?

In Russia, they say the past is unpredictable. In India, from our recent experience with school history textbooks, we know how true that is. Now all 'pseudo-secularists' have been reduced to hoping that archaeologists digging under the Babri Masjid wouldn't find the ruins of a Ram temple. But even if it were true that there is a Hindu temple under every mosque in India, what was under the temple? Perhaps another Hindu temple to another god. Perhaps a Buddhist stupa. Most likely an Adivasi shrine. History didn't begin with Savarna Hinduism, did it? How deep shall we dig? How much should we overturn? And why is it that while Muslims—who are socially, culturally and economically an unalienable part of India—are called outsiders and invaders and are cruelly targeted, the government is busy signing corporate deals and contracts for development aid with a government that colonized us for centuries? Between 1876 and 1902, millions of Indians died of starvation while the British government continued to export food and raw materials to England. Historical records put the figure at 12.2 to 29.3 million people.[30] That should figure somewhere in the politics of revenge, should it not? Or is vengeance only fun when its victims are vulnerable and easy to target?

Successful fascism takes hard work. And so does Creating a Good Investment Climate. Do the two work well together? Historically, corporations have not been shy of fascists. Corporations like Siemens, I.G. Farben, Bayer, IBM and Ford did business with the Nazis.[31] We have the more recent example of our own Confederation of Indian Industry (CII) abasing itself to the Gujarat government after the pogrom in 2002.[32] As long as our markets are open, a little home-grown fascism won't come in the way of a good business deal.

It's interesting that just around the time Manmohan Singh, then the finance minister, was preparing India's markets for neo-liberalism, L.K. Advani was making his first Rath Yatra, fuelling communal passion and preparing us for neo-fascism.[33] In December 1992, rampaging mobs destroyed the Babri Masjid. In 1993, the Congress government of Maharashtra signed a power purchase agreement with Enron. It was the first private power project in India. The Enron contract, disastrous as it has turned out, kick-started the era of privatization in India.[34] Now, as the Congress whines from the sidelines, the Bharatiya Janata Party (BJP) has wrested the baton from its hands. The government is conducting an extraordinary dual orchestra. While one arm is busy selling off the nation's assets in chunks, the other, to divert attention, is arranging a baying, howling, deranged chorus of cultural nationalism. The inexorable ruthlessness of one process feeds directly into the insanity of the other.

Economically, too, the dual orchestra is a viable model. Part of the enormous profits generated by the process of indiscriminate privatization (and the accruals of 'India Shining') goes into financing Hindutva's vast army—the RSS, the VHP, the Bajrang Dal and the myriad other charities and trusts that run schools, hospitals and social services. Between them they have tens of thousands of shakhas across the country. The hatred they preach, combined with the unmanageable frustration generated by the relentless impoverishment and dispossession of the corporate globalization project, fuels the violence of poor on poor—the perfect smoke screen to keep the structures of power intact and unchallenged.

However, directing people's frustrations into violence is not always enough. In order to Create a Good Investment Climate, the state often needs to intervene directly. In recent years, the police has repeatedly opened fire on unarmed people, mostly Adivasis, at peaceful demonstrations. In Nagarnar, Jharkhand; in Mehndi Kheda, Madhya Pradesh; in Umergaon, Gujarat; in Rayagada and Chilika, Orissa; in Muthanga, Kerala. People are killed for encroaching on forest land, as well as when they're trying to protect forest land from dams, mining operations, steel plants. The repression goes on and on. Jambudwip island, Bengal; Maikanj village, Orissa. In almost every instance of police firing, those who have been fired on are immediately called militants.[35]

~

When victims refuse to be victims, they are called terrorists and are dealt with as such. POTA is the broad-spectrum antibiotic for the disease of dissent. There are other, more specific steps that are being taken—court judgments that in effect curtail free speech, the right to strike, the right to life and livelihood.

This year, one hundred and eighty-one countries voted in the United Nations for increased protection of human rights in the era of the War on Terror. Even the United States voted in favour of the resolution. India abstained.[36] The stage is being set for a full-scale assault on human rights.

So how can ordinary people counter the assault of an increasingly violent state?

The space for nonviolent civil disobedience has atrophied. After struggling for several years, several nonviolent people's resistance movements have come up against a wall and feel, quite rightly, they have to now change direction. Views about what that direction should be are deeply polarized. There are some who believe that an armed struggle is the only avenue left. Leaving aside Kashmir and the northeast, huge swathes of territory, whole districts in Jharkhand, Bihar, Chhattisgarh, Orissa and Madhya Pradesh are controlled by those who hold that view.[37] Others are increasingly beginning to feel they must participate in electoral politics—enter the system, negotiate from within. (Similar, is it not, to the choices people face in Kashmir?) The thing to remember is that while their methods differ radically, both sides share the belief that, to put it crudely, Enough is Enough. *Ya Basta.*

There is no debate taking place in India that is more crucial than this one. Its outcome will, for better or for worse, change the quality of life in this country. For everyone. Rich, poor, rural, urban.

Armed struggle provokes a massive escalation of violence from the state. We have seen the morass it has led to in Kashmir and across the northeast. So then, should we do what our prime minister suggests we do? Renounce dissent and enter the fray of electoral politics? Join the road show? Participate in the shrill exchange of meaningless insults which serve only to hide what is otherwise an almost absolute consensus? Let's not forget that on every major issue—nuclear bombs, big dams, the Babri Masjid controversy and privatization—the Congress sowed the seeds and the BJP swept in to reap the hideous harvest.

This does not mean that the Parliament is of no consequence and elections should be ignored. Of course there is a difference between an overtly communal party with fascist leanings and an opportunistically communal party. Of course there is a difference between a politics that openly, proudly preaches hatred and a politics that slyly pits people against each other.

But the legacy of one has led us to the horror of the other. Between them, they have eroded any real choice that parliamentary democracy is supposed to provide. The frenzy, the fairground atmosphere created around elections, takes centre stage in the media because everybody is secure in the knowledge that regardless of who wins, the status quo will essentially remain unchallenged. (After the impassioned speeches in Parliament, repealing POTA doesn't seem to be a priority in any party's election campaign. They all know they need it, in one form or another.)[38] Whatever they say during elections or when they're in the opposition, no state or national government, and no political party—right, left, centre or sideways—has managed to stay the hand of neo-liberalism. There will be no radical change from 'within'.

Personally, I don't believe that entering the electoral fray is a path to alternative politics. Not because of that middle-class squeamishness—'politics is dirty' or 'all politicians are corrupt'—but because I believe that strategically battles must be waged from positions of strength, not weakness.

The targets of the dual assault of neo-liberalism and communal fascism are the poor and the minority communities. As neo-liberalism drives its wedge between the rich and the poor, between India Shining and India, it becomes increasingly absurd for any mainstream political party to pretend to represent the interests of both the rich and the poor, because the interests of one can only be represented at the *cost* of the other. My 'interests' as a wealthy Indian (were I to pursue them) would hardly coincide with the interests of a poor farmer in Andhra Pradesh.

A political party that represents the poor will be a poor party. A party with very meagre funds. Today it isn't possible to fight an election without funds. Putting a couple of well-known social activists into Parliament is interesting, but not really politically meaningful. Not a process worth channeling all our energies into. Individual charisma, personality politics, cannot effect radical change.

However, being poor is not the same as being weak. The strength of the poor is not indoors in office buildings and courtrooms. It's outdoors, in the fields, the mountains, the river valleys, the city streets and university campuses of this country. That's where negotiations must be held. That's where the battle must be waged.

Right now, those spaces have been ceded to the Hindu Right. Whatever anyone might think of their politics, it cannot be denied that they're out there, working extremely hard. As the state abrogates its responsibilities and withdraws funds from health, education and essential public services, the foot soldiers of the Sangh Parivar have moved in. Alongside their tens of thousands of shakhas disseminating deadly propaganda, they run schools, hospitals, clinics, ambulance services, disaster management cells. They understand powerlessness. They also understand that people, and particularly powerless people, have needs and desires that are not only practical, humdrum day-to-day needs, but emotional, spiritual, recreational. They have fashioned a hideous crucible into which the anger, the frustration, the indignity of daily life—and dreams of a different future—can be decanted and directed to deadly purpose. Meanwhile, the traditional, mainstream Left still dreams of 'seizing power', but remains strangely unbending, unwilling to address the times. It has laid siege to itself and retreated into an inaccessible intellectual space where ancient arguments are proffered in an archaic language that few can understand.

The only ones who present some semblance of a challenge to the onslaught of the Sangh Parivar are the grassroots resistance movements scattered across the country, fighting the dispossession and violation of fundamental rights caused by our current model of 'development'. Most of these movements are isolated and, despite the relentless accusation that they are 'foreign funded agents', work with almost no money or resources at all. They're magnificent firefighters. They have their backs to the wall. But they have their ears to the ground, and they are in touch with grim reality. If they got together, if they were supported and strengthened, they could grow into a force to reckon with. Their battle, when it is fought, will have to be an idealistic one—not a rigidly ideological one.

At a time when opportunism is everything, when hope seems lost, when everything boils down to a cynical business deal, we must find the courage to dream. To reclaim romance. The romance of believing in justice, in freedom, and in dignity. For everybody. We have to make common cause, and to do this we need to understand how this big old machine works—who it works for and who it works against. Who pays, who profits.

Many nonviolent resistance movements fighting isolated, single-issue battles across the country have realized that their kind of special interest politics, which had its time and place, is no longer enough. That they feel cornered and ineffectual is not good enough reason to abandon nonviolent resistance as a strategy. It is, however, good enough reason to do some serious introspection. We need vision. We need to make sure that those of us who say we want to reclaim democracy are egalitarian and democratic in our own methods of functioning. If our struggle is to be an idealistic one, we cannot really make caveats for the internal injustices that we perpetrate on one another, on women, on children. For example, those fighting communalism cannot turn a blind eye to economic injustices. Those fighting dams or development projects cannot elide issues of communalism or caste politics in their spheres of influence—even at the cost of short-term success in their immediate campaign. If opportunism and expediency come at the cost of our beliefs, then there is nothing to separate us from mainstream politicians. If it is justice that we want, it must be justice and equal rights for all—not only for special interest groups with special interest prejudices. That is non-negotiable. We have allowed nonviolent resistance to atrophy into feel-good political theatre, which at its most successful is a photo opportunity for the media, and at its least successful is simply ignored.

We need to look up and urgently discuss strategies of resistance, wage real battles, and inflict real damage. We must remember that the Dandi March was not just fine political theatre. It was a strike at the economic underpinning of the British Empire.

We need to redefine the meaning of politics. The 'NGO-ization' of civil society initiatives is taking us in exactly the opposite direction.[39] It's depoliticizing us. Making us dependent on aid and handouts. We need to re-imagine the meaning of civil disobedience.

Perhaps we need an elected shadow Parliament *outside* the Lok Sabha, without whose support and affirmation Parliament cannot easily function. A shadow Parliament that keeps up an underground drumbeat, that shares intelligence and information (all of which is increasingly unavailable in the mainstream media). Fearlessly, but nonviolently, we must disable the working parts of this machine that is consuming us.

We're running out of time. Even as we speak, the circle of violence is closing in. Either way, change will come. It could be bloody, or it could be beautiful. It depends on us.

'AND HIS LIFE SHOULD BECOME EXTINCT'

THE VERY STRANGE STORY OF THE ATTACK ON THE INDIAN PARLIAMENT

This essay first appeared in Outlook *magazine (India) on 30 October 2006.*

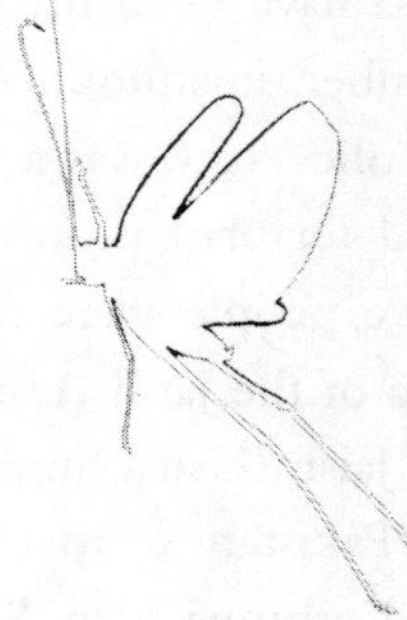

WE KNOW this much: On 13 December 2001, the Indian Parliament was in its winter session. (The National Democratic Alliance government was under attack for yet another corruption scandal.) At 11:30 in the morning, five armed men in a white Ambassador car fitted out with an Improvised Explosive Device drove through the gates of Parliament House in New Delhi. When they were challenged, they jumped out of the car and opened fire. In the gun battle that followed, all the attackers were killed. Eight security personnel and a gardener were killed, too. The dead terrorists, the police said, had enough explosives to blow up the Parliament building, and enough ammunition to take on a whole battalion of soldiers.[1] Unlike most terrorists, these five left behind a thick trail of evidence—weapons, mobile phones, phone numbers, ID cards, photographs, packets of dry fruit and even a love letter.[2]

Not surprisingly, Prime Minister A.B. Vajpayee seized the opportunity to compare the assault to the September 11 attacks in the United States that had happened only three months previously.

On 14 December 2001, the day after the attack on Parliament, the Special Cell of the Delhi police claimed it had tracked down several people suspected to have been involved in the conspiracy. A day later, on 15 December, it announced that it had 'cracked the case': the attack, the police said, was a joint operation carried out by two Pakistan-based terrorist groups, Lashkar-e-Toiba and Jaish-e-Mohammad. Twelve people were named as being part of the conspiracy. Ghazi Baba of the Jaish (Usual Suspect I); Maulana Masood Azhar, also of the Jaish (Usual Suspect II); Tariq Ahmed (a 'Pakistani'); five deceased 'Pakistani terrorists' (we still don't know who they are). And three Kashmiri men, S.A.R. Geelani, Shaukat Hussain Guru and Mohammad Afzal; and Shaukat's wife, Afsan Guru. These were the only four to be arrested.[3]

In the tense days that followed, Parliament was adjourned. On 21 December, India recalled its high commissioner from Pakistan, suspended air, rail and bus communications, and banned over-flights. It put into motion a massive mobilization of its war machinery, and moved more than half a million troops to the Pakistan border. Foreign embassies evacuated their staff, and tourists travelling to India were issued cautionary travel advisories. The world watched with bated breath as the subcontinent was taken to the brink of nuclear war.[4] All this cost India an estimated one hundred billion rupees ($2 billion) of public money. A few hundred soldiers died just in the panicky process of mobilization.

Almost three-and-a-half years later, on 4 August 2005, the Supreme Court delivered its final judgment in the case. It endorsed the view that the Parliament attack be looked on as an act of war. It said, 'The attempted attack on Parliament is an undoubted invasion of the sovereign attribute of the State including the government of India which is its alter ego . . . the deceased terrorists were roused and impelled to action by a strong anti-Indian feeling as the writing on the fake home ministry sticker found on the car (Ex PW1/8) reveals.' It went on to say 'the modus operandi adopted by the hardcore "fidayeens" are all demonstrative of launching a war against the Government of India.'

The text on the fake home ministry sticker read as follows:

> 'INDIA IS A VERY BAD COUNTRY AND WE HATE INDIA WE WANT TO DESTROY INDIA AND WITH THE GRACE OF GOD WE WILL DO IT GOD IS WITH US AND WE WILL TRY OUR BEST. THIS EDIET WAJPAI AND ADVANI WE WILL KILL THEM. THEY HAVE KILLED MANY INNOCENT PEOPLE AND THEY ARE VERY BAD PERSONS THERE BROTHER BUSH IS ALSO A VERY BAD PERSON HE WILL BE NEXT TARGET HE IS ALSO THE KILLER OF INNOCENT PEOPLE HE HAVE TO DIE AND WE WILL DO IT.'[5]

This subtly worded sticker-manifesto was displayed on the windscreen of the car bomb as it drove into Parliament. (Given the amount of text, it's a wonder the driver could see anything at all. Maybe that's why he collided with the vice president's cavalcade?)

The police charge sheet was filed in a special fast-track Trial Court designated for cases under the Prevention of Terrorism Act (POTA). On 16 December 2002, the Trial Court sentenced Geelani, Shaukat and Afzal to death. Afsan Guru was sentenced to five years of rigorous imprisonment. A year later the high court acquitted Geelani and Afsan, but it upheld Shaukat's and Afzal's death sentence. Eventually, the Supreme Court too upheld the acquittals, and reduced Shaukat's punishment to ten years of rigorous imprisonment. However it not just confirmed, but enhanced Mohammad Afzal's sentence. He has been given three life sentences and a double death sentence.

In its 4 August 2005 judgment, the Supreme Court clearly says that there was no evidence that Mohammad Afzal belonged to any terrorist group or organization. But it also says, 'As is the case with most of the conspiracies, there is and could be no direct evidence of the agreement amounting to criminal conspiracy. However, the circumstances, cumulatively weighed, would unerringly point to the collaboration of the accused Afzal with the slain "fidayeen" terrorists.'

So no direct evidence, but yes, circumstantial evidence.

A controversial paragraph in the judgment goes on to say, 'The incident, which resulted in heavy casualties, had shaken the entire nation, and the collective conscience of the society will only be satisfied if capital punishment is awarded to the offender.'[6]

To invoke the 'collective conscience of the society' to validate ritual murder, which is what the death penalty is, skates precariously close to valorizing lynch law. It's chilling to think that this has been laid upon us not by predatory politicians or sensation-seeking journalists (though they too have done that), but as an edict from the highest court in the land.

Spelling out the reasons for awarding Afzal the death penalty, the judgment goes on to say, 'The appellant, who is a surrendered militant and who was bent on repeating the acts of treason against the nation, is a menace to the society and his life should become extinct.'

This sentence combines flawed logic with absolute ignorance of what it means to be a 'surrendered militant' in Kashmir today.

So: Should Mohammad Afzal's life become extinct?

A small, but influential minority of intellectuals, activists, editors, lawyers and public figures have objected to the death sentence as a matter of moral principle. They also argue that there is no empirical evidence to suggest that the death sentence works as a deterrent to terrorists. (How can it, when, in this age of fidayeen and suicide bombers, death seems to be the main attraction?)

If opinion polls, letters-to-the-editor and the reactions of live audiences in TV studios are a correct gauge of public opinion in India, then the lynch mob is expanding by the hour. It looks as though an overwhelming majority of Indian citizens would like to see Mohammad Afzal hanged every day, weekends included, for the next few years. L.K. Advani, leader of the opposition, displaying an unseemly sense of urgency, wants him to be hanged as soon as possible, without a moment's delay.[7]

Meanwhile in Kashmir, public opinion is equally overwhelming. Huge angry protests make it increasingly obvious that if Afzal is hanged, the consequences will be political. Some protest what they see as a miscarriage of justice, but even as they protest, they do not expect justice from Indian courts. They have lived through too much brutality to believe in courts, affidavits and justice any more. Others would like to see Mohammad Afzal march to the gallows like Maqbool Butt, a proud martyr to the cause of Kashmir's freedom struggle.[8] On the whole, most Kashmiris see Mohammad Afzal as a sort of prisoner-of-war being tried in the courts of an occupying power. (Which it undoubtedly is.) Naturally, political parties, in India as well as in Kashmir, have sniffed the breeze and are cynically closing in for the kill.

Sadly, in the midst of the frenzy, Afzal seems to have forfeited the right to be an individual, a real person any more. He's become a vehicle for everybody's fantasies—nationalists, separatists and anti-capital punishment activists. He has become India's great villain and Kashmir's great hero—proving only that whatever our pundits, policy-makers and peace gurus say, all these years later, the war in Kashmir has by no means ended.

In a situation as fraught and politicized as this, it's tempting to believe that the time to intervene has come and gone. After all, the judicial process lasted forty months, and the Supreme Court has examined the evidence before it. It has convicted two of the accused and acquitted the other two. Surely this in itself is proof of judicial objectivity? What more remains to be said? There's another way of looking at it. Isn't it odd that the prosecution's case, proved to be so egregiously wrong in one half, has been so gloriously vindicated in the other?

~

The story of Mohammad Afzal is fascinating precisely because he is *not* Maqbool Butt. Yet his story too is inextricably entwined with the story of the Kashmir Valley. It's a story whose coordinates range far beyond the confines of courtrooms and the limited imagination of people who live in the secure heart of a self-declared 'superpower'. Mohammad Afzal's story has its origins in a war zone whose laws are beyond the pale of the fine arguments and delicate sensibilities of normal jurisprudence.

For all these reasons it is critical that we consider carefully the strange, sad and utterly sinister story of the 13 December Parliament attack. It tells us a great deal about the way the world's largest 'democracy' really works. It connects the biggest things to the smallest. It traces the pathways that connect what happens in the shadowy grottoes of our police stations to what goes on in the cold, snowy streets of Paradise Valley; from there to the impersonal malign furies that bring nations to the brink of nuclear war. It raises specific questions that deserve specific—not ideological or rhetorical—answers.

On 4 October this year, I was one among a very small group of people who had gathered at Jantar Mantar in New Delhi to protest against Mohammad Afzal's death sentence. I was there because I believe Mohammad Afzal is only a pawn in a very sinister game. He's not the Dragon he's being made out to be, he's only the Dragon's footprint. And if the footprint is made to 'become extinct', we'll never know who the Dragon was. Is.

Not surprisingly, that afternoon there were more journalists and TV crews than there were protesters. Most of the attention was on Ghalib, Afzal's angelic looking little son. Kind-hearted people, not sure of what to do with a young boy whose father was going to the gallows, were plying him with ice-creams and cold drinks. As I looked around at the people gathered there, I noted a sad little fact. The convener of the protest, the small, stocky man who was nervously introducing the speakers and making the announcements, was S.A.R. Geelani, a young lecturer in Arabic literature at Delhi University. Accused Number Three in the Parliament attack case. He was arrested on 14 December 2001, a day after the attack, by the Special Cell of the Delhi police. Though Geelani was brutally tortured in custody, though his family—his wife, young children and brother—were illegally detained, he refused to confess to a crime he hadn't committed. Of course you wouldn't know this if you read newspapers in the days following his arrest. They carried detailed descriptions of an entirely imaginary, non-existent confession. The Delhi police portrayed Geelani as the evil mastermind of the Indian end of the conspiracy. Its scriptwriters orchestrated a hateful propaganda campaign against him, which was eagerly amplified and embellished by a hyper-nationalistic, thrill-seeking media. The police knew perfectly well that in criminal trials, judges are not supposed to take cognizance of media reports. So they knew that their entirely cold-blooded fabrication of a profile for these 'terrorists' would mould public opinion, and create a climate for the trial. But it would not come in for any legal scrutiny.

Here are some of the malicious, outright lies that appeared in the mainstream press:

'Case Cracked: Jaish Behind Attack', Neeta Sharma and Arun Joshi, *The Hindustan Times*, 16 December 2001:

> In Delhi, the Special Cell detectives detained a Lecturer in Arabic, who teaches at Zakir Hussain College (Evening) . . . after it was established that he had received a call made by militants on his mobile phone.

'DU Lecturer was Terror Plan Hub', *The Times of India*, 17 December 2001:

> The attack on Parliament on December 13 was a joint operation of the Jaish-e-Mohammad (JeM) and Lashkar-e-Toiba (LeT) terrorist groups in which a Delhi University lecturer, Syed A.R. Gilani [sic], was one of the key facilitators in Delhi, Police Commissioner Ajai Raj Sharma said on Sunday.

'Professor Guided the "Fidayeen",' Devesh K. Pandey, *The Hindu*, 17 December 2001:

> During interrogation Geelani disclosed that he was in the know of the conspiracy since the day the "fidayeen" attack was planned.

'Don Lectured on Terror in Free Time', Sutirtho Patranobis, *The Hindustan Times*, 17 December 2001:

> Investigations have revealed that by evening he was at the college teaching Arabic literature. In his free time, behind closed doors, either at his house or at Shaukat Hussain's, another suspect to be arrested, he took and gave lessons on terrorism.

'Professor's Proceeds', *The Hindustan Times*, 17 December 2001:

> Geelani recently purchased a house for 22 lakhs [2,200,000 rupees ($44,300)] in West Delhi. Delhi Police are investigating how he came upon such a windfall.

'Aligarh se England tak chaatron mein aatankwaad ke beej bo raha tha Geelani' (From Aligarh to England Geelani Sowed the Seeds of Terrorism), Sujit Thakur, *Rashtriya Sahara*, December 18, 2001:

> According to sources and information collected by investigation agencies, Geelani has made a statement to the police that he was an agent of Jaish-e-Mohammad for a long time . . . It was because of Geelani's articulation, style of working and sound planning that in 2000 Jaish-e-Mohammad gave him the responsibility of spreading intellectual terrorism. [Translation mine.]

'Terror suspect frequent visitor to Pak[istan] Mission' Swati Chaturvedi, *The Hindustan Times*, December 21, 2001:

> During interrogation, Geelani has admitted that he had made frequent calls to Pakistan and was in touch with militants belonging to Jaish-e-Mohammad . . . Geelani said that he had been provided with funds by some members of the Jaish and told to buy two flats that could be used in militant operations.

'Person of the Week', *Sunday Times of India*, 23 December 2001:

> A cellphone proved his undoing. Delhi University's Syed A.R. Geelani was the first to be arrested in the December 13 case—a shocking reminder that the roots of terrorism go far and deep.

Zee TV trumped them all. It produced a film called *December 13th*, a 'docudrama' that claimed to be the 'truth based on the police charge-sheet.' (A contradiction in terms, wouldn't you say?) The film was privately screened for Prime Minister A.B. Vajpayee and Home Minister L.K. Advani. Both men applauded the film. Their approbation was widely reported by the media.[9]

The Supreme Court dismissed an appeal to stay the broadcast of the film on the grounds that judges are not influenced by the media.[10] (Would the Supreme Court concede that even if judges are beyond being influenced by media reports, the 'collective conscience of the society' might not be?) *December 13th* was broadcast on Zee TV's national network a few days before the fast-track trial court sentenced Geelani, Afzal and Shaukat to death. Geelani eventually spent eighteen months in jail, many of them in solitary confinement, on death row.

He was released when the High Court acquitted him and Afsan Guru. (Afsan, who was pregnant when she was arrested, had her baby in prison. Her experience broke her. She now suffers from a serious psychiatric condition.) The Supreme Court upheld the acquittal. It found absolutely no evidence to link Geelani with the Parliament attack or with any terrorist organization. *Not a single newspaper or journalist or TV channel has seen fit to apologize to S.A.R. Geelani for their lies.* But his troubles didn't end there. His acquittal left the Special Cell with a plot, but no 'mastermind'. This, as we shall see, becomes something of a problem.

More importantly, Geelani was a free man now—free to meet the press, talk to lawyers, clear his name. On the evening of 8 February 2005, during the course of the final hearings at the Supreme Court, Geelani was making his way to his lawyer's house. A mysterious gunman appeared from the shadows and fired five bullets into his body.[11] Miraculously, he survived. It was an unbelievable new twist to the story. Clearly somebody was worried about what he knew, what he would say. One would imagine that the police would give this investigation top priority, hoping it would throw up some vital new leads into the Parliament attack case. Instead, the Special Cell treated Geelani as though he was the prime suspect in his own assassination. They confiscated his computer and took away his car. Hundreds of activists gathered outside the hospital and called for an inquiry into the assassination attempt, which would include an investigation into the Special Cell itself. (Of course that never happened. More than a year has passed, nobody shows any interest in pursuing the matter. Odd.)

So here he was now, S.A.R. Geelani, having survived this terrible ordeal, standing up in public at Jantar Mantar, saying that Mohammad Afzal didn't deserve a death sentence. How much easier it would be for him to keep his head down, stay at home. I was profoundly moved, humbled, by this quiet display of courage.

Across the line from S.A.R. Geelani, in the jostling crowd of journalists and photographers, trying his best to look inconspicuous in a lemon T-shirt and gabardine pants, holding a little tape-recorder, was another Gilani. Iftikhar Gilani. He had been in prison too. He was arrested and taken into police custody on 9 June 2002. At the time he was a reporter for the Jammu-based *Kashmir Times*. He was charged under the Official Secrets Act.[12] His 'crime' was that he possessed obsolete information on Indian troop deployment in 'Indian-held Kashmir.' (This 'information', it turns out, was a published monograph by a Pakistani research institute, and was freely available on the Internet for anybody who wished to download it.) Iftikhar Gilani's computer was seized. IB officials tampered with his hard drive, meddled with the downloaded file, changed the words 'Indian-held Kashmir' to 'Jammu and Kashmir' to make it sound like an Indian document, and added the words 'Only for Reference. Strictly Not For Circulation', to make it seem like a secret document smuggled out of the home ministry. The directorate general of military intelligence—though it had been given a photocopy of the monograph—ignored repeated appeals from Iftikhar Gilani's counsel, kept quiet, and refused to clarify the matter for a whole six months.

Once again the malicious lies put out by the Special Cell were obediently reproduced in the newspapers. Here are a few of the lies they told:

> 'Iftikhar Gilani, 35-year-old son-in-law of Hurriyat hardliner Syed Ali Shah Geelani, is believed to have admitted in a city court that he was an agent of Pakistan's spy agency.'—Neeta Sharma, *The Hindustan Times,* June 11, 2002
>
> 'Iftikhar Gilani was the pin-point man of Syed Salahuddin of Hizbul Mujahideen. Investigations have revealed that Iftikhar used to pass information to Salahuddin about the moves of Indian security agencies. He had camouflaged his real motives behind his journalist's facade so well that it took

years to unmask him, well-placed sources said.'—Pramod Kumar Singh, *The Pioneer,* June 2002

'Geelani ke damaad ke ghar aaykar chhaapon mein behisaab sampati wa samwaidansheil dastaweiz baramad' (Unaccounted for wealth and sensitive documents recovered from the house of Geelani's son-in-law during income tax raids).—*Hindustan*, June 10, 2002

Never mind that the police charge sheet recorded a recovery of only Rs 3,450 ($69) from his house. Meanwhile, other media reports said that he had a three-bedroom flat, an undisclosed income of Rs 2,200,000 ($44,300), had evaded income tax of Rs 7,900,000 ($159,000), that he and his wife were absconding to evade arrest.

But arrested he was. In jail, Iftikhar Gilani was beaten, abjectly humiliated. In his book *My Days In Prison* he tells of how, among other things, he was made to clean the toilet with his shirt and then wear the same shirt for days.[13] After several months of court arguments and lobbying by his colleagues, when it became obvious that if the case against him continued it would lead to serious embarrassment, he was released.[14]

Here he was now. A free man, a reporter come to Jantar Mantar to cover a story. It occurred to me that S.A.R. Geelani, Iftikhar Gilani and Mohammad Afzal would have been in Tihar jail at the same time. (Along with scores of other less well known Kashmiris whose stories we may never learn.)

It can and will be argued that the cases of both S.A.R. Geelani and Iftikhar Gilani serve only to demonstrate the objectivity of the Indian judicial system and its capacity for self-correction, they do not discredit it. That's only partly true. Both Iftikhar Gilani and S.A.R. Geelani are fortunate to be Delhi-based Kashmiris with a community of articulate, middle-class peers; journalists and university teachers, who knew them well and rallied around them in their time of need. S.A.R. Geelani's lawyer Nandita Haksar put together an All India Defense Committee for S.A.R. Geelani (of which I was a member).[15] There was a coordinated campaign by activists, lawyers and journalists to rally behind Geelani. Well-known lawyers Ram Jethmalani, K.G. Kannabiran and Vrinda Grover represented him. They showed up the case for what it was—a pack of absurd assumptions, suppositions and outright lies, bolstered by fabricated evidence. So *of course* judicial objectivity exists. But it's a shy beast that lives somewhere deep in the labyrinth of our legal system. It shows itself rarely. It takes whole teams of top lawyers to coax it out of its lair and make it come out and play. It's what in newspaper-speak would be called a Herculean task. Mohammad Afzal did not have Hercules on his side.

~

For five months, from the time he was arrested to the day the police charge sheet was filed, Mohammad Afzal, lodged in a high-security prison, had no legal defense, no legal advice. No top lawyers, no defence committee (in India or Kashmir), and no campaign. Of all the four accused, he was the most vulnerable. His case was far more complicated than Geelani's. Significantly, during much of this time, Afzal's younger brother Hilal was illegally detained by the Special Operations Group (SOG) in Kashmir. He was released after the charge sheet was filed. (This is a piece of the puzzle that will only fall into place as the story unfolds.)

In a serious lapse of procedure, on 20 December 2001, the investigating officer, Assistant Commissioner of Police (ACP) Rajbir Singh (affectionately known as Delhi's 'encounter specialist' for the number of 'terrorists' he has killed in 'encounters'), called a press conference at the Special Cell.[16] Mohammad Afzal was made to 'confess' before the media. Deputy Commissioner of Police (DCP) Ashok Chand told the press that Afzal had already confessed to the police. This turned out to be untrue. Afzal's formal confession to the police took place only the next day (after which he continued to remain in police custody—and vulnerable to torture—another serious procedural lapse). In his media 'confession' Afzal incriminated himself in the Parliament attack completely.[17]

During the course of this 'media confession' a curious thing happened. In an answer to a direct question, Afzal clearly said that Geelani had nothing to do with the attack and was completely innocent. At this point, ACP Rajbir Singh shouted at him and forced him to shut up, and requested the media not to carry this part of Afzal's 'confession'. *And they obeyed!* The story came out only three months later when the television channel Aaj Tak re-broadcast the 'confession' in a program called *Hamle Ke Sau Din* (*Hundred Days of the Attack*) and somehow kept this part in. But in the eyes of the general public—who know little about the law and criminal procedure—Afzal's public 'confession' only confirmed his guilt. The verdict of the 'collective conscience of the society' would not have been hard to second guess.

The day after this 'media' confession, Afzal's 'official' confession was extracted from him. The flawlessly structured, perfectly fluent narrative dictated in articulate English to DCP Ashok Chand (in the DCP's words, 'he kept on narrating and I kept on writing') was delivered in a sealed envelope to a judicial magistrate. In this confession, Afzal, now the sheet-anchor of the prosecution's case, weaves a masterful tale that connected Ghazi Baba, Maulana Masood Azhar, a man called Tariq and the five dead terrorists; their equipment, arms and ammunition, home ministry passes, a laptop and fake ID cards; detailed lists of exactly how many kilos of what chemical he bought from where, the exact ratio in which they were mixed to make explosives; and the exact times at which he made and received calls on which mobile number. (For some reason, by then Afzal had also changed his mind about Geelani and implicated him completely in the conspiracy.)

Each point of the 'confession' corresponded perfectly with the evidence that the police had already gathered. In other words, Afzal's confessional statement slipped perfectly into the version that the police had already offered the press days ago, like Cinderella's foot into the glass slipper. (If it were a film, you could say it was a screenplay, which came with its own box of props. Actually, as we know now, it was made into a film. Zee TV owes Afzal some royalty payments.)

Eventually, both the high court and the Supreme Court set aside Afzal's confession citing 'lapses and violations of procedural safeguards'. But Afzal's confession somehow survives, the phantom keystone in the prosecution's case. And before it was technically and legally set aside, the confessional document had already served a major extra-legal purpose: On 21 December 2001, when the government of India launched its war effort against Pakistan it said it had 'clear and incontrovertible proof' of Pakistan's involvement.[18] Afzal's confession was the only 'proof' of Pakistan's involvement that the government had! Afzal's confession. And the sticker-manifesto. Think about it. On the basis of this illegal confession extracted under torture, hundreds of thousands of soldiers were moved to the Pakistan border at huge cost to the public exchequer, and the subcontinent devolved into a game of nuclear brinkmanship in which the whole world was held hostage.

Big Whispered Question: Could it have been the other way around? Did the confession precipitate the war, or did the need for a war precipitate the need for the confession?

Later, when Afzal's confession was set aside by the higher courts, all talk of Jaish-e-Mohammad and Lashkar-e-Toiba ceased. The only other link to Pakistan was the identity of the five dead fidayeen. Mohammad Afzal, still in police custody, identified them as Mohammed, Rana, Raja, Hamza and Haider. The home minister said they 'looked like Pakistanis,' the police said they were Pakistanis, the trial court judge said they were Pakistanis.[19] And there the matter rests. (Had we been told that their names were Happy, Bouncy, Lucky, Jolly and Kidingamani from Scandinavia, we would have had to accept that too).

We still don't know who they really are, or where they're from. Is anyone curious? Doesn't look like it. The high court said the 'identity of the five deceased thus stands established. Even otherwise it makes no difference. What is relevant is the association of the accused with the said five persons and not their names.'

In his Statement of the Accused (which, unlike the confession, is made in court and not police custody) Afzal says:'I had not identified any terrorist. Police told me the names of terrorists and forced me to identify them.'[20] But by then it was too late for him. On the first day of the trial, the lawyer appointed by the trial court judge *agreed to accept Afzal's identification of the bodies and the post-mortem reports as undisputed evidence without formal proof!* This baffling move was to have serious consequences for Afzal. To quote from the Supreme Court judgment, 'The *first circumstance* against the accused Afzal is that Afzal knew who the deceased terrorists were. He identified the dead bodies of the deceased terrorists. On this aspect the evidence remains unshattered.'

Of course it's possible that the dead terrorists were foreign militants. But it is just as possible that they were not. Killing people and falsely identifying them as 'foreign terrorists', or falsely identifying dead people as 'foreign terrorists', or falsely identifying living people as terrorists, is not uncommon among the police or security forces either in Kashmir or even on the streets of Delhi.[21]

The best known among the many well-documented cases in Kashmir, one that went on to become an international scandal, is the killing that took place after the Chattisinghpora massacre. On the night of 20 April 2000, just before the US president Bill Clinton arrived in New Delhi, thirty-five Sikhs were killed in the village of Chattisinghpora by 'unidentified gunmen' wearing Indian army uniforms.[22] (In Kashmir many people suspected that Indian security forces were behind the massacre.) Five days later the SOG and the Rashtriya Rifles, a counter-insurgency unit of the army, killed five people in a joint operation outside a village called Pathribal.[23] The next morning they announced that the men were the Pakistan-based foreign militants who had killed the Sikhs in Chattisinghpora. The bodies were found burned and disfigured. Under their (unburned) army uniforms, they were in ordinary civilian clothes. It turned out that they were all local people, rounded up from Anantnag district and brutally killed in cold blood.

There are others:

20 October 2003: The Srinagar newspaper *Al-safa* printed a picture of a 'Pakistani militant' who the Eighteenth Rashtriya Rifles claimed they had killed while he was trying to storm an

army camp. A baker in Kupwara, Wali Khan, saw the picture and recognized it as his son, Farooq Ahmed Khan, who had been picked up by soldiers in a Gypsy two months earlier. His body was finally exhumed more than a year later.[24]

20 April 2004: The Eighteenth Rashtriya Rifles posted in the Lolab valley claimed it had killed four foreign militants in a fierce encounter. It later turned out that all four were ordinary labourers from Jammu, hired by the army and taken to Kupwara. An anonymous letter tipped off the labourers' families who travelled to Kupwara and eventually had the bodies exhumed.[25]

9 November 2004: The army showcased forty-seven surrendered 'militants' to the press at Nagrota, Jammu, in the presence of the General Officer Commanding Sixteenth Corps of the Indian Army and the Director General of Police, Jammu and Kashmir. The Jammu and Kashmir police later found that twenty-seven of them were just unemployed men who had been given fake names and fake aliases and promised government jobs in return for playing their part in the charade.[26]

These are just a few quick examples to illustrate the fact that in the absence of any other evidence, the police's word is *just not good enough*.

~

The hearings in the fast-track trial court began in May 2002. Let's not forget the climate in which the trial took place. The frenzy over the 9/11 attacks was still in the air. The United States was gloating over its victory in Afghanistan. Gujarat was convulsed by communal frenzy. A few months previously, coach S-6 of the Sabarmati Express had been set on fire and fifty-eight Hindu pilgrims had been burned alive inside. As 'revenge', in an orchestrated pogrom, more than two thousand Muslims were publicly butchered and more than one hundred and fifty thousand driven from their homes.

For Afzal, everything that could go wrong went wrong. He was incarcerated in a high-security prison, with no access to the outside world, and no money to hire a lawyer professionally. Three weeks into the trial the lawyer appointed by the court asked to be discharged from the case because she had now been professionally hired to be on the team of lawyers for S.A.R. Geelani's defence. The court appointed her junior, a lawyer with very little experience, to represent Afzal. He did not once visit his client in jail to take instructions. He did not summon a single witness for Afzal's defense and barely cross-questioned any of the prosecution witnesses. Five days after he was appointed, on 8 July, Afzal asked the court for another lawyer and gave the court a list of lawyers whom he hoped the court might hire for him. Each of them refused. (Given the frenzy of propaganda in the media, it was hardly surprising. At a later stage of the trial, when senior advocate Ram Jethmalani agreed to represent Geelani, Shiv Sena mobs ransacked his Mumbai office.)[27] The judge expressed his inability to do anything about this, and gave Afzal the right to cross-examine witnesses. It's astonishing for the judge to expect a layperson to be able to cross-examine witnesses in a criminal trial. It's a virtually impossible task for someone who does not have a sophisticated understanding of criminal law, including new laws that had just been passed, like POTA, and the amendments to the Evidence Act and the Telegraph Act. Even experienced lawyers were having to work overtime to bring themselves up to date.

The case against Afzal was built up in the trial court on the strength of the testimonies of almost eighty prosecution witnesses: landlords, shopkeepers, technicians from cellphone companies, the police themselves. This was a crucial period of the trial, when the legal foundation of the case was being laid. It required meticulous, back-breaking legal work in which evidence needed to be amassed and put on record, witnesses for the defence summoned and testimonies from prosecution witnesses cross-questioned. Even if the verdict of the trial court went against the accused (trial courts are notoriously conservative), the evidence could then be worked on by lawyers in the higher courts. Through this absolutely critical period, Afzal went virtually undefended. It was at this stage that the bottom fell out of his case, and the noose tightened around his neck.

Even then, during the trial, the skeletons began to clatter out of the Special Cell's cupboard in an embarrassing heap. It became clear that the accumulation of lies, fabrications, forged documents and serious lapses in procedure began from the very first day of the investigation. While the Delhi High Court and Supreme Court judgements have pointed these things out, they have just wagged an admonitory finger at the police, or occasionally called it a 'disturbing feature', which is a disturbing feature in itself. At no point in the trial has the police been seriously reprimanded, leave alone penalized. In fact, almost every step of the way, the Special Cell displayed an egregious disregard for procedural norms. The shoddy callousness with which the investigations were carried out demonstrate a worrying belief that they wouldn't be 'found out', and if they were, it wouldn't matter very much. Their confidence does not seem to have been misplaced.

There is fudging in almost every part of the investigation.[28]

Consider the time and place of the arrests and seizures: The Delhi police said that Afzal and Shaukat were arrested in Srinagar, based on information given to them by Geelani following his arrest. The court records show that the message to look out for Shaukat and Afzal was flashed to the Srinagar police on 15 December at 5.45 a.m. But according to the Delhi police's records Geelani was only arrested in Delhi on 15 December at 10 a.m.—four hours *after* they had started looking for Afzal and Shaukat in Srinagar. They haven't been able to explain this discrepancy. The high court judgment puts it on record that the police version contains a 'material contradiction' and cannot be true. It goes down as a 'disturbing feature'. Why the Delhi police needed to lie remains unasked, and unanswered.

When the police arrest somebody, procedure requires them to have public witnesses for the arrest who sign an Arrest Memo and a Seizure Memo for what they may have 'seized' from those who have been arrested—goods, cash, documents, whatever. The police claim they arrested Afzal and Shaukat together on 15 December at 11 a.m. in Srinagar. They say they 'seized' the truck the two men were fleeing in (it was registered in the name of Shaukat's wife). They also say they seized a Nokia mobile phone, a laptop and one million rupees ($20,100) from Afzal. In his Statement of the Accused, Afzal says he was arrested at a bus stop in Srinagar and that no laptop, mobile phone or money was 'seized' from him.

Scandalously, the Arrest Memos for both Afzal and Shaukat have been signed in Delhi, by Bismillah, Geelani's younger brother, who was at the time being held in illegal confinement at the Lodhi Road Police Station. Meanwhile, the two witnesses who signed the Seizure Memo for the phone, the laptop and the one million rupees ($20,100) are both from the Jammu and Kashmir police. One of them is Head Constable Mohammed Akbar (Prosecution Witness 62) who, as we shall see later, is no stranger to Mohammad Afzal, and is not just any old policeman who happened to be passing by. Even by the Jammu and Kashmir police's own admission, they first located Afzal and Shaukat in Parimpura Fruit Mandi. For reasons they don't state, the police didn't arrest them there. They say they followed them to a less public place—where there were no public witnesses.

So here's another serious inconsistency in the prosecution's case. Of this the high court judgment says 'the time of arrest of accused persons has been seriously dented.' Shockingly, it is *at this contested time and place of arrest that the police claim to have recovered the most vital evidence that implicates Afzal in the conspiracy*: the mobile phone and the laptop. Once again, in the matter of the date and time of the arrests, and in the alleged seizure of the incriminating laptop and the one million rupees ($20,100), we have only the word of the police, against the word of a 'terrorist'.

The seizures continued: The seized laptop, the police said, contained the files that created the fake home ministry pass and the fake identity cards. It contained no other useful information. They claimed that Afzal was carrying it to Srinagar in order to return it to Ghazi Baba. The Investigating Officer, ACP Rajbir Singh, said that the hard disk of the computer had been sealed on 16 January 2002 (a whole month after the seizure). But the computer shows that it was accessed even after that date. The courts have considered this but taken no cognizance of it.

(On a speculative note, isn't it strange that the only incriminating information found on the computer were the files used to make the fake passes and ID cards? And a Zee TV film clip showing the Parliament building. If other incriminating information had been deleted, why wasn't this? And why did Ghazi Baba, chief of operations of an international terrorist organization, need a laptop—with bad artwork on it—so urgently?)

Consider the mobile phone call records: Stared at for long enough, a lot of the 'hard evidence' produced by the Special Cell begins to look dubious. The backbone of the prosecution's case has to do with the recovery of mobile phones, SIM cards, computerized call records, and the testimonies of officials from cellphone companies and shopkeepers who sold the phones and SIM cards to Afzal and his accomplices. The call records that were produced to show that Shaukat, Afzal, Geelani and Mohammad (one of the dead militants) had all been in touch with each other very close to the time of the attack were uncertified computer printouts, not even copies of primary documents. They were outputs of the billing system stored as text files that could have been easily doctored and at any time. For example, the call records that were produced show that two calls had been made at exactly the same time from the same SIM card, but from *separate* handsets with *separate* IMEI numbers. This means that either the SIM card had been cloned or the call records were doctored.

Consider the SIM card: To prop up its version of the story, the prosecution relies heavily on one particular mobile phone number—9811489429. The police say it was Afzal's number—the number that connected Afzal to Mohammad, Afzal to Shaukat, and Shaukat to Geelani. The police also say that this number was written on the back of the identity tags found on the dead terrorists. Pretty convenient. *Lost Kitten! Call Mom at 9811489429.*

It's worth mentioning that normal procedure requires evidence gathered at the scene of a crime to be sealed. The ID cards were never sealed and remained in the custody of the police and could have been tampered with at any time.

The only evidence the police have that 9811489429 was indeed Afzal's number is Afzal's confession, which as we have seen is no evidence at all. The SIM card has never been found. The police produced a prosecution witness, Kamal Kishore, who identified Afzal and said that he had sold him a Motorola phone and a SIM card on 4 December 2001. However, the call records the prosecution relied on show that that particular SIM card was already in use on 6 November, *a whole month before Afzal is supposed to have bought it!* So either the witness is lying, or the call records are false. The high court glosses over this discrepancy by saying that Kamal Kishore had only said that he sold Afzal a SIM card, not *this* particular SIM card. The Supreme Court judgment loftily says 'The SIM card should necessarily have been sold to Afzal prior to 4.12.2001.'

Consider the Identification of the Accused: A series of prosecution witnesses, most of them shopkeepers, identified Afzal as the man to whom they had sold various things: ammonium nitrate, aluminum powder, sulfur, a Sujata mixer-grinder, packets of dry fruit and so on. Normal procedure would require these shopkeepers to pick Afzal out from a number of people in a test identification parade. This didn't happen. Instead, Afzal was identified by them when he 'led' the police to these shops while he was in police custody and introduced to the witnesses as an Accused in the Parliament attack. (Are we allowed to speculate about whether he led the police or the police led *him* to the shops? After all he was still in their custody, still vulnerable to torture. If his confession under these circumstances is legally suspect, then why not all of this?)

The judges have pondered the violation of these procedural norms but have not taken them very seriously. They said that they did not see why ordinary members of the public would have reason to falsely implicate an innocent person. But does this hold true, given the orgy of media propaganda that ordinary members of the public were subjected to, particularly in this case? Does this hold true, if you take into account the fact that ordinary shopkeepers, particularly those who sell electronic goods without receipts in the 'grey market', are completely beholden to the Delhi police?

None of the inconsistencies that I have written about so far are the result of spectacular detective work on my part. A lot of them are documented in an excellent book called *December 13: Terror Over Democracy* by Nirmalangshu Mukherji; in two reports (*Trial of Errors* and *Balancing Act*) published by the Peoples' Union for Democratic Rights, Delhi; and most important of all, in the three thick volumes of judgments of the Trial Court, the High Court and the Supreme Court.[29] All these are public documents, lying on my desk. Why is it that when there is this whole murky universe begging to be revealed, our TV channels are busy staging hollow debates between uninformed people and grasping politicians? Why is it that apart from a few sporadic independent commentators, our newspapers carry front-page stories about who the hangman is going to be, and macabre details about the length (60 feet) and weight (3.75 kilograms) of the rope that will be used to hang Mohammad Afzal?[30] Shall we pause for a moment to say a few hosannas for the Free Press?

~

It's not an easy thing for most people to do, but if you can, unmoor yourself conceptually, if only for a moment, from the Police are Good/Terrorists are Evil ideology. The evidence on offer *minus its ideological trappings* opens up a chasm of terrifying possibilities. It points in directions which most of us would prefer not to look.

The prize for the Most Ignored Legal Document in the entire case goes to the Statement of the Accused Mohammad Afzal under Section 313 of the Criminal Procedure Code. In this document, the evidence against him is put to him by the court in the form of questions. He can either accept the evidence or dispute it, and has the opportunity to put down his version of his story in his own words. In Afzal's case, given that he has never had any real opportunity to be heard, this document tells his story in his voice.

In this document, Afzal accepts certain charges made against him by the prosecution. He accepts that he met a man called Tariq. He accepts that Tariq introduced him to a man called Mohammad. He accepts that he helped Mohammad come to Delhi and helped him to buy a second-hand white Ambassador car. He accepts that Mohammad was one of the five fidayeen who was killed in the Attack. The important thing about Afzal's Statement of the Accused is that he makes no effort to completely absolve himself or claim innocence. But he puts his actions in a context that is devastating. Afzal's statement explains the peripheral part he played in the Parliament attack. But it also ushers us towards an understanding of some possible reasons for why the investigation was so shoddy, why it pulls up short at the most crucial junctures and why it is vital that we do not dismiss this as just incompetence and shoddiness. Even if we don't believe Afzal, given what we do know about the trial and the role of the Special Cell, it is inexcusable not to look in the direction he's pointing. He gives specific information—names, places, dates. (This could not have been easy, given that his family, his brothers, his wife and young son live in Kashmir and are easy meat for the people he mentions in his deposition.)

In Afzal's words:

> I live in Sopre [Sopore] Jammu and Kasmir [Jammu and Kashmir] and in the year 2000 when I was there Army used to harass me almost daily . . . One Raja Mohan Rai used to

tell me that I should give information to him about militants. I was a surrendered militant and all militants have to mark Attendance at Army Camp every Sunday. I was not being physically torture . . . He used to only just threatened me. I used to give him small information which I used to gather from newspaper, in order to save myself. In June/July 2000 I migrated from my village and went to town Baramullah. I was having a shop of distribution of Surgical instruments which I was running on commission basis. One day when I was going on my scooter S.T.F (Special Task Force) people came and picked me up and they continuously tortured me for five days. Somebody had given information to S.T.F that I was again indulging in militant activities. That person was confronted with me and released in my presence. Then I was kept by them in custody for about 25 days and I got myself released by paying rupees 1 lakh [one hundred thousand rupees ($2,000)]. Special Cell People had confirmed this incident. Thereafter I was given a certificate by the S.T.F and they made me a Special Police Officer for six months. They were knowing I will not work for them. Tariq met me in Palhalan S.T.F camp where I was in custody of S.T.F. Tariq met me later on in Sri Nagar and told me he was basically working for S.T.F. I told him I was also working for S.T.F. Mohammad who was killed in Attack on Parliament was along with Tariq. Tariq told me he was from Keran sector of Kashmir and he told me that I should take Mohammad to Delhi as Mohammad has to go out of country from Delhi after some time. I don't know why I was caught by the police of Sri Nagar on 15.12.2001 [December 15, 2001]. I was boarding bus at Sri Nagar bus stop, for going home

> when police caught me. Witness Akbar who had deposed in the court that he had apprehended Shaukat and me in Sri Nagar had conducted a raid at my shop about a year prior to December 2001 and told me that I was selling fake surgical instruments and he took rupees 5,000/- [roughly $100] from me. I was tortured at Special Cell and one Bhoop Singh even compelled me to take urine and I saw family of S.A.R. Geelani also there, Geelani was in miserable condition. He was not in a position to stand. We were taken to Doctor for examination but instructions used to be issued that we have to tell Doctor that everything was alright with a threat that if we do not do so we be again tortured.

He then asks the court's permission to add some more information.

> Mohammad the slain terrorist of Parliament attack had come along with me from Kashmir. The person who handed him over to me is Tariq. Tariq is working with Security Force and S.T.F JK Police. Tariq told me that if I face any problem due to Mohammad he will help me as he knew the security forces and S.T.F very well . . . Tariq had told me that I just have to drop Mohammad at Delhi and do nothing else. And if I would not take Mohammad with me to Delhi I would be implicated in some other case. I under these circumstances brought Mohammad to Delhi under a compulsion without knowing he was a terrorist.

So now we have a picture emerging of someone who could be a key player. 'Witness Akbar' (Prosecution Witness 62), Mohd Akbar, head constable, Parimpora Police Station, the Jammu and

Kashmir policeman who signed the Seizure Memo at the time of Afzal's arrest. In a letter to Sushil Kumar, his Supreme Court lawyer, Afzal describes a chilling moment at one point in the trial. In the court, Witness Akbar, who had come from Srinagar to testify about the Seizure Memo, reassured Afzal in Kashmiri that 'his family was alright.' Afzal immediately recognized that this was a veiled threat. Afzal also says that after he was arrested in Srinagar he was taken to the Parimpora police station and beaten, and plainly told that his wife and family would suffer dire consequences if he did not cooperate. (We already know that Afzal's brother Hilal had been held in illegal detention by the SOG during some crucial months.)

In this letter, Afzal describes how he was tortured in the STF camp—with electrodes on his genitals and chillies and petrol in his anus. He mentions the name of Deputy Superintendent of Police Dravinder Singh who said he needed him to do a 'small job' for him in Delhi. He also says that some of the phone numbers mentioned in the charge sheet can be traced to an STF camp in Kashmir.

It is Afzal's story that gives us a glimpse into what life is really like in the Kashmir Valley. It's only in the Noddy book version we read about in our newspapers that Security Forces battle Militants and innocent Kashmiris are caught in the crossfire. In the adult version, Kashmir is a valley awash with militants, renegades, security forces, double-crossers, informers, spooks, blackmailers, blackmailees, extortionists, spies, both Indian and Pakistani intelligence agencies, human rights activists, NGOs, and unimaginable amounts of unaccounted-for money and weapons. There are not always clear lines that demarcate the boundaries between all these things and people. It's not easy to tell who is working for whom.

Truth, in Kashmir, is probably more dangerous than anything else. The deeper you dig, the worse it gets. At the bottom of the pit is the SOG and STF that Afzal talks about. These are the most ruthless, undisciplined and dreaded elements of the Indian security apparatus in Kashmir. Unlike the more formal forces, they operate in a twilight zone where policemen, surrendered militants, renegades and common criminals do business. They prey on the local population, particularly in rural Kashmir. Their primary victims are the thousands of young Kashmiri men who rose up in revolt in the anarchic uprising of the early 1990s and have since surrendered and are trying to live normal lives.

In 1989, when Afzal crossed the border to be trained as a militant, he was only twenty years old. He returned with no training, disillusioned with his experience. He put down his gun and enrolled himself in Delhi University. In 1993 without ever having been a practising militant, he *voluntarily* surrendered to the Border Security Force (BSF). Illogically enough, it was at this point that his nightmares began. His surrender was treated as a crime and his life became a hell. Can young Kashmiri men be blamed if the lesson they draw from Afzal's story is that it would be not just stupid, but insane to surrender their weapons and submit to the vast range of myriad cruelties the Indian state has on offer for them?

The story of Mohammad Afzal has enraged Kashmiris because his story is their story too. What has happened to him could have happened, is happening and has happened to thousands of young Kashmiri men and their families. The only difference is that their stories are played out in the dingy bowels of joint interrogation centres, army camps and police stations where they have been burned, beaten, electrocuted, blackmailed and killed, their bodies thrown out of the backs of trucks for passers-by to find. Whereas Afzal's story is being performed like a piece of medieval theatre on the national stage, in the clear light of day, with the legal sanction of a 'fair trial', the hollow benefits of a 'free press' and all the pomp and ceremony of a so-called democracy.

If Afzal is hanged, we'll never know the answer to the real question: Who attacked the Indian Parliament? Was it Lashkar-e-Toiba? Jaish-e-Mohammad? Or does the answer lie somewhere deep in the secret heart of this country that we all live in and love and hate in our own beautiful, intricate, various and thorny ways?

There ought to be a Parliamentary Inquiry into the December 13 attack on Parliament. While the inquiry is pending, Afzal's family in Sopore must be protected because they are vulnerable hostages in this bizarre story.

To hang Mohammad Afzal without knowing what really happened is a misdeed that will not easily be forgotten. Or forgiven. Nor should it be.

Notwithstanding the 10 per cent Growth Rate.

BREAKING THE NEWS

This essay first appeared as an introduction to 13 December—A Reader: The Strange Case of the Attack on the Indian Parliament *(New Delhi: Penguin Books India, 2006), a collection of writings by a group of lawyers, academics, journalists and writers about the controversies surrounding the Parliament attack.*

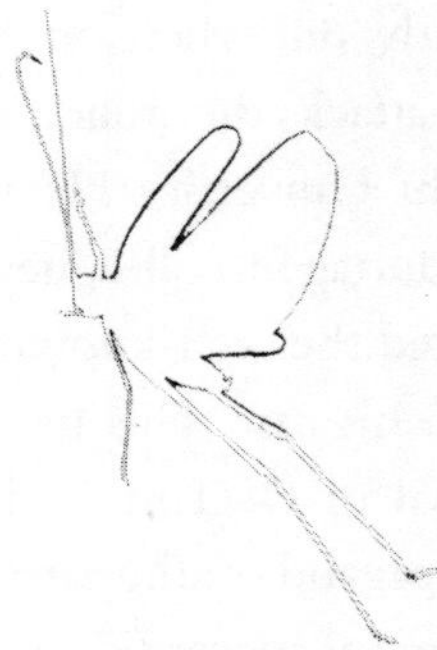

THIS READER [*13 December—A Reader: The Strange Case of the Attack on the Indian Parliament*: 2006] goes to press almost five years to the day since 13 December 2001, when five men (some say six) drove through the gates of the Indian Parliament in a white Ambassador car and attempted what looked like an astonishingly incompetent terrorist strike.

Consummate competence appeared to be the hallmark of everything that followed: the gathering of evidence, the speed of the investigation by the Special Cell of the Delhi Police, the arrest and charge sheeting of the accused, and the forty-month-long judicial process that began with the fast-track trial court.

The operative phrase in all of this is 'appeared to be'. If you follow the story carefully, you'll encounter two sets of masks. First the mask of consummate competence (accused arrested, 'case cracked' in two days flat), and then, when things began to come undone, the benign mask of shambling incompetence (shoddy evidence, procedural flaws, material contradictions). But underneath all of this, as each of the essays in this collection shows, is something more sinister, more worrying. Over the last few years the worries have grown into a mountain of misgivings, impossible to ignore.

The doubts set in early on, when on 14 December 2001, the day after the Parliament attack, the police arrested S.A.R. Geelani, a young lecturer in Delhi University. He was one of four people who were arrested. His outraged colleagues and friends, certain he had been framed, contacted the well-known lawyer Nandita Haksar and asked her to take on his case. This marked the beginning of a campaign for the fair trial of Geelani. It flew in the face of mass hysteria and corrosive propaganda enthusiastically disseminated by the mass media. The campaign was successful, and Geelani was eventually acquitted, along with Afsan Guru, co-accused in the same case.

Geelani's acquittal blew a gaping hole in the prosecution's version of the Parliament attack. But in some odd way, in the public mind, the acquittal of two of the accused only confirmed the guilt of the other two. When the government announced that Mohammad Afzal Guru, Accused Number One in the case, would be hanged on 20 October 2006, it seemed as though most people welcomed the news not just with approval, but morbid excitement. But then, once again, the questions resurfaced.

To see through the Prosecution's case against Geelani was relatively easy. He was plucked out of thin air and transplanted into the centre of the 'conspiracy' as its kingpin. Afzal was different. He had been extruded through the sewage system of the hell that Kashmir has become. He surfaced through a manhole, covered in shit (and when he emerged, policemen in the Special Cell pissed on him.[1]) The first thing they made him do was a 'media confession' in which he implicated himself completely in the attack.[2] The speed with which this happened made many of us believe that he was indeed guilty as charged. It was only much later that the circumstances under which this 'confession' was made were revealed, and even the Supreme Court was to set it aside saying that the police had violated legal safeguards.[3]

From the very beginning there was nothing pristine or simple about Afzal's case. Even today Afzal does not claim complete innocence. It is the *nature* of his involvement that is being contested. For instance, was he coerced, tortured and blackmailed into playing even the peripheral part he played? He didn't have a lawyer to put out his version of the story, or help anyone to sift through the tangle of lies and fabrications. Various individuals worked it out for themselves. These essays by a group of lawyers, academics, journalists and writers represent that body of work. It has fractured what—only recently—appeared to be a national consensus interwoven with mass hysteria. We're late at the barricades, but we're here.

Most people, or let's say many people, when they encounter real facts and a logical argument, *do* begin to ask the right questions. This is exactly what has begun to happen in the Parliament attack case. The questions have created public pressure. The pressure has created fissures, and through these fissures those who have come under the scanner—shadowy individuals, counter-intelligence and security agencies, political parties—are beginning to surface. They wave flags, hurl abuse, issue hot denials and cover their tracks with more and more untruths. Thus they reveal themselves.

Public unease continues to grow. A group of citizens have come together as a committee (chaired by Nirmala Deshpande) to publicly demand a parliamentary inquiry into the episode.[4] There is an online petition demanding the same thing.[5] Thousands of people have signed on. Every day new articles appear in the papers, on the net. At least half a dozen websites are following the developments closely. They raise questions about how Mohammad Afzal, who never had proper legal representation, can be sentenced to death, without having had an opportunity to be heard, without a fair trial. They raise questions about fabricated evidence, procedural flaws and the outright lies that were presented in court and published in newspapers. They show how there is hardly a single piece of evidence that stands up to scrutiny.

And then, there are even more disturbing questions that have been raised, which range beyond the fate of Mohammad Afzal. Here are thirteen questions for 13 December:

Question 1: For months before the Attack on Parliament, both the government and the police had been saying that Parliament could be attacked. On 12 December 2001, at an informal meeting, Prime Minister Atal Bihari Vajpayee warned of an imminent attack on Parliament.[6] On 13 December, Parliament was attacked. Given that there was an 'improved security drill', how did a car bomb packed with explosives enter the Parliament complex?

Question 2: Within days of the attack, the Special Cell of Delhi Police said it was a meticulously planned joint operation of Jaish-e-Mohammad and Lashkar-e-Toiba. They said the attack was led by a man called 'Mohammad' who was also involved in the hijacking of IC-814 in 1998. (This was later refuted by the CBI.[7]) None of this was ever proved in court. What evidence did the Special Cell have for its claim?

Question 3: The entire attack was recorded live on closed circuit TV (CCTV). Congress Party MP Kapil Sibal demanded in Parliament that the CCTV recording be shown to the members. He was supported by the Deputy Chairman of the Rajya Sabha, Najma Heptullah, who said that there was confusion about the details of the event. The chief whip of the Congress Party, Priya Ranjan Dasmunshi, said, 'I counted six men getting out of the car.

But only five were killed. The closed circuit TV camera recording clearly showed the six men.'[8] If Dasmunshi was right, why did the police say that there were only five people in the car? Who was the sixth person? Where is he now? Why was the CCTV recording not produced by the prosecution as evidence in the trial? Why was it not released for public viewing?

Question 4: Why was Parliament adjourned after some of these questions were raised?

Question 5: A few days after 13 December, the government declared that it had 'incontrovertible proof' of Pakistan's involvement in the attack, and announced a massive mobilization of almost half a million soldiers to the Indo-Pakistan border. The subcontinent was pushed to the brink of nuclear war. Apart from Afzal's 'confession', extracted under torture (and later set aside by the Supreme Court), what was the 'incontrovertible proof'?

Question 6: Is it true that the military mobilization to the Pakistan border had begun long before the 13 December attack?

Question 7: How much did this military standoff, which lasted for nearly a year, cost? How many soldiers died in the process? How many soldiers and civilians died because of mishandled landmines, and how many peasants lost their homes and land because trucks and tanks were rolling through their villages and landmines were being planted in their fields?

Question 8: In a criminal investigation it is vital for the police to show how the evidence gathered at the scene of the attack led them to the accused. How did the police reach Mohammad Afzal? The Special Cell says S.A.R. Geelani led them to Afzal.[9] But the message to look out for Afzal was actually flashed to the Srinagar police *before* Geelani was arrested. So how did the Special Cell connect Afzal to the 13 December attack?

Question 9: The courts acknowledge that Afzal was a surrendered militant who was in regular contact with the security forces, particularly the Special Task Force (STF) of the Jammu and Kashmir police. How do the security forces explain the fact that a person under their surveillance was able to conspire in a major militant operation?

Question 10: Is it plausible that organizations like Lashkar-e-Toiba or Jaish-e-Mohammad would rely on a person who had been in and out of STF torture chambers, and was under constant police surveillance, as the principal link for a major operation?

Question 11: In his Statement before the court, Afzal says that he was introduced to 'Mohammad' and instructed to take him to Delhi by a man called Tariq, who was working with the STF. Tariq was named in the police charge sheet. Who is Tariq and where is he now?

Question 12: On 19 December 2001, six days after the Parliament attack, Police Commissioner, Thane (Maharashtra), S.M. Shangari identified one of the attackers killed in the Parliament attack as Mohammad Yasin Fateh Mohammed (alias Abu Hamza) of the Lashkar-e-Toiba, who had been arrested in Mumbai in November 2000, and immediately handed over to the Jammu and Kashmir police. He gave detailed descriptions to support his statement. If Police Commissioner Shangari was right, how did Mohammad Yasin, a man in the custody of the Jammu and Kashmir police, end up participating in the Parliament attack? If he was wrong, where is Mohammad Yasin now?

Question 13: Why is it that we still don't know who the five dead 'terrorists' killed in the Parliament attack are?

These questions, examined cumulatively, point to something far more serious than incompetence. The words that come to mind are Complicity, Collusion, Involvement. There's no need for us to feign shock, or shrink from thinking these thoughts and saying them out loud. Governments and their intelligence agencies have a hoary tradition of using strategies like this to further their own ends. (Look up the burning of the Reichstag and the rise of Nazi power in Germany, 1933; or Operation Gladio, in which European Intelligence Agencies 'created' acts of terrorism, especially in Italy, in order to discredit militant groups like the Red Brigade.[10])

The official response to all of these questions has been dead silence. As things stand, the execution of Afzal has been postponed while the president considers his clemency petition. Meanwhile the Bharatiya Janata Party announced that it would turn 'Hang Afzal' into a national campaign.[11] The campaign was fuelled by the usual stale cocktail of religious chauvinism, nationalism and strategic falsehoods. But it doesn't seem to have taken off. Now other avenues are being explored. M.S. Bitta of the All India Anti-Terrorist Front is parading around the families of some of the security personnel who were killed during the Attack. They have threatened to return the government's posthumous bravery medals if Afzal is not hanged by December 13. (On balance, it might not be a bad idea for them to turn those medals in until they really know who the attackers were working for.)

The main strategy seems to be to create confusion and polarize the debate on communal lines. The editor of *The Pioneer* newspaper writes in his columns that Mohammad Afzal was actually one of the men who attacked Parliament, that he was the first to open fire and kill at least three security guards.*[12] The columnist Swapan Dasgupta, in an article titled 'You Can't Be Good to Evil', suggests that if Afzal

---

*Chandan Mitra, editor of the *Pioneer* newspaper reviewed the book *13 December: A Reader* in *India Today* (22 January 2007, 'Trapped in Half-Truths'). An edited version of my letter in response was published in the Letters section of *India Today* (5 February 2007). Here is the full text:

is not hanged there would be no point in celebrating the victory of Good over Evil at Dussehra or Durga Puja.[13] It's hard to believe that falsehoods like this stem only from a poor grasp of facts.

Sir—This is regarding Chandan Mitra's review of the book *13 December: A Reader.* An interesting choice of reviewer—someone who has brazenly falsified facts on the Parliament attack case and has been exposed for doing so in the book he reviews. He asks for a 'source' for my statement: 'On December 12, 2001, at an informal meeting, Prime Minister Atal Bihari Vajpayee warned of an imminent attack on Parliament.'

Please refer to the speech made by the Prime Minster Manmohan Singh, (then leader of the opposition) on December 18, 2001, in the Rajya Sabha. He said: 'Yes, it is a fact that an attack on Parliament was quite anticipated . . . In fact, one day before this attack took place, i.e. on 12th December, while speaking at Mumbai, the Hon. Prime Minister himself had referred to the existence of this threat, such a threat to our Parliament.'

In his own article, 'Celebrating Treason' (*The Pioneer,* October 7, 2006) cited in my Introduction, Chandan Mitra says, 'Afzal Guru was one of the terrorists who stormed Parliament House on December 13th 2001 and it was he who first opened fire on security personnel, apparently killing three of the six who died protecting the majesty of democracy that morning.'

None of the three court judgments sentencing Mohammad Afzal to death have accused him (leave alone found him guilty) of killing anybody, of being directly involved in the attack on Parliament, or indeed of being anywhere near the Parliament building on December 13, 2001. Even the police chargesheet clearly states that at the time of the attack, Afzal was somewhere else. The Supreme Court judgment explicitly says there was no direct evidence against him, nor any evidence that he was a member of a terrorist organization. Can Chandan Mitra cite a source for his outlandish assertion? Or tell us how he knows what the police and the courts do not? And why he has suppressed this 'evidence' for all these years?

In the business of spreading confusion, the mass media, particularly television journalists, can be counted on to be perfect collaborators. On discussions, chat shows and 'special reports', we have television anchors playing around with crucial facts, like young children in a sandpit. Torturers, estranged brothers, senior police officers and politicians are emerging from the woodwork and talking. The more they talk, the more interesting it all becomes.

At the end of November 2006, Afzal's older brother Aijaz made it on to a national news channel (CNN-IBN).[14] He was featured on hidden camera, on what was meant to be a 'sting' operation, making—we were asked to believe—stunning revelations. Aijaz's story had already been on offer to various journalists on the streets of Delhi for weeks. People were wary of him because his rift with his brother's wife and family is well known. More significantly, in Kashmir he is known to have a relationship with the STF. More than one person has suggested an audit of his new-found assets.

But here he was now, on the national news, endorsing the Supreme Court decision to hang his brother. Then saying Afzal had never surrendered, and that it was *he* (Aijaz), who surrendered his brother's weapon to the BSF! And since he had never surrendered, Aijaz was able to 'confirm' that Afzal was an active militant with the Jaish-e-Mohammad, and that Ghazi Baba, chief of operations of the Jaish, used to regularly hold meetings in their home. (Aijaz claims that when Ghazi Baba was killed, it was he who the police called in to identify the body). On the whole, it sounded as though there had been a case of mistaken identity—and that given how much he knew, and all he was admitting, Aijaz should have been the one in custody instead of Afzal!

Of course we must keep in mind that behind both Aijaz and Afzal's 'media confessions', spaced five years apart, is the invisible hand of the STF, the dreaded counter-insurgency outfit in Kashmir. They can make anyone say anything at any time. Their methods (both punitive and remunerative) are familiar to every man, woman and child in the Kashmir Valley. At a time like this, for a responsible news channel to announce that their 'investigation finds that Afzal was a Jaish militant', based on totally unreliable testimony, is dangerous and irresponsible. (Since when did what our brothers say about us become admissible evidence? My brother, for instance, will testify that I'm God's Gift to the Universe. I could dredge up a couple of aunts who'd say I'm a Jaish militant. For a price.) How can family feuds be dressed up as Breaking News?

The other character who is rapidly emerging from the shadowy periphery and wading on to center stage is Deputy Superintendent of Police Dravinder Singh of the STF. He is the man who Afzal has named as the police officer who held him in illegal detention and tortured him in the STF camp at Humhama in Srinagar, only a few months before the Parliament attack. In a letter to his lawyer Sushil Kumar, Afzal says that several of the calls made to him and Mohammad (the man killed in the Attack) can be traced to Dravinder Singh. Of course no attempt was made to trace these calls.

Dravinder Singh was also showcased on the CNN-IBN show, on the by-now ubiquitous low-angle shots, camera shake and all.[15] It seemed a bit unnecessary, because Dravinder Singh has been talking a lot these days. He's done recorded interviews, on the phone as well as face-to-face, saying exactly the same shocking things. Weeks before the sting operation, in a recorded interview to Parvaiz Bukhari, at that time a freelance journalist based in Srinagar, he said:

> I did interrogate and torture him [Afzal] at my camp for several days. And we never recorded his arrest in the books

> anywhere. His description of torture at my camp is true. That was the procedure those days and we did pour petrol in his ass and gave him electric shocks. But I could not break him. He did not reveal anything to me despite our hardest possible interrogation. We tortured him enough for Ghazi Baba but he did not break. He looked like a 'bhondu' those days, what you call a 'chootya' type. And I had a reputation for torture, interrogation and breaking suspects. If anybody came out of my interrogation clean, nobody would ever touch him again. He would be considered clean for good by the whole department.[16]

On TV this boasting spiralled into policy-making. 'Torture is the only deterrent for terrorism,' he said, 'I do it for the nation.' He didn't bother to explain why or how the 'bhondu' that he tortured and subsequently released, allegedly went on to become the diabolical mastermind of the Parliament attack. Dravinder Singh then said that Afzal was a Jaish militant. If this is true, why wasn't the evidence placed before the courts? And why on earth was Afzal released? Why wasn't he watched? There is a definite attempt to try and dismiss this as incompetence. But given everything we know now, it would take all of Dravinder Singh's delicate professional skills to make some of us believe that.

Meanwhile right-wing commentators have consistently taken to referring to Afzal as a Jaish-e-Mohammad militant. It's as though instructions have been issued that this is to be the party line. They have absolutely no evidence to back their claim, but they know that repeating something often enough makes it the 'truth'. As part of the campaign to portray Afzal as an 'active' militant, and not a surrendered militant, S.M. Sahai, Inspector General, Kashmir,

Jammu and Kashmir police, appeared on TV to say that he had found no evidence in his records that Afzal had surrendered. It would have been odd if he had, because in 1993 Afzal surrendered not to the Jammu and Kashmir police, but to the BSF. But why would a TV journalist bother with that kind of detail? And why does a senior police officer need to become part of this game of smoke and mirrors?

The official version of the story of the Parliament attack is very quickly coming apart at the seams.

Even the Supreme Court judgment, with all its flaws of logic and leaps of faith, does not accuse Mohammad Afzal of being the mastermind of the attack. So who *was* the mastermind? If Mohammad Afzal is hanged we may never know. But L.K. Advani, leader of the opposition wants him hanged at once. Even a day's delay, he says, is against the national interest.[17] Why? What's the hurry? The man is locked up in a high-security cell on death row. He's not allowed out of his cell for even five minutes a day. What harm can he do? Talk? Write, perhaps? Surely, (even in L.K. Advani's own narrow interpretation of the term) it's in the national interest *not* to hang Afzal? At least not until there is an inquiry that reveals what the real story is, and who actually attacked Parliament?

Among the people who have appealed against Mohammad Afzal's death sentence are those who are opposed to capital punishment in principle. They have asked that his death sentence be commuted to a life sentence. To sentence a man who has not had a fair trial, and has not had the opportunity to be heard, to a life sentence, is less cruel, but just as arbitrary as sentencing him to death. The right thing to do would be to order a retrial of Afzal's case, and an impartial, transparent inquiry into the 13 December Parliament attack. It is utterly demonic to leave a man locked up alone in a prison cell, day after day, week after week, leaving him and his family to guess which day will be the last day of his life.

A genuine inquiry would have to mean far more than just a political witch-hunt. It would have to look into the part played by intelligence, counter-insurgency and security agencies as well. Offences such as the fabrication of evidence and the blatant violation of procedural norms have already been established in the courts, but they look very much like just the tip of the iceberg.[18] We now have a police officer admitting (boasting) on record that he was involved in the illegal detention and torture of a fellow citizen. Is all of this acceptable to the people, the government and the courts of this country?

Given the track record of Indian governments (past and present, right, left and centre) it is naïve—perhaps *utopian* is a better word—to hope that it will ever have the courage to institute an inquiry that will, once and for all, uncover the real story. A maintenance dose of pusillanimity is probably encrypted in all governments. But hope has little to do with reason.

Therefore, this book, offered in hope.

CUSTODIAL CONFESSIONS, THE MEDIA AND THE LAW

This essay was first published in the Hindustan Times *on 22 December 2006.*

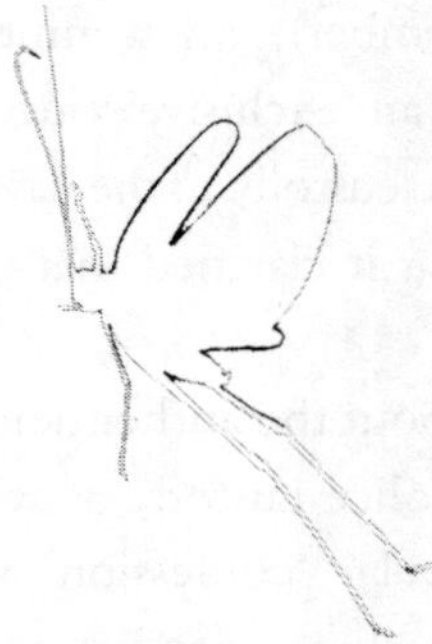

THE SUPREME COURT of India has sentenced Mohammad Afzal, Accused Number One in the Parliament attack case, to death. It acknowledged that the evidence against him was not direct, only circumstantial, but in its now famously controversial statement it said: 'The incident, which resulted in heavy casualties has shaken the entire nation, and the collective conscience of the society will only be satisfied if capital punishment is awarded to the offender.'[1]

Is the 'collective conscience' the same as majority opinion? Would it be fair to say that it is fashioned by the information we receive? And therefore, that in this case, the mass media has played a pivotal role in determining the final court verdict? If so, has it been accurate and truthful?

Now, five years later, when disturbing questions are being raised about the Parliament attack, is the Special Cell, once again, cleverly exploiting the frantic hunt for 'breaking news'? Suddenly spurious 'exposes' are finding their way onto prime-time TV. Unfortunately, some of India's best, most responsible news channels have been caught up in this game in which carelessness and incomprehension is as deadly as malice. (A few weeks ago we had a fiasco on CNN-IBN.)

Last week (16 December), on a ninety-minute prime-time show, NDTV showcased an 'exclusive' video of Mohammad Afzal's 'confession' made in police custody, in the days immediately following his arrest. At no point was it clarified that the 'confession' was five years old.[2]

Much has been said about the authenticity, reliability and legality of confessions taken in police custody, as well as the circumstances under which this particular 'confession' was extracted. Because of the very real danger that custodial torture will replace real investigation, the Indian Penal Code does not admit confessions made in police custody as legal evidence in a criminal trial. POTA was considered an outrage on civil rights and was eventually withdrawn primarily because it made confessions obtained in police custody admissible as legal evidence. In fact, in the case of Afzal's 'confession', the Supreme Court said the Special Cell had violated even the tenuous safeguards provided under POTA, and set it aside it as being illegal and unreliable. Even before this, the High Court had already reprimanded the Special Cell sharply for forcing Afzal to incriminate himself publicly in a 'media confession'.[3]

So what made NDTV showcase this thoroughly discredited old 'confession' all over again? Why now? How did the Special Cell video find its way into their hands? Does it have something to do with the fact that Afzal's clemency petition is pending with the president of India and a curative petition asking for a retrial is pending in the Supreme Court? In her column in the *Hindustan Times*, Barkha Dutt, Managing Editor of NDTV, said the channel spent many hours 'debating what the fairest way' was to show this video.[4] Clearly it was a serious decision and demands to be discussed seriously.

At the start of the show, for several minutes the image of Afzal 'confessing' was inset in a text that said 'Afzal ne court mein gunah qabool kiya tha' (Afzal has admitted his guilt in Court). This is blatantly untrue. Then, for a full fifteen minutes the 'confession' ran without comment. After this, an anchor came on and said 'Sansad par hamle ki kahani, Afzal ki zubaani' (The story of the Parliament attack, in Afzal's words.) This, too, is a travesty of the truth. Well into the program a reporter informed us that Afzal had since withdrawn this 'confession' and had claimed it had been extracted under torture. The smirking anchor then turned to one of the panelists, S.A.R. Geelani, who was also one of the accused in the case, (and who knows a thing or two about torture and the Special Cell) and remarked that if this confession was 'forced', then Afzal was a very good actor.

(The anchor has clearly never experienced torture. Or even read the wonderful Uruguayan writer, Eduardo Galeano—'The electric cattle prod turns anyone into a prolific storyteller.' Nor has he known what it's like to be held in police custody in Delhi while his family was hostage—as Afzal's was—in the war zone that is Kashmir.)

Later on, the 'confession' was juxtaposed with what the channel said was Afzal's statement to the Court, but was actually the text of a letter he wrote to his high court lawyer in which he implicates the State Task Force (STF) in Kashmir and describes how in the months before the Parliament attack he was illegally detained and tortured by the STF. NDTV does not tell us that a Deputy Superintendent of the STF has since confirmed that he did illegally detain and torture Afzal. Instead it uses Afzal's letter to discredit him further. The bold caption at the bottom of the frame read: 'Afzal ka badalta hua baiyan' (Afzal's changing statements).

There is another serious ethical issue. In Afzal's confession to the Special Cell in December 2001 (as opposed to his 'media confession'), he implicated S.A.R. Geelani and said he was the mastermind of the conspiracy. While this was in line with the Special Cell's charge sheet, it turned out to be false, and Geelani was acquitted by the Supreme Court. Why was this portion of Afzal's confession left out? So that the confession would seem less constructed, more plausible? Who made that decision to leave it out? NDTV or the Special Cell?

All this makes the broadcast of this programme a seriously prejudicial act. It wasn't surprising to watch the 'collective conscience' of society forming its opinion as the show unfolded. The SMS messages on the ticker tape said:

> Afzal ko boti boti mein kaat ke kutton ko khila do. (Cut him into bits and feed him to the dogs.)
> Afzal ke haath aur taang kaat ke, road mein bheek mangvani chahiye. (Cut off his arms and legs and make him beg on the streets.)

Then in English: Hang him by his balls in Lal Chowk. Hang him and hang those who are supporting him.

Even without Sharia courts, we seem to be doing just fine.

For the record, the reporter Neeta Sharma, credited several times on the programme for procuring the video has been previously exposed for publishing falsehoods: on the 'encounter' in Ansal Plaza[5]; on the Iftikhar Gilani case[6]; on the S.A.R. Geelani case; and now on this one. Neeta Sharma was formerly a reporter with the *Hindustan Times*. Publishing Special Cell handouts seems to have got her a promotion—from print journalism to TV.

This kind of thing really makes you wonder whether media houses have an inside track on the police and intelligence agencies, or whether it's the other way around.

The quietest guest on the panel was M.K. Dhar, a former Joint Director of the Intelligence Bureau. He was pretty enigmatic. He certainly didn't repeat what he has said in his astonishingly frank book *Open Secrets: India's Intelligence Unveiled*: 'Some day or the other, taking advantage of the weakening fabric of our democracy, some unscrupulous intelligence men may gang up with ambitious Army brass and change the political texture of the nation.'[7]

Weakening fabric of our democracy. I couldn't have put it better.

BABY BUSH, GO HOME

This essay first appeared in The Hindu *on 28 February 2006, and on the website of* The Nation *on 27 February 2006.*

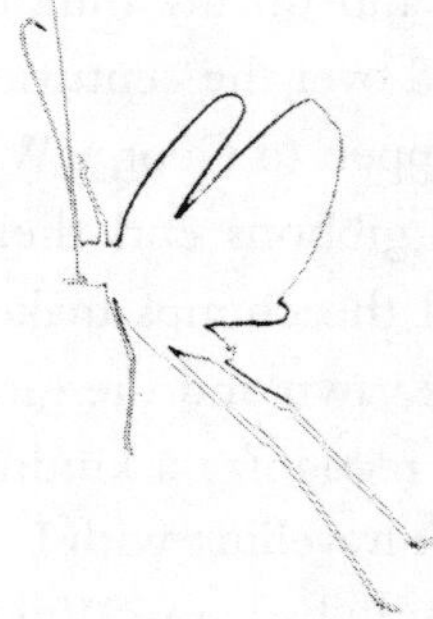

ON HIS triumphalist tour of India and Pakistan, where he hopes to wave imperiously at people he considers potential subjects, President Bush's itinerary is getting curiouser and curiouser.

For his 2 March pit stop in New Delhi, the Indian government tried very hard to have Bush address our Parliament. A not inconsequential number of MPs threatened to heckle him, so Plan One was hastily shelved. Plan Two was that Bush address the masses from the ramparts of the magnificent Red Fort, where the Indian prime minister traditionally delivers his Independence Day address. But the Red Fort, surrounded as it is by the predominantly Muslim population of Old Delhi, was considered a security nightmare. So now we're into Plan Three: President George Bush speaks from Purana Qila, the Old Fort.[1]

Ironic isn't it, that the only safe public space for a man who has recently been so enthusiastic about India's modernity should be a crumbling medieval fort?

Since the Purana Qila also houses the Delhi zoo, George Bush's audience will be a few hundred caged animals and an approved list of caged human beings, who in India go under the category of 'eminent persons'. They're mostly rich folk who live in our poor country like captive animals, incarcerated by their own wealth, locked and barred in their gilded cages, protecting themselves from the threat of the vulgar and unruly multitudes whom they have systematically dispossessed over the centuries.

So what's going to happen to George W. Bush? Will the gorillas cheer him on? Will the gibbons curl their lips? Will the brow-antlered deer sneer? Will the chimps make rude noises? Will the owls hoot? Will the lions yawn and the giraffes bat their beautiful eyelashes? Will the crocs recognize a kindred soul? Will the quails give thanks that Bush isn't travelling with Dick Cheney, his hunting partner with the notoriously bad aim? Will the CEOs agree?

Oh, and on 2 March, Bush will be taken to visit Gandhi's memorial in Rajghat.[2] He's by no means the only war criminal who has been invited by the Indian government to lay flowers at Rajghat. (Only recently we had the Burmese dictator General Than Shwe, no shrinking violet himself.[3]) But when George Bush places flowers on that famous slab of highly polished stone, millions of Indians will wince. It will be as though he has poured a pint of blood on the memory of Gandhi.

We really would prefer that he didn't.

It is not in our power to stop Bush's visit. It is in our power to protest it, and we will. The government, the police and the corporate press will do everything they can to minimize the extent of our outrage. Nothing the happy-newspapers say can change the fact that for millions of us from all over India, from the biggest cities to the smallest villages, in public places and private homes, George W. Bush, the President of the United States of America, world nightmare incarnate, is just not welcome.

ANIMAL FARM II

IN WHICH GEORGE BUSH SAYS WHAT HE REALLY MEANS

In March 2006, George Bush came on a state visit to India and was greeted by massive public protests. In the days before his visit, 'Animal Farm II' was written in place of a lecture, and performed at a late night, open-air student meeting at New Delhi's Jawaharlal Nehru University on 28 February 2006.

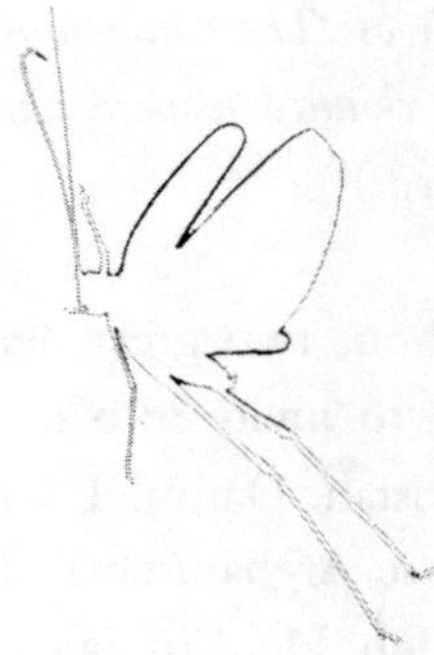

Ext. Day. Purana Qila. The Delhi Zoo.

It's spring. The neem trees have come into new leaf. The silk cotton and the kachnaar are in full bloom. The car park is packed with Mercs with their engines running and their air conditioners on. Bored uniformed chauffeurs are listening to Hindi film songs on swanky car stereos.

Inside the zoo the animals' cages have been recently cleaned and smell of phenyl. Tiny American and Indian flags flutter from the bars. There are heavily armed US security guards with muscles and sunglasses on top of every cage. They search the crowd and the cages for the first sign of trouble. They seem particularly uneasy about the pangolin.

George Bush is standing in a bulletproof cage and addressing a gathering of rich industrialists, MPs and a few film stars. They all wear lots of rings and have faded red thread wrapped around their wrists.

GEORGE BUSH: Hello all you lucky people! Thank you for taking time off your busy schedules to come and listen to the President of the United States.

(The Hoolock Gibbon hoots. The Orangutan doesn't even look up from his flea-hunt. The clouded leopard paces up and down. The Slow Loris looks surprised.)

I'm here today to talk about two great democracies in Asia, both of whom I have decided to invite into my Harem. Innia . . . and Afghanistan—sorry—Pakistan. Damn! I knew it had a Stan in it somewhere—but of course Afghanistan's already *in* my harem, so how can I invite her in. Heh! Heh! Innia's a democracy because the people voted for a government that obeys me. Pakistan's a democracy because General Musharraf has my vote. So do the bigots in Central Asia and Saudi Arabia. Palestine's not a democracy because they voted for people I don't like. But Innia's my favourite democracy.

More than five centuries ago the famous mass murderer and founder of our nation—Christopher Columbus—set out to discover Innia and proved the world was round. Now my friend Tom Friedman says its flat. Frankly, I don't really care what shape it is, as long as it belongs to me and I can play with it all day long. But as you know, Chris Columbus discovered America instead of Innia. Fortunately there were lots of Innians there too. With God on our side we killed them all—forty to sixty million of them—I don't recall the actual figure, my office will send out a statement later. But let's not quibble, what's a little genocide between friends? The good thing is that we now have the country to ourselves. Land of the Free, Home of the Brave. We have more newcooler weapons than any of you could possibly imagine. I could destroy the whole world in a minute if I'm in a bad mood. Heh! Heh! Jus' kiddin'. I'm not really a moody guy. Besides . . . I'm on your side for now. I mean, I'm on your side now. I'm not your enemy, am I? Do I look like that kind of guy? Have you seen *Sleeping with the Enemy*? I have, and I said to Laura, the film's okay, but the question is, who gets fucked? Ha!

Looks around with that sneering, triumphant look we have all come to know and love.

I'm sorry Laura's not here. She's doing a photo-op with some orphans down at Mother Treezer's. I have truly enjoyed meeting your prime minister—the guy with the turban and the funny high voice. I'm trying to get him to hand over the couple of newcooler bombs you peoples have in your little cupboard, so that I can look after them for you. Your prime minister is a good man—he went to Oxford, didn't he? But still . . . he *does* wear that funny turban, and when I look around me I see all kinds of funnily dressed people, some of them even have beards and look like Muzzlims. People who live in hot countries smell funny and don't use deodorant. My favourite deodorant is called Freedom, it has a lovely lemony smell. I don't think funnily dressed people should have newcooler weapons. So those bombs in your cupboard—just hand them over, folks.

In the United States we don't keep bombs in our cupboards. Only skeletons. Our favourite skellies have pet names. They're called Peace, Democracy and the Free Market. Their real names are Cruise Missile, Daisy Cutter and Bunker Buster. We like Cluster Bomb too. We call her Claire. She's real pretty and kids like to play with her and then she explodes in their faces and maims or kills them. That's a real hoot. But don't tell my mom I said that. She'll make me wash my tongue with soap.

I'm here today because Asia is transforming very quickly, and I want to be part of all the spiralling violence and environmental destruction. I love that sort of stuff—as those morons in Kyoto have no doubt been bleating about to you. I believe there isn't a single river left in Innia with potable water and the water table is plummeting. But you can have Coke instead, it's cooler and tastes better. And you're getting those lovely gigantic malls where you can buy anything if you have the cash. It gives me a thrill to know that the lives of rich Innians are improving rapidly and that Innian CEOs' salaries are beginning to match their Western counterparts. That's lovely. In the United States we subsidize our CEOs. We spoil them rotten because we love them. We love our corporate farmers too. We give them billions of dollars of subsidies because they're really good people. They're not like your farmers—thin and poor and suicidal. Your farmers don't deserve subsidies because they're not good people. You should put them on Prozac. That would bring in some more revenue to US drug companies.

As I was saying last week at the Asia Society, its good to know that rich Innians are buying air conditioners, kitchen appliances and washing machines made by US companies like General Electric, Whirlpool and Westinghouse. Younger Innians are developing a taste for Dominos Pizza and revolting hamburgers. This is wonderful news because Americans are tired of being the only people in the world with obesity problems and a truly disgusting cuisine.

But all bad things have a good apcess. The good apcess. (*An aide leans forward and whispers, 'Aspect,* Mr President.*'*) That's what I said, Henry—the good aspect of our terrible food is that it strengthens our resolve and commitment in our war against Muzzlims—I beg your pardon—against terrorists. I love Muzzlims. The good ones that is, the ones who aren't terrorists, but work in call centres. My friend Tom Friedman tells me that Innian Muzzlims are real nice folks. To defeat terrorists our intelligence agencies are spying on all of you all the time. You have no idea how much we know about you. We have surveillance cameras and wireless devices and software we have put into your computers so that we can watch you all the time. We know where you go, what you buy, who you sleep with.

I hate terrorists because they think they have a right to kill people too. But when I was small, my mother *and* my grandmother—you say *Naani* in Hindi, right? My mom and my naani told me that the only person who has the right to kill people, bomb countries and use chemical and newcooler weapons is the President of the United States. And guess who that is!

Begins to whoop and hoot and startle all the animals. The zoo erupts with alarm calls.

I'm very glad to be here because I love animals. I love hunting animals, especially when they are in cages and can't bite me. Once when I was small a bee bit me and I cried. I also love fighting wars against countries after they have been starved and forced to disarm. You know how clever we were about all that in Eye-raq. I love bombs because you don't have to see who you've killed which really suits cowards like me. But you needn't worry, I'm not here to bomb you or starve you—because you Innians are starving anyway. Ha! Ha!

Looks around triumphantly and looks contrite when he realizes he's made a boo-boo.

Oops . . . that's what my granny calls a boo boo! Sorry. The reason I'm here is that I like rich Innians. The reason I like rich Innians is that they are obedient and brainy and that is a pretty rare combination. In the United States we consider them model immigrants. I like obedient brainy rich Innians because they bring additional brainpower to help solve problems and provide executives in the United States with critical information about the needs of their consumers and customers overseas. Innia is important as a market for US products. It has one billion people for us to exploit. The best part is that the Innian government lets us take Innia's own stuff—coal, bauxite, minerals, even water and electricity and sell it back to them at huge profits. That's really fun. I love the Innian government.

Unfortunately out of these one billion people, most of them are poor. I hate poor people because they have no money to buy anything. I wish they would just disappear. I was glad to hear that tens of thousands of Innian farmers are committing suicide. In the United States we called that irresponsible self-destructive behaviour. But if we could just speed that up a bit, put it on a fast track trajectory, we could turn things around real fast. But poor people make good maidservants and wage labourers so we need to keep them going.

Soon we hope that US corporations will own all Innian seeds, plants, biodiversity, essential infrastructure and even their new ideas. As I said, Innians are quite brainy and sometimes have good ideas. We can't afford to let them own their own ideas. We can't allow farmers to owns seeds. Everybody ought to ask us about everything. I love it when everybody needs my permission. Dick says the key word is control.

One of the US corporations that we're proudest of was started by Bill Gates. He visits Innia often. He is a wonderful and generous man. He gives the Innian government millions of dollars to fight HIV-Aids. I don't like people who have HIV-Aids because they're mostly blacks and homos. I like the companies who make Aids drugs that no one can afford. I love that kind of dark, edgy humour. But I was talking about Bill. In return for Bill Gates' millions the Innian government buys hundreds of millions of dollars worth of computer technology from him. He's so rich I'm afraid he might burst. I always wear an apron when I'm around him.

I'm quite rich too. So are my friends and my friends' friends and my friends' friends' friends. Especially Dick Cheney. We work on our filthy deals together. Oil, weapons—all that. Shame about what happened to Enron. But it was good while it lasted. I love Dick especially because he tells me what to say at press conferences. I miss him. But I'll never go hunting with him. He might shoot me with his illegal gun, and I don't know what I'll do when I'm dead.

I'm looking forward to bombing Eye-ran. We have some new weapons we want to test. It should be fun. I hope Innia will send some soldiers to help us. There are so many of you, it won't matter much if you lose a few. And you're committing suicide in droves anyway, which is illegal. Why not get killed legally in Eye-ran or Eye-raq? We could arrange posthumous green cards. We'd have them laminated. But that would be charged to their account. Think about it.

Thank you for your time. 'Bye now. Jay Hind. Catcha later.

CAVEAT: In this age of copyright, intellectual property, piracy and plagiarism, I want to acknowledge that this play is entirely derivative. The ideas have all come from the public speeches and actions of the famous poet, pacifist, flower child, freethinker and social activist George W. Bush. Much of the play is based on the text of his recent speech in the Asia Society in Washington DC.[1] *All money from ticket sales should be sent directly to him.*

SCANDAL
IN THE
PALACE

This essay first appeared in Outlook *magazine (India) on 26 September 2007.*

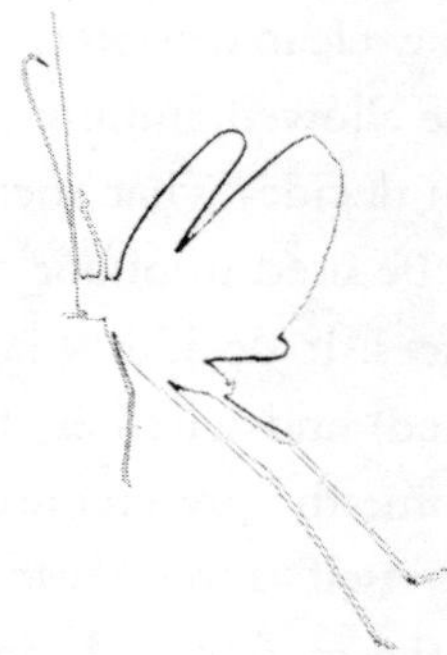

SCANDALS CAN be fun. Especially those that knock preachers from their pulpits and flick halos off saintly heads. But some scandals can be corrosive and more damaging for the scandalized than the scandalee. Right now we're in the midst of one such.

At its epicentre is Y.K. Sabharwal, former chief justice of India, who until recently headed the most powerful institution in this country—the Supreme Court. When there's a scandal about a former chief justice and his tenure in office, it's a little difficult to surgically excise the man and spare the institution. But then commenting adversely on the institution can lead you straight to a prison cell as some of us have learned to our cost. It's like having to take the wolf and the chicken and the sack of grain across the river, one by one. The river's high and the boat's leaking. Wish me luck.

The higher judiciary, the Supreme Court in particular, doesn't just uphold the law, it micromanages our lives. Its judgments range through matters great and small. It decides what's good for the environment and what isn't, whether dams should be built, rivers linked, mountains moved, forests felled. It decides what our cities should look like and who has the right to live in them. It decides whether slums should be cleared, streets widened, shops sealed, whether strikes should be allowed, industries should be shut down, relocated, or privatized. It decides what goes into school textbooks, what sort of fuel should be used in public transport and schedules of fines for traffic offences. It decides what colour the lights on judges' cars should be (red) and whether they should flash or not (they should). It has become the premier arbiter of public policy in this country that markets itself as the World's Largest Democracy.

Ironically, judicial activism first rode in on a tide of popular discontent with politicians and their venal ways. Around 1980, the courts opened their doors to ordinary citizens and people's movements seeking justice for underprivileged and marginalized people. This was the beginning of the era of Public Interest Litigation, a brief window of hope and real expectation.[1] While Public Interest Litigation gave people access to courts, it also did the opposite. It gave courts access to people and to issues that had been outside the judiciary's sphere of influence so far. So it could be argued that it was Public Interest Litigation that made the courts as powerful as they are. Over the last fifteen years or so, through a series of significant judgments, the judiciary has dramatically enhanced the scope of its own authority.

Today, as neo-liberalism sinks its teeth deeper into our lives and imagination, as millions of people are being pauperized and dispossessed in order to keep India's Tryst with Destiny (the un-Hindu 10 per cent rate of growth), the state has to resort to elaborate methods to contain growing unrest. One of its techniques is to invoke what the middle and upper classes fondly call the Rule of Law. The Rule of Law is a precept that is distinct, and can often be far removed from the principle of justice. The Rule of Law is a phrase that derives its meaning from the context in which it operates. It depends on what the laws are and who they're designed to protect.

For instance, from the early 1990s, we have seen the systematic dismantling of laws that protect workers' rights and the fundamental rights of ordinary people (the right to shelter/health/education/water). International financial institutions like the International Monetary Fund (IMF), the World Bank and the Asian Development Bank (ADB) demand these not just as a precondition, but as a condition, set down in black and white, before they agree to sanction loans. (The polite term for it is 'structural adjustment'.) What does the Rule of Law mean in a situation like this?

Howard Zinn, author of *A People's History of the United States*, puts it beautifully: 'The rule of law does not do away with unequal distribution of wealth and power, but reinforces that inequality with the authority of law. It allocates wealth and poverty . . . in such complicated and indirect ways as to leave the victim bewildered.'[2]

As it becomes more and more complicated for elected governments to be seen to be making unpopular decisions (decisions, for example, that displace millions of people from their villages, from their cities, from their jobs), it has increasingly fallen to the courts to make these decisions, to uphold the Rule of Law. The expansion of judicial powers has not been accompanied by an increase in its accountability. Far from it. The judiciary has managed to foil every attempt to put in place any system of checks and balances that other institutions in democracies are usually bound by. It has opposed the suggestion by the Committee for Judicial Accountability[3] that an independent disciplinary body be created to look into matters of judicial misconduct. It has decreed that an FIR cannot be registered against a sitting judge without the consent of the chief justice (which has never ever been given). It has so far successfully insulated itself against the Right to Information Act. The most effective weapon in its arsenal is, of course, the Contempt of Court Act which makes it a criminal offence to do or say anything that 'scandalizes' or 'lowers the authority' of the court. Though the act is framed in arcane language more suited to medieval ideas of feminine modesty, it actually arms the judiciary with formidable, arbitrary powers to silence its critics and to imprison anyone who asks uncomfortable questions. Small wonder then that the media pulls up short when it comes to reporting issues of judicial corruption and uncovering the scandals that must rock through our courtrooms on a daily basis. There are not many journalists who are willing to risk a long criminal trial and a prison sentence. Until recently, under the Law of Contempt, even truth was not considered a valid defence. So suppose, for instance, we had prima facie evidence that a judge has assaulted or raped someone, or accepted a bribe in return for a favourable judgment, it would be a criminal offence to make the evidence public because that would 'scandalise, or tend to scandalise' or 'lower, or tend to lower' the authority of the court.[4]

Yes, things have changed, but only a little. Last year, Parliament amended the Contempt of Court Act so that truth becomes a valid defence in a contempt of court charge. But in most cases (such as in the case of the Sabharwal . . . er . . . shall we say 'affair') in order to prove something it would have to be investigated. But obviously when you ask for an investigation you have to state your case, and when you state your case you will be imputing dishonourable motives to a judge for which you can be convicted for contempt. So: nothing can be proved unless it is investigated and nothing can be investigated unless it has been proved.

The only practical option that's on offer is for us to think Pure Thoughts.

For example:

a. Judges in India are divine beings.
b. Decency, wholesomeness, morality, transparency and integrity are encrypted in their DNA.
c. This is proved by the fact that no judge in the history of our republic has ever been impeached or disciplined in any way.
d. Jai Judiciary, Jai Hind.

It all becomes a bit puzzling when ex-chief justices like Justice S.P. Bharucha go about making public statements about widespread corruption in the judiciary.[5] Perhaps we should wear ear plugs on these occasions or chant a mantra.

It may hurt our pride and curb our free spirits to admit it, but the fact is that we live in a sort of judicial dictatorship. And now there's a scandal in the palace.

For people in Delhi 2006 was a hard year. The Supreme Court passed a series of orders that changed the face of the city, a city that has over the years expanded organically, extra-legally, haphazardly. A division bench headed by Y.K. Sabharwal, chief justice at the time, ordered the sealing of thousands of shops, houses and commercial complexes that housed what the court called 'illegal' businesses. These had been functioning, in some cases for decades, out of residential areas in violation of the old master plan. It's true that according to the designated land-use in the old master plan, these businesses were non-conforming. But the municipal authorities in charge of implementing the plan had developed only about a quarter of the commercial areas they were supposed to. So they looked away while people made their own arrangements (and put their lives' savings into them.) Then suddenly Delhi became the capital city of the new emerging Superpower. It had to be dressed up to look the part. The easiest way was to invoke the Rule of Law.

The sealing affected the lives and livelihoods of tens of thousands of people. There were protests, there was rioting. The city burned. The Rapid Action Force was called in. Dismayed by the seething rage and despair of the people, the Delhi government beseeched the court to reconsider its decision. It submitted a new '2021 Master Plan', which allowed mixed land-use and commercial activity in several areas that had until now been designated 'residential'. Justice Sabharwal remained unmoved. The bench he headed ordered the sealing to continue.[6]

Around the same time, another bench of the Supreme Court ordered the demolition of Nangla Maachi and other jhuggi squatter colonies, which left hundreds of thousands homeless, living on top of the debris of their broken homes, in the scorching summer sun.[7] Yet another bench ordered the removal of all 'unlicensed' vendors from the city's streets. Even as Delhi was being purged of its poor, a new kind of city was springing up around us. A glittering city of air-conditioned corporate malls and multiplexes where multinational corporations showcased their newest products. The better off among those whose shops and offices had been sealed queued up for space in these malls. Prices shot up. The mall business boomed, it was the newest game in town.

Some of these malls, mini-cities in themselves, were also illegal constructions and did not have the requisite permissions. But here the Supreme Court viewed their misdemeanours through a different lens. The Rule of Law winked and went off for a tea break. In its judgment on the writ petition against the Vasant Kunj Mall dated 17 October 2006 (in which it allowed the construction of the mall to go right ahead), Justices Arijit Pasayat and S.H. Kapadia said:

> Had such parties inkling of an idea that such clearances were not obtained by DDA, they would not have invested such huge sums of money. The stand that wherever constructions have been made unauthorizedly demolition is the only option cannot apply to the present cases, more particularly, when they unlike, where some private individuals or private limited companies or firms being allotted to have made contraventions, are corporate bodies and institutions and the question of their having indulged in any malpractices in getting the approval or sanction does not arise.[8]

It's a bit complicated, I know. A friend and I sat down and translated it into ordinary English. Basically,

a. Even though in this present case the construction may be unauthorized and may not have the proper clearances, huge amounts of money have been invested and demolition is not the only option.
b. Unlike private individuals or private limited companies who have been allotted land and may have flouted the law, these allottees are corporate bodies and institutions and there is no question of their having indulged in any malpractice in order to get sanctions or approval.

The question of corporate bodies having indulged in malpractice in getting approval or sanction does not arise. So says the Indian Supreme Court.[9] What should we say to those shrill hysterical people protesting out there on the streets, accusing the court of being an outpost of the New Corporate Empire? Shall we shout them down? Shall we say 'Enron zindabad'? Long live Enron. 'Bechtel, Halliburton zindabad'? 'Tata, Birla, Mittals, Reliance, Vedanta,

Alcan zindabad'? 'Coca-Cola aage badho, hum tumhaare saath hain'? This then was the ideological climate in the Supreme Court at the time the Sabharwal 'affair' took place.

It's important to make it clear that Justice Sabharwal's orders were not substantially different or ideologically at loggerheads with the orders of other judges who have not been touched by scandal and whose personal integrity is not in question. But the ideological bias of a judge is quite a different matter from the personal motivations and conflict of interest that could have informed Justice Sabharwal's orders. That is the substance of this story.

In his final statement to the media before he retired in January 2007, Justice Sabharwal said that the decision to implement the sealing in Delhi was the most difficult decision he had made during his tenure as chief justice. Perhaps it was. Tough Love can't be easy.

In May 2007, the Delhi edition of the evening paper *Mid Day* published detailed investigative stories (and a cartoon) alleging serious judicial misconduct on the part of Justice Sabharwal. The articles are available on the Internet. The charges *Mid Day* made have subsequently been corroborated by the Committee for Judicial Accountability, an organization that counts senior lawyers, retired judges, professors, journalists and activists as its patrons.[10]

The charges in brief are:

1. That Y.K. Sabharwal's sons Chetan and Nitin had three companies: Pawan Impex, Sabs Exports and Sug Exports whose registered offices were initially at their family home in 3/81, Punjabi Bagh, New Delhi and were then shifted to their father's official residence at 6, Motilal Nehru Marg, New Delhi.
2. That while he was a judge in the Supreme Court but before he became chief justice, he called for and dealt with the sealing of commercial properties case in Delhi. (This was impropriety. Only

the chief justice is empowered to call for cases that are pending before a different bench.)

3. That at exactly this time, Justice Sabharwal's sons went into partnership with two major mall and commercial complex developers, Purshottam Bagheria (of the fashionable Square 1 Mall fame) and Kabul Chawla of Business Park Town Planners (BPTP) Ltd. That as a result of Justice Sabharwal's sealing orders, people were forced to move their shops and businesses to malls and commercial complexes, which pushed up prices, thereby benefiting Justice Sabharwal's sons and their partners financially and materially.
4. That the Union Bank gave a two hundred and eighty million rupees ($5.6 million) loan to Pawan Impex on collateral security which turned out to be non-existent. (Justice Sabharwal says his sons' companies had credit facilities of up to seven hundred and fifty million rupees [$15.1 million].)
5. That because of obvious conflict of interest, he should have recused himself from hearing the sealing case (instead of doing the opposite—calling the case to himself).
6. That a number of industrial and commercial plots of land in NOIDA were allotted to his sons' companies at throwaway prices by the Mulayam Singh/Amar Singh government while Justice Sabharwal was the sitting judge on the case of the Amar Singh phone tapes (in which he issued an order restricting their publication).
7. That his sons bought a house in Maharani Bagh for Rs 154,600,000 ($3.1 million). The source of this money is unexplained. In the deeds they have put down their father's name as Yogesh Kumar (uncharacteristic coyness for boys who don't mind running their businesses out of their judge father's official residence).

All these charges are backed by what looks like watertight, unimpeachable documentation. Registration deeds, documents from the Union ministry of company affairs, certificates of incorporation of the various companies, published lists of shareholders, notices declaring increased share capital in Nitin and Chetan's companies, notices from the Income Tax department and a CD of recorded phone conversations between the investigating journalist and the judge himself.

These documents seem to indicate that while Delhi burned, while thousands of shops and businesses were sealed and their owners and employees deprived of their livelihood, Justice Sabharwal's sons and their partners were raking in the bucks. They read like an instruction manual for how the New India works.

When the story became public, another retired chief justice, J.S. Verma, appeared on *India Tonight*, Karan Thapar's interview show on CNBC. He brought all the prudence and caution of a former judge to bear on what he said: 'if it is true, this is the height of impropriety . . . every one who holds any public office is ultimately accountable in democracy to the people, therefore, the people have right to know how they are functioning, and higher is the office that you hold, greater is the accountability'. Justice Verma went on to say that if the facts were correct, it would constitute a clear case of conflict of interest and that Justice Sabharwal's orders on the sealing case must be set aside and the case heard all over again.[11]

This is the heart of the matter. This is what makes this scandal such a corrosive one. Hundreds of thousands of lives have been devastated. If it is true that the judgment that caused this stands vitiated, then amends must be made.

But are the facts correct?

Scandals about powerful and well-known people can be, and often are, malicious, motivated and untrue. God knows that judges make mortal enemies—after all, in each case they adjudicate there is a winner and a loser. There's little doubt that Justice Y.K. Sabharwal would have made his fair share of enemies. If I were him, and if I really had nothing to hide, I would actually welcome an investigation. In fact, I would beg the chief justice to set up a commission of inquiry. I would make it a point to go after those who had fabricated evidence against me and made all these outrageous allegations.

What I certainly wouldn't do is to make things worse by writing an ineffective, sappy defence of myself which doesn't address the allegations and doesn't convince anyone.[12]

Equally, if I were the sitting chief justice or anybody else who claims to be genuinely interested in 'upholding the dignity' of the court (fortunately this is not my line of work), I would know that to shovel the dirt under the carpet at this late stage, or to try and silence or intimidate the whistle-blowers, is counterproductive. It wouldn't take me very long to work out that if I didn't order an inquiry and order it quickly, what started out as a scandal about a particular individual could quickly burgeon into a scandal about the entire judiciary.

But, of course, not everybody sees it that way. Days after *Mid Day* went public with its allegations, the Delhi high court issued *suo motu* notice charging the editor, the resident editor, the publisher and the cartoonist of *Mid Day* with Contempt of Court.[13] Three months later, on 11 September 2007, it passed an order holding them guilty of criminal Contempt of Court. They have been summoned for sentencing on 21 September.

What was *Mid Day*'s crime? An unusual display of courage? The high court order makes absolutely no comment on the factual accuracy of the allegations that *Mid Day* levelled against Justice Sabharwal. Instead, in an extraordinary, almost yogic manoeuvre, it makes out that the real targets of the *Mid Day* article were the judges sitting with Justice Sabharwal on the division bench, judges who are still in service (and therefore imputing motives to them constitutes Criminal Contempt):

> We find the manner in which the entire incidence has been projected appears as if the Supreme Court permitted itself to be led into fulfilling an ulterior motive of one of its members. The nature of the revelations and the context in which they appear, though purporting to single out former Chief Justice of India, tarnishes the image of the Supreme Court. It tends to erode the confidence of the general public in the institution itself. The Supreme Court sits in divisions and every order is of a bench. By imputing motive to its presiding member automatically sends a signal that the other members were dummies or were party to fulfill the ulterior design.

Nowhere in the *Mid Day* articles has any other judge been so much as mentioned. So the journalists are in the dock for an imagined insult. What this means is that if there are several judges sitting on a bench and you have proof that one of them has given an opinion or an order based on corrupt considerations or is judging a case in which he or she has a clear conflict of interest, it's not enough. You don't have a case unless you can prove that all of them are corrupt or that all of them have a conflict of interest and all of them have left a trail of evidence in their wake. Actually, even this is not enough. You must also be able to state your case without casting any aspersions whatsoever on the court. (Purely for the sake of argument: What if two judges on a bench decide to take turns to be corrupt? What would we do then?)

So now we're saddled with a whole new school of thought on Contempt of Court: Fevered interpretations of imagined insults against unnamed judges. Phew! We're in La-la Land.

In most other countries, the definition of Criminal Contempt of Court is limited to anything that threatens to be a clear and present danger to the administration of justice. This business of 'scandalising' and 'lowering the authority' of the court is an absurd, dangerous form of censorship and an insult to our collective intelligence.

The journalists who broke the story in *Mid Day* have done an important and courageous thing. Some newspapers acting in solidarity have followed up the story. A number of people have come together and made a public statement further bolstering that support. It's all happening. The lid is off, and about time too.

LISTENING TO GRASS-HOPPERS

GENOCIDE, DENIAL AND CELEBRATION

This article was delivered as a lecture in Istanbul on 18 January 2008, to commemorate the first anniversary of the assassination of Hrant Dink, editor of the Turkish-Armenian paper Agos. *It appeared in* Outlook *magazine (India) on 4 February 2008, and* International Socialist Review, *Issue 58, March–April 2008.*

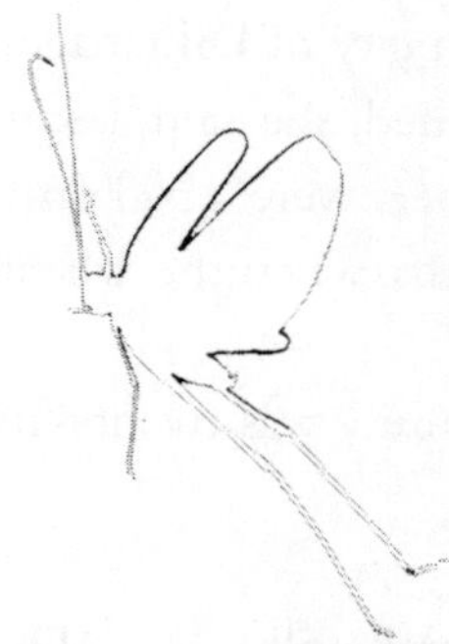

I NEVER met Hrant Dink, a misfortune that will be mine for time to come. From what I know of him, of what he wrote, what he said and did, how he lived his life, I know that had I been here in Istanbul a year ago, I would have been among the one hundred thousand people who walked with his coffin in dead silence through the wintry streets of this city, with banners saying 'We are all Armenians', 'We are all Hrant Dink'. Perhaps I'd have carried the one that said 'One and a half million plus one'.†[1]

I wonder what thoughts would have gone through my head as I walked beside his coffin. Maybe I would have heard a reprise of the voice of Araxie Barsamian, mother of my friend David Barsamian, telling the story of what happened to her and her family. She was ten years old in 1915. She remembered the swarms of grasshoppers that arrived in her village, Dubne, which was north

†One and a half million is the number of Armenians who were systematically murdered by the Ottoman Empire in the genocide in Anatolia in the spring of 1915. The Armenians, the largest Christian minority living under Islamic Turkic rule in the area, had lived in Anatolia for more than two thousand five hundred years.

of the historic Armenian city of Dikranagert, now Diyarbakir. The village elders were alarmed, she said, because they knew in their bones that the grasshoppers were a bad omen. They were right; the end came in a few months, when the wheat in the fields was ready for harvesting.

'When we left, my family was twenty-five in the family,' Araxie Barsamian says.

> They took all the men folks . . . . They asked my father, 'Where is your ammunition?' He says, 'I sold it.' So they says, 'Go get it.' So when he went to the Kurd town, to get it, they beat him and took him all his clothes. And when he came back there—this is my mother tells me story—when he came back there, naked body, he went in the jail, they cut his arms . . . . So he die in the jail . . . . They took all the mens in the field, they tied their hands, and they shooted, killed every one of them.[2]

Araxie, her mother and three younger brothers were deported. All of them perished except Araxie. She was the lone survivor. This is, of course, a single testimony that comes from a history that is denied by the Turkish government, and many Turks as well.

I have not come here to play the global intellectual, to lecture you, or to fill the silence in this country that surrounds the memory (or the forgetting) of the events that took place in Anatolia in 1915. That is what Hrant Dink tried to do, and paid for with his life.

The day I arrived in Istanbul, I walked the streets for many hours, and as I looked around, envying the people of Istanbul their beautiful, mysterious, thrilling city, a friend pointed out to me young boys in white caps who seemed to have suddenly appeared like a rash in the city. He explained that they were expressing their solidarity with the child-assassin who was wearing a white cap when he killed Hrant. Obviously the assassination was meant both as a punishment for Hrant and a warning to others in this country who might have been inspired by his courage—not just to say the unsayable, but to think the unthinkable.

This was the message written on the bullet that killed Hrant Dink. This is the message in the death threats received by Orhan Pamuk, Elif Shafak and others who have dared to differ with the Turkish government's view.[3] Before he was killed, Hrant Dink was tried three times under Article 301 of the Turkish Penal Code, which makes publicly denigrating 'Turkishness' a criminal offence. Each of these trials was a signal from the Turkish state to Turkey's fascist right wing that Hrant Dink was an acceptable target. How can telling the truth denigrate Turkishness? Who has the right to limit and define what Turkishness is?

Hrant Dink has been silenced. But those who celebrate his murder should know that what they did was counterproductive. Instead of silence, it has raised a great noise. Hrant's voice has become a shout that can never be silenced again, not by bullets, or prison sentences, or insults. It shouts, it whispers, it sings, it shatters the bullying silence that has begun to gather once again like an army that was routed and is regrouping. It has made the world curious about something that happened in Anatolia more than ninety years ago. Something that Hrant's enemies wanted to bury. To forget. Well . . . speaking for myself, my first reaction was to find out what I could about 1915, to read history, to listen to testimonies. Something I might not otherwise have done. Now I have an opinion, an informed opinion about it, but, as I said, that is not what I'm here to inflict on you.

The battle with the cap-wearers of Istanbul, of Turkey, is not my battle, it's yours. I have my own battles to fight against other kinds of cap-wearers and torch-bearers in my country. In a way, the battles are not all that different. There is one crucial difference, though. While in Turkey there is silence, in India there's celebration, and I really don't know which is worse. I think that silence suggests shame, and shame suggests conscience. Is that too naïve and generous an interpretation? Perhaps, but why not be naïve and generous? Celebration, unfortunately, does not lend itself to interpretation. It is what it says it is.

Lessons from your past have given me an insight into our future. My talk today is not about the past, it's about the future. I want to talk about the foundations that are being laid for the future of India, a country being celebrated all over the world as a role model of progress and democracy.

~

In the state of Gujarat, there was genocide against the Muslim community in 2002. I use the word genocide advisedly, and in keeping with its definition contained in Article 2 of the United Nations Convention on the Prevention and Punishment of the Crime of Genocide. The genocide began as collective punishment for an unsolved crime—the burning of a railway coach in which fifty-three Hindu pilgrims were burned to death. In a carefully planned orgy of supposed retaliation, two thousand Muslims were slaughtered in broad daylight by squads of armed killers, organized by fascist militias, and backed by the Gujarat government and the administration of the day. Muslim women were gang-raped and burned alive. Muslim shops, Muslim businesses and Muslim shrines and mosques were systematically destroyed. One hundred and fifty thousand people were driven from their homes.

Even today, many of them live in ghettos—some built on garbage heaps—with no water supply, no drainage, no street lights, no health care. They live as second-class citizens, boycotted socially and economically.[4] Meanwhile, the killers, police as well as civilian, have been embraced, rewarded, promoted. This state of affairs is now considered 'normal'. To seal the 'normality', in 2004 both Ratan Tata and Mukesh Ambani, India's leading industrialists, praised Gujarat for being a dream destination for finance capital.[5]

The initial outcry in the national press has settled down. In Gujarat, the genocide has been brazenly celebrated as the epitome of Gujarati pride, Hindu-ness, even Indian-ness. This poisonous brew has been used twice in a row to win state elections, with campaigns that have cleverly used the language and apparatus of modernity and democracy. The helmsman, Narendra Modi, has become a folk hero, called in by the Bharatiya Janata Party (BJP) to campaign on its behalf in other Indian states.

As genocides go, the Gujarat genocide cannot compare with the people killed in the Congo, Rwanda and Bosnia, where the numbers run into millions, nor is it by any means the first that has occurred in India. (In 1984, for instance, three thousand Sikhs were massacred on the streets of Delhi with similar impunity, by killers overseen by the Congress Party.[6]) But the Gujarat genocide is part of a larger, more elaborate and systematic vision. It tells us that the wheat is ripening and the grasshoppers have landed in mainland India.

It's an old human habit, genocide is. It has played a sterling part in the march of civilization. Among the earliest recorded genocides is thought to be the destruction of Carthage at the end of the Third

Punic War in 149 BC. The word itself—genocide—was coined by Raphael Lemkin only in 1943, and adopted by the United Nations in 1948, after the Nazi Holocaust. Article 2 of the United Nations Convention on the Prevention and Punishment of the Crime of Genocide defines it as:

> any of the following acts committed with intent to destroy, in whole or in part, a national, ethnic, racial or religious group, as such:
> (a) Killing members of the group;
> (b) Causing serious bodily or mental harm to members of the group;
> (c) Deliberately inflicting on the group conditions of life calculated to bring about its physical destruction in whole or in part;
> (d) Imposing measures intending to prevent births within the group;
> (e) Forcibly transferring children of the group to another group.[7]

Since this definition leaves out the persecution of political dissidents, 'enemies of the people', real or imagined, it does not include some of the greatest mass murders in history. Personally I think the definition by Frank Chalk and Kurt Jonassohn, authors of *The History and Sociology of Genocide*, is more apt. Genocide, they say, 'is a form of one-sided mass killing in which a state or other authority intends to destroy a group, as that group and membership in it are defined by the perpetrator'.[8] Defined like this, genocide would include for example, the millions killed and the monumental crimes committed by Suharto in Indonesia, Pol Pot in Cambodia, Stalin in the Soviet Union and Mao in China.

All things considered, the word extermination, with its crude evocation of pests and vermin, of infestations, is perhaps the more honest, more apposite word. When a set of perpetrators faces its victims, in order to go about its business of wanton killing, it must first sever any human connection with it. It must see its victims as subhuman, as parasites whose eradication would be a service to society. Here, for example, is an account of the massacre of Pequot Indians by English Puritans led by John Mason in Connecticut in 1636:

> Those that scaped the fire were slaine with the sword; some hewed to peeces, others rune throw with their rapiers, so as they were quickly dispatchte, and very few escaped. It was conceived they thus destroyed about four hundred at this time. It was a fearful sight to see them thus frying in the fyer, and the streams of blood quenching the same, and horrible was the stincke and sente there of, but the victory seemed a sweete sacrifice.[9]

And here, approximately four centuries later, is Babu Bajrangi, one of the major lynchpins of the Gujarat genocide, recorded on camera in the sting operation mounted by the Indian newsmagazine *Tehelka* a few months ago:

> We didn't spare a single Muslim shop, we set everything on fire, we set them on fire and killed them . . . . hacked, burnt, set on fire . . . . We believe in setting them on fire because these bastards don't want to be cremated, they're afraid of it . . . .[10]

I hardly need to say that Babu Bajrangi had the blessings of Narendra Modi, the protection of the police, and the love of his people. He continues to work and prosper as a free man in Gujarat. The one crime he cannot be accused of is Genocide Denial.

Genocide Denial is a radical variation on the theme of the old, frankly racist, bloodthirsty triumphalism. It was probably evolved as an answer to the somewhat patchy, dual morality that arose in the nineteenth century, when Europe was developing limited but new forms of democracy and citizens' rights at home while simultaneously exterminating people in their millions in her colonies. Suddenly countries and governments began to deny or attempt to hide the genocides they had committed. 'Denial is saying, in effect,' Robert J. Lifton observes, that 'the murderers didn't murder. The victims weren't killed. The direct consequence of denial is that it invites future genocide.'[11]

Of course, today, when genocide politics meets the Free Market, official recognition—or denial—of holocausts and genocides is a multinational business enterprise. It rarely has anything to do to with historical fact or forensic evidence. Morality certainly does not enter the picture. It is an aggressive process of high-end bargaining that belongs more to the World Trade Organization than to the United Nations. The currency is geopolitics, the fluctuating market for natural resources, that curious thing called futures trading, and plain old economic and military might.

In other words, genocides are often denied for the same set of reasons genocides are prosecuted. Economic determinism marinated in racial/ethnic/religious/national discrimination. Crudely, the lowering or raising of the price of a barrel of oil (or a ton of uranium), permission granted for a military base, or the opening up of a country's economy could be the decisive factor when governments adjudicate on whether a genocide did or did not occur. Or indeed whether genocide will or will not occur. And if it does, whether it will or will not be reported, and if it is, then what slant that reportage will take. For example, the death of millions in the Congo goes virtually unreported.[12] Why? And was the death of a million Iraqis under the sanctions regime, prior to the US invasion in 2003, genocide (which is what UN Humanitarian Coordinator for Iraq, Denis Halliday called it) or was it 'worth it', as Madeleine Albright, the US ambassador to the United Nations, claimed?[13] It depends on who makes the rules. Bill Clinton? Or an Iraqi mother who has lost her child?

Since the United States is the richest and most powerful country in the world, in the Genocide Denial seedings it is the World's Number One. It continues to celebrate Columbus Day, the day Christopher Columbus arrived in the Americas, which marks the beginning of a holocaust that wiped out millions of Native Indians, about 90 per cent of the original population. Lord Amherst, the man whose idea it was to distribute blankets infected with smallpox virus to Indians, has a university town in Massachusetts, and a prestigious liberal arts college, named after him.

In America's second holocaust, almost thirty million Africans were kidnapped and sold into slavery. Well near half of them died during transportation. But in 2001, the US delegation could still walk out of the World Conference Against Racism in Durban, refusing to acknowledge that slavery and the slave trade were crimes. Slavery, they insisted, was legal at the time.[14] The United States has also refused to accept that the bombing of Tokyo, Hiroshima, Nagasaki, Dresden and Hamburg—which killed hundreds of thousands of civilians—were crimes, let alone acts of genocide. (The argument here is that the government didn't intend to kill civilians. This was an early stage of the development of the concept of 'collateral damage'.)[15] Since its first foreign conquest of Mexico in 1848, the US government has militarily intervened abroad, whether overtly or covertly, countless times. Its invasion of Vietnam, with excellent intentions of course, led to the deaths of millions of people in Indochina.[16]

None of these actions have been acknowledged as war crimes or genocidal acts. 'How much evil,' asks Robert McNamara, whose career graph took him from the bombing of Tokyo in 1945 (one hundred thousand dead overnight), to being the architect of the war in Vietnam, to president of the World Bank, now sitting in his comfortable chair in his comfortable home in his comfortable country, 'must we do in order to do good?'[17]

Could there be a more perfect illustration of Robert J. Lifton's point that the denial of genocide invites more genocide?

As a friendly gesture to the government of Turkey, its ally in the volatile politics of the Middle East, the US government concurs with the Turkish government's denial of the Armenian genocide. So does the government of Israel.[18] For the same reasons. For them the Armenian people are suffering a collective hallucination.

And what when the victims become perpetrators, as they did in the Congo and in Rwanda? What remains to be said about Israel, created out of the debris of one of the cruelest genocides in human history? What of its actions in the Occupied Territories? Its burgeoning settlements, its colonization of water, its new 'Security Wall' that separates Palestinian people from their farms, from their work, from their relatives, from their children's schools, from hospitals and health care? It is genocide in a fishbowl, genocide in slow motion—meant especially to illustrate that section of Article 2 of the United Nations Convention on the Prevention and Punishment of the Crime of Genocide, that says genocide is any act that is designed to 'deliberately inflict on the group conditions of life, calculated to bring about its physical destruction in whole or part'.

Perhaps the ugliest aspect of the Genocide Game is that genocides have been ranked and seeded like tennis players on the international circuit. Their victims are categorized into worthy or unworthy ones. Take, for example, the best-known, best-documented, most condemned genocide by far—the Jewish Holocaust, which took the lives of six million Jews. (Less publicized in books and films and Holocaust literature is the fact that the Nazis also liquidated thousands of gypsies, communists, homosexuals and millions of Russian prisoners of war, not all of them Jewish.[19]) The Nazi genocide of Jews has been universally accepted as the most horrifying event of the twentieth century. In the face of this, some historians call the Armenian genocide the Forgotten Genocide, and in their fight to remind the world about it, frequently refer to it as the first genocide of the twentieth century. Peter Balakian, one of the most knowledgeable scholars of the Armenian genocide, and author of *The Burning Tigris: The Armenian Genocide and America's Response*, says that 'the Armenian genocide is a landmark event. It changed history. It was unprecedented. It began the age of genocide, which we must acknowledge the twentieth century indeed was.'[20]

The professor is in error. The 'era of genocide' had begun long ago. The Herero people, for example, were exterminated by the Germans in South-West Africa only a few years into the twentieth century. In October 1904, General Adolf Lebrecht von Trotha ordered that the Herero be exterminated.[21] They were driven into the desert, cut off from food and water, and in this way annihilated. Meanwhile, in other parts of the African continent, genocide was proceeding apace. The French, the British, the Belgians were all busy. King Leopold of Belgium was well into his 'experiment in commercial expansion' in search of slaves, rubber and ivory in the Congo.[22] The price of his experiment: ten million human lives. It was one of the most brutal genocides of all time. (The battle to control Africa's mineral wealth rages on—scratch the surface of contemporary horrors in Africa, in Rwanda, the Congo, Nigeria, pick your country, and chances are that you will be able to trace the story back to the old colonial interests of Europe and the new colonial interests of the United States.)

In Asia, by the last quarter of the nineteenth century, the British had finished exterminating the aboriginal people in Tasmania, and most of Australia, starving them out, hunting them down. British convicts were given five pounds for every native they hunted down. The last Tasmanian woman, Truganina, died in 1876. (Her skeleton was kept in a museum for years. It was finally given back to her people in 1976 and she was put to rest with respect and ceremony.) The Spanish, the French and the British, of course, had by then almost finished God's Work in the Americas.

In the genocide sweepstakes, while pleading for justice for one people, it is so easy to inadvertently do away with the suffering of others. This is the slippery morality of the international politics of genocide. Genocide within genocide, denial within denial, on and on, like Matryoshka dolls.

The history of genocide tells us that it's not an aberration, an anomaly, a glitch in the human system. It's a habit as old, as persistent, as much part of the human condition as love and art and agriculture. Most of the genocidal killing from the fifteenth century onwards has been an integral part of Europe's search for what the Germans famously called *lebensraum*, living space. Lebensraum was a word coined by the German geographer and zoologist Friedrich Ratzel to describe what he thought of as dominant human species' natural impulse to expand their territory in their search for not just space, but sustenance. This impulse to expansion would naturally be at the cost of a less dominant species, a weaker species that Nazi ideologues believed should give way, or be made to give way, to the stronger one.

The idea of lebensraum was set out in precise terms in 1901, but Europe had already begun her quest for lebensraum four hundred years earlier, when Columbus landed in America.

Sven Lindqvist, author of *Exterminate All the Brutes*, argues that it was Hitler's quest for lebensraum—in a world that had already been carved up by other European countries—that led the Nazis to push through Eastern Europe and on towards Russia.[23] The Jews of Eastern Europe and western Russia stood in the way of Hitler's colonial ambitions. Therefore, like the native peoples of Africa and America and Asia, they had to be enslaved or liquidated. So, Lindqvist says, the Nazis' racist dehumanization of Jews cannot be dismissed as a paroxysm of insane evil. Once again, it is a product of the familiar mix: economic determinism well marinated in age-old racism—very much in keeping with European tradition of the time.

It's not a coincidence that the political party that carried out the Armenian genocide in the Ottoman Empire was called the Committee for Union and Progress. 'Union' (racial/ethnic/religious/national) and 'Progress' (economic determinism) have long been the twin coordinates of genocide.

Armed with this reading of history, is it reasonable to worry about whether a country that is poised on the threshold of 'progress' is also poised on the threshold of genocide? Could the India being celebrated all over the world as a miracle of progress and democracy possibly be poised on the verge of committing genocide? The mere suggestion might sound outlandish and at this point of time, the use of the word genocide surely unwarranted. However, if we look to the future, and if the Tsars of Development believe in their own publicity, if they believe that There Is No Alternative to their chosen model for Progress, then they will inevitably have to kill, and kill in large numbers, in order to get their way.

In bits and pieces, as the news trickles in, it seems clear that the killing and the dying has already begun.

~

It was in 1989, soon after the collapse of the Soviet Union, that the Government of India turned in its membership in the Non-Aligned Movement and signed up for membership in the Completely Aligned, often referring to itself as the 'natural ally' of Israel and the United States. (They have at least this one thing in common, all three are engaged in overt, neocolonial military occupations: India in Kashmir, Israel in Palestine, the United States in Iraq and Afghanistan.)

Almost like clockwork, the two major national political parties, the BJP and the Congress, embarked on a joint programme to advance India's version of Union and Progress, whose modern-day euphemisms are Nationalism and Development. Every now and then, particularly during elections, they stage some noisy familial squabbles, but have managed to gather into their fold even grumbling relatives, like the Communist Party of India (Marxist).

The Union project offers Hindu Nationalism (which seeks to unite the Hindu vote, vital, you will admit, for a great democracy like India). The Progress project aims at a 10 per cent annual growth rate. Both projects are encrypted with genocidal potential.

The Union project has been largely entrusted to the Rashtriya Swayamsevak Sangh (RSS), the ideological heart, the holding company of the BJP and its militias, the Vishwa Hindu Parishad (VHP) and the Bajrang Dal. The RSS was founded in 1925. By the 1930s, its founder, Dr K.B. Hedgewar, a fan of Benito Mussolini's, had begun to model it overtly along the lines of Italian fascism.

Hitler, too, was and is, an inspirational figure. Here are some excerpts from the RSS bible, *We, or, Our Nationhood Defined* by M.S. Golwalker, who succeeded Dr Hedgewar as head of the RSS in 1940:

> Ever since that evil day, when Moslems first landed in Hindustan, right up to the present moment, the Hindu Nation has been gallantly fighting on to take on these despoilers. The Race Spirit has been awakening.

Then:

> In Hindustan, land of the Hindus, lives and should live the Hindu Nation . . . .
>
> All others are traitors and enemies to the National Cause, or, to take a charitable view, idiots . . . . The foreign races in Hindustan . . . may stay in the country, wholly subordinated to the Hindu Nation, claiming nothing, deserving no privileges, far less any preferential treatment—not even citizen's rights.

And again:

> To keep up the purity of its race and culture, Germany shocked the world by her purging the country of the Semitic races—the Jews. Race pride at its highest has been manifested here . . . a good lesson for us in Hindustan to learn and profit by.

How do you combat this kind of organized hatred? Certainly not with goofy preachings of secular love.

By the year 2000, the RSS had more than sixty thousand shakhas (branches) and an army of more than four million swayamsevaks (volunteers) preaching its doctrine across India.[24] They include India's former prime minister Atal Bihari Vajpayee, the former home minister and current leader of the opposition L.K. Advani, and, of course, the three times Gujarat chief minister Narendra Modi. It also includes senior people in the media, the police, the army, the intelligence agencies, the judiciary and the administrative services who are informal devotees of Hindutva—the RSS ideology. These people, unlike politicians who come and go, are permanent members of government machinery.

But the RSS's real power lies in the fact that it has put in decades of hard work and has created a network of organizations at every level of society, something that no other political or cultural group in India can match. The BJP is its political front. It has a trade union wing (Bharatiya Mazdoor Sangh), women's wing (Rashtriya Sevika Samiti), student wing (Akhil Bharatiya Vidyarthi Parishad), and economic wing (Swadeshi Jagran Manch).

Its front organization Vidya Bharati is the largest educational organization in the non-governmental sector. It has thirteen thousand educational institutes, including the Saraswati Vidya Mandir schools with seventy thousand teachers and more than 1.7 million students. It has organizations working with tribals (Vanavasi Kalyan Ashram), literature (Akhil Bharatiya Sahitya Parishad), intellectuals (Pragya Bharati, Deendayal Research Institute), historians (Bharatiya Itihaas Sankalan Yojanalaya), language (Sanskrit Bharti), slum dwellers (Seva Bharati, Hindu Seva Prathishtan), health (Swami Vivekanand Medical Mission, National Medicos Organization), leprosy patients (Bharatiya Kushta Nivarak Sangh), cooperatives (Sahkar Bharati), publication of newspapers and other propaganda material (Bharat Prakashan, Suruchi Prakashan, Lokhit Prakashan, Gyanganga Prakashan, Archana Prakashan, Bharatiya Vichar Sadhana, Sadhana Pustak and Akashvani Sadhana), caste integration (Samajik Samrasta Manch), religion and proselytization (Vivekananda Kendra, Vishwa

Hindu Parishad, Hindu Jagran Manch, Bajrang Dal). The list goes on and on.

In 1986, Prime Minister Rajiv Gandhi gave the RSS a gift. He was obliging enough to open the locks of the disputed Babri Masjid in Ayodhya, which the RSS claimed was the birthplace of Lord Ram. At the national executive meeting of the BJP on 11 June 1989, the party passed a resolution to demolish the mosque and build a temple in Ayodhya. Immediately after the meeting, L.K. Advani said, 'I'm sure the resolution will translate into votes,' and the following year he went on his Rath Yatra. He crisscrossed the country on his Chariot of Fire, demanding the demolition of the Babri Masjid, leaving riots and bloodshed in his wake. In 1991, the party won one hundred and twenty seats in Parliament. (It had won two in 1984.) The hysteria orchestrated by Advani peaked in 1992, when the mosque was brought down by a marauding mob. By 1998, the BJP was in power at the Centre.

Its first act in office was to conduct a series of nuclear tests. Across the country, fascists and corporates, princes and paupers alike, celebrated India's Hindu Bomb. Hindutva had transcended petty party politics. In 2002, Narendra Modi's government planned and executed the Gujarat genocide. In the elections that took place a few months after the genocide, he was returned to power with an overwhelming majority. He ensured complete impunity for those who had participated in the killings. In the rare case where there has been a conviction, it is of course the lowly foot soldiers and not the masterminds who stand in the dock. Impunity is an essential prerequisite for genocidal killing. India has a great tradition of granting impunity to mass killers. I could fill volumes with the details.

In a democracy, for impunity after genocide, you have to 'apply through proper channels'. Procedure is everything. To begin with, of the two hundred and eighty seven people accused, booked under the Prevention of Terrorism Act, two hundred and eighty six are Muslim and one is Sikh.[25] No bail for them, so they're still in prison. In the case of several massacres, the lawyers that the Gujarat government appointed as public prosecutors had actually already appeared for the accused. Several of them belonged to the RSS or the VHP and were openly hostile to those they were supposedly representing. Survivor witnesses found that, when they went to the police to file reports, the police would record their statements inaccurately or refuse to record the names of the perpetrators. In several cases, when survivors had seen members of their families being killed (and burned alive so their bodies could not be found), the police would refuse to register cases of murder.

Ehsan Jaffri, the Congress politician and poet who had made the mistake of campaigning against Modi in the Rajkot elections, was publicly butchered. (By a mob led by a fellow Congress Party worker.) In the words of a man who took part in the savagery: 'Five people held him, then someone struck him with a sword . . . chopped off his hand, then his legs . . . then everything else . . . [and] after cutting him to pieces, they put him on the wood they'd piled and set him on fire. Burned him alive.' While the mob that lynched Jaffri, murdered seventy people, and gang-raped twelve women—before burning them alive—was gathering, the Ahmedabad commissioner of police, P.C. Pandey, was kind enough to visit the neighbourhood. After Modi was re-elected, Pandey was promoted and made Gujarat's Director General of police. The entire killing apparatus remains in place.

The Supreme Court in Delhi made a few threatening noises, but eventually put the matter into cold storage. The Congress and the Communist parties made a great deal of noise, but did nothing.

In the *Tehelka* sting operation, broadcast recently on a news channel at prime time, apart from Babu Bajrangi, killer after killer recounted how the genocide had been planned and executed, how Modi and senior politicians and police officers had been personally involved. None of this information was new, but there they were, the butchers, on the news networks, not just admitting to but boasting about their crimes. The overwhelming public reaction to the sting was not outrage, but suspicion about its timing. Most people believed that the exposé would help Modi win the elections again. Some even believed, quite outlandishly, that he had engineered the sting. He did win the elections. And this time, on the ticket of Union and Progress. A committee all unto himself. At BJP rallies, thousands of adoring supporters now wear plastic Modi masks, chanting slogans of death. The fascist democrat has physically mutated into a million little fascists. These are the joys of democracy. (Who in Nazi Germany would have dared to put on a Hitler mask?) Preparations to recreate the 'Gujarat blueprint' are currently in different stages in the BJP-ruled states of Orissa, Chhattisgarh, Jharkhand, Rajasthan, Madhya Pradesh and Karnataka.

To commit genocide, says Peter Balakian, scholar of the Armenian genocide, you have to marginalize a subgroup for a long time. This criterion has been well met in India. The Muslims of India have been systematically marginalized and have now joined the Adivasis and Dalits, who have not just been marginalized but dehumanized by caste Hindu society and its scriptures for years, for centuries. (There was a time when they were dehumanized in order to be put to work doing things that caste Hindus would not do. Now, with technology, even that labour is becoming redundant.) The RSS also pits Dalits against Muslims and Adivasis against Dalits as part of its larger project.

While the 'people' were engaged with the Union project and its doctrine of hatred, India's Progress project was proceeding apace. The new regime of privatization and liberalization resulted in the sale of the country's natural resources and public infrastructure to private corporations. It has created an unimaginably wealthy upper class and growing middle class who have naturally became militant evangelists for the new dispensation.

The Progress project has its own tradition of impunity and subterfuge, no less horrific than the elaborate machinery of the Union project. At the heart of it lies the most powerful institution in India, the Supreme Court, which is rapidly becoming a pillar of Corporate Power, issuing order after order allowing for the building of dams, the interlinking of rivers, indiscriminate mining, the destruction of forests and water systems. All of this could be described as ecocide—a prelude perhaps to genocide. (And to criticize the court is a criminal offence, punishable by imprisonment.)

Ironically, the era of the free market has led to the most successful secessionist struggle ever waged in India—the secession of the middle and upper classes to a country of their own, somewhere up in the stratosphere where they merge with the rest of the world's elite. This Kingdom in the Sky is a complete universe in itself, hermetically sealed from the rest of India. It has its own newspapers, films, television programs, morality plays, transport systems, malls and intellectuals. And in case you are beginning to think it's all joy-joy, you're wrong. It also has its own tragedies, its own environmental issues (parking problems, urban air pollution), its own class struggles. An organization called Youth for Equality, for example, has taken up the issue of reservations (affirmative action), because it feels Upper Castes are discriminated against by India's pulverized Lower Castes. This India has its own People's Movements and candlelight vigils

(Justice for Jessica, the model who was shot in a bar) and even its own People's Car (the Wagon for the Volks launched by the Tata Group recently). It even has its own dreams that take the form of TV advertisements in which Indian CEOs (smeared with Fair & Lovely Face Cream) buy international corporations, including an imaginary East India Company. They are ushered to their plush new offices by fawning white women (who look as though they're longing to be laid, the final prize of conquest) and applauding white men, ready to make way for the new kings. Meanwhile the crowd in the stadium roars to its feet (with credit cards in their pockets) chanting 'India! India!'

But there is a problem, and the problem is lebensraum. A Kingdom needs its lebensraum. Where will the Kingdom in the Sky find lebensraum? The Sky Citizens look toward the Old Nation. They see Adivasis sitting on the bauxite mountains of Orissa, on the iron ore in Jharkhand and Chhattisgarh. They see the people of Nandigram (Muslims, Dalits) sitting on prime land, which really ought to be a chemical hub.[26] They see thousands of acres of farmland, and think: These really ought to be Special Economic Zones for our industries. They see the rich fields of Singur and know this really ought to be a car factory for the Tata Nano, the People's Car. They think: That's our bauxite, our iron ore, our uranium. What are these people doing on our land? What's our water doing in their rivers? What's our timber doing in their trees?

If you look at a map of India's forests, its mineral wealth, and the homelands of the Adivasi people, you'll see that they're stacked up over each other. So in reality, those who we call poor are the truly wealthy. But when the Sky Citizens cast their eyes over the land, they see superfluous people sitting on precious resources. The Nazis had a phrase for them—*überzähligen Essern*, superfluous eaters.

The struggle for lebensraum, Friedrich Ratzel said, after closely observing the struggle between native Indians and their European colonizers in North America, is 'an annihilating struggle'.[27] Annihilation doesn't necessarily mean the physical extermination of people—by bludgeoning, beating, burning, bayoneting, gassing, bombing, or shooting them. (Except sometimes. Particularly when they try to put up a fight. Because then they become Terrorists.) Historically, the most efficient form of genocide has been to displace people from their homes, herd them together, and block their access to food and water. Under these conditions, they die without obvious violence and often in far greater numbers. 'The Nazis gave the Jews a star on their coats and crowded them into "reserves",' Sven Lindqvist writes, 'just as the Indians, the Hereros, the Bushmen, the Amandebele, and all the other children of the stars had been crowded together. They died on their own when food supply to the reserves was cut off.'

The historian Mike Davis writes that 12.2 to 29.3 million people starved to death in India in the famines between 1876 and 1902, while Britain continued to export food and raw material from India.[28] In a democracy, as Amartya Sen says, we are unlikely to have famine. So in place of China's Great Famine, we have India's Great Malnutrition. (India hosts more than a third of the world's undernourished children.)[29]

With the possible exception of China, India today has the largest population of internally displaced people in the world. Dams alone have displaced more than thirty million people.[30] The displacement is being enforced with court decrees or at gunpoint by policemen, by government-controlled militias, or corporate thugs. (In Nandigram, even the Communist Party of India [Marxist] has its own armed militia.) The displaced are being herded into tenements, camps and resettlement colonies where, cut off from a means of earning a living, they spiral into poverty.

In the state of Chhattisgarh, being targeted by corporates for its wealth of iron ore, there's a different technique. In the name of fighting Maoist rebels, hundreds of villages have been forcibly evacuated and almost forty thousand people moved into police camps. The government is arming some of them, and has created Salwa Judum, the supposedly anti-Maoist 'peoples' militia, created and funded by the state government.[31] While the poor fight the poor, in conditions that approach civil war, the Tata and Essar groups have been quietly negotiating for the rights to mine iron ore in Chhattisgarh. (Can we establish a connection? We wouldn't dream of it. Even though the Salwa Judum was announced a day after the Memorandum of Understanding between the Tata Group and the government was signed.)[32]

It's not surprising that very little of this account of events makes it into the version of the New India currently on the market. That's because what is on sale is another form of denial—the creation of what Robert J. Lifton calls a 'counterfeit universe'.[33] In this universe, systemic horrors are converted into temporary lapses, attributable to flawed individuals, and a more 'balanced', happier world is presented in place of the real one. The balance is spurious: often Union and Progress are set off against each other, a liberal secular critique of the Union project being used to legitimize the depredations of the Progress project. Those at the top of the food chain, those who have no reason to want to alter the status quo, are most likely to be the manufacturers of the 'counterfeit universe'. Their job is to patrol the border, diffuse rage, delegitimize anger and negotiate a ceasefire.

Consider the response of Shahrukh Khan (Bollywood superstar, heartthrob of millions) to a question about Narendra Modi. 'I don't know him personally, I have no opinion,' he says. 'Personally they have never been unkind to me.'[34] Ramachandra Guha, liberal historian and founding member of the New India Foundation, advises us in his new book, *India After Gandhi: The History of the World's Largest Democracy*, that to describe the BJP regime—in power both in Gujarat and at the Centre during the 2002 genocide—as fascist would be to 'overestimate its powers and to underestimate the democratic traditions of the Indian people'. To substantiate his point, Guha reminds us that in the 2004 general elections, the BJP alliance at the Centre was voted out of office. 'When was the last time a "fascist" regime permitted such an orderly transfer of power?' he asks. He omits to mention that in the Gujarat state elections held soon after the genocide (which Guha calls 'the Gujarat riots') Narendra Modi was voted to power for a second term and then, five years later, for a third term. So far, in Gujarat, there has been no transfer of power, 'orderly' or otherwise.[35]

Editors and commentators in the 'secular' national press, having got over their outrage at the Gujarat genocide, now assess Modi's administrative skills, which most of them are uniformly impressed by. The editor of the *Hindustan Times* said, 'Modi may be a mass murderer, but he's our mass murderer,' and went on to air his dilemmas about how to deal with a mass murderer who is also a 'good' chief minister.[36]

In this 'counterfeit' version of India, in the realm of culture, in the new Bollywood cinema, in the boom in Indo-Anglian literature, the poor, for the most part, are simply absent. They have been erased in advance. (They only put in an appearance as the smiling beneficiaries of microcredit loans, development schemes and charity meted out by NGOs.)

Last summer, I happened to wander into a cool room in which four beautiful young girls with straightened hair and porcelain skin were lounging, introducing their puppies to one another. One of them turned to me and said, 'I was on holiday with my family and I found an old essay of yours about dams and stuff? I was asking my brother if he knew about what a bad time these Dalits and Adivasis were having, being displaced and all . . . . I mean just being kicked out of their homes 'n' stuff like that? And you know, my brother's such a jerk, he said they're the ones who are holding India back. They should be exterminated. Can you imagine?'

The trouble is, I could. I can.

The puppies were sweet. I wondered whether dogs could ever imagine exterminating each other. They're probably not progressive enough.

That evening, I watched Amitabh Bachchan (*another* Bollywood superstar, heartthrob of millions) on TV, appearing in a commercial for the *Times of India*'s 'India Poised' campaign. The TV anchor introducing the campaign said it was meant to inspire people to leave behind the 'constraining ghosts of the past'. To choose optimism over pessimism.

'There are two Indias in this country,' Amitabh Bachchan said, in his famous baritone:

> One India is straining at the leash, eager to spring forth and live up to all the adjectives that the world has been recently showering upon us. The Other India is the leash.
>
> One India says, 'Give me a chance and I'll prove myself.' The Other India says, 'Prove yourself first, and maybe then, you'll have a chance.'
>
> One India lives in the optimism of our hearts. The Other

> India lurks in the skepticism of our minds. One India wants, the Other India hopes.
>
> One India leads, the Other India follows.
>
> These conversions are on the rise. With each passing day, more and more people from the Other India are coming over to this side. And quietly, while the world is not looking, a pulsating, dynamic new India is emerging.

And finally:

> Now in our sixtieth year as a free nation, the ride has brought us to the edge of time's great precipice. And one India, a tiny little voice in the back of the head, is looking down at the bottom of the ravine and hesitating. The Other India is looking up at the sky and saying, 'It's time to fly.'[37]

Here is the counterfeit universe laid bare. It tells us that the rich don't have a choice (There Is No Alternative) but the poor do. They can choose to become rich. If they don't, it's because they are choosing pessimism over optimism, hesitation over confidence, want over hope. In other words, they're choosing to be poor. It's their fault. They are weak. (And we know what the seekers of lebensraum think of the weak.) They are the 'Constraining Ghost of the Past'. They're already ghosts. 'Within an ongoing counterfeit universe,' Robert J. Lifton says, 'genocide becomes easy, almost natural.'[38]

The poor, the so-called poor, have only one choice: To resist or to succumb. Bachchan is right: they are crossing over, quietly, while the world's not looking. Not to where he thinks, but across another ravine, to another side. The side of armed struggle. From there they look back at the Tsars of Development and mimic their regretful slogan: 'There Is No Alternative.'

They have watched the great Gandhian peoples' movements being reduced and humiliated, floundering in the quagmire of court cases, hunger strikes and counter-hunger strikes. Perhaps these many million Constraining Ghosts of the Past wonder what advice Gandhi would have given the Indians of the Americas, the slaves of Africa, the Tasmanians, the Hereros, the Hottentots, the Armenians, the Jews of Germany, the Muslims of Gujarat? Perhaps they wonder how they can go on hunger strike when they're already starving. How they can boycott foreign goods when they have no money to buy any goods. How they can refuse to pay taxes when they have no earnings.

People who have taken to arms have done it with full knowledge of what the consequences of that decision will be. They have done so knowing that they are on their own. They know that the new laws of the land criminalize the poor and conflate resistance with terrorism. They know that appeals to conscience, liberal morality, and sympathetic press coverage will not help them now. They know no international marches, no globalized dissent, no famous writers will be around when the bullets fly. Hundreds of thousands have broken faith with the institutions of India's democracy. Large swathes of the country have fallen out of the government's control. (At last count it was supposed to be 25 per cent.)[39] The battle stinks of death. It's by no means pretty. How can it be when the helmsman of the army of Constraining Ghosts is the ghost of Chairman Mao himself? (The ray of hope is that many of the foot soldiers don't know who he is. Or what he did. More Genocide Denial? Maybe.) Are they Idealists fighting for a Better World? Well . . . anything is better than annihilation.

The prime minister has declared that the Maoist resistance is the 'single largest threat' to internal security.[40] There have even been appeals to call out the army. The media is agog with breathless condemnation.

Here's a typical newspaper column. Nothing out of the ordinary. 'Stamp Out Naxals', it is called:

> This government is at last showing some sense in tackling Naxalism.
>
> Less than a month ago Prime Minister Manmohan Singh asked state governments to 'choke' Naxal infrastructure and 'cripple' their activities through a dedicated force to eliminate the 'virus.' It signaled a realization that the focus on tackling Naxalism must be through enforcement of law, rather than wasteful expense on development.[41]

'Choke.' 'Cripple.' 'Virus.' 'Infested.' 'Eliminate.' 'Stamp out.' Yes. The idea of extermination is in the air.

And people believe that faced with extermination they have the right to fight back. By any means necessary.

Perhaps they've been listening to the grasshoppers.

AZADI

This essay first appeared in The Guardian *(London) on 22 August 2008, and in* Outlook *magazine (India) on 1 September 2008.*

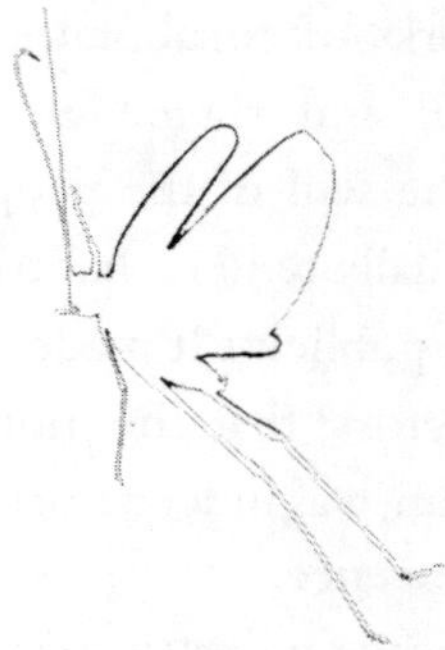

FOR THE past sixty days or so, since about the end of June, the people of Kashmir have been free. Free in the most profound sense. They have shrugged off the terror of living their lives in the gunsights of half a million heavily armed soldiers, in the most densely militarized zone in the world.

After eighteen years of administering a military occupation, the Indian government's worst nightmare has come true. Having declared that the militant movement has been crushed, it is now faced with a nonviolent mass protest, but not the kind it knows how to manage.[1] This one is nourished by peoples' memory of years of repression in which tens of thousands have been killed, thousands have been 'disappeared', hundreds of thousands tortured, injured and humiliated.[2] That kind of rage, once it finds utterance cannot easily be tamed, re-bottled and sent back to where it came from.

For all these years the Indian state, known among the knowing as the 'deep state', has done everything it can to subvert, suppress, represent, misrepresent, discredit, interpret, intimidate, purchase—and simply snuff out the voice of the Kashmiri people. It has used money (lots of it), violence (lots of it), disinformation, propaganda, torture, elaborate networks of collaborators and informers, terror, imprisonment, blackmail and rigged elections to subdue what democrats would call 'the will of the people'. But now the deep state, as deep states eventually tend to, has tripped on its own hubris and bought into its own publicity. It made the mistake of believing that domination was victory, that the 'normalcy' it had enforced through the barrel of a gun, was indeed normal, and that the peoples' sullen silence was acquiescence.

The well-endowed peace industry, speaking on peoples' behalf, informed us that 'Kashmiris are tired of violence and want peace.' What kind of peace they were willing to settle for was never clarified. Meanwhile Bollywood's cache of Kashmir/Muslim-terrorist films has brainwashed most Indians into believing that all of Kashmir's sorrows could be laid at the door of evil, people-hating terrorists.

To anybody who cared to ask, or, more importantly, to listen, it was always clear that even in their darkest moments, people in Kashmir had kept the fires burning and that it was not peace alone they yearned for, but freedom too. Over the last two months the carefully confected picture of an innocent people trapped between 'two guns', both equally hated, has, pardon the pun, been shot to hell.

A sudden twist of fate, an ill-conceived move over the transfer of nearly one hundred acres of state forest land to the Amarnath Shrine Board (which manages the annual Hindu pilgrimage to a cave deep in the Kashmir Himalayas) suddenly became the equivalent of tossing a lit match into a barrel of petrol.[3] Until 1989 the Amarnath pilgrimage used to attract about twenty thousand people who travelled to the Amarnath cave over a period of about two weeks. In 1990, when the overtly Islamic militant uprising in the valley coincided with the spread of virulent Hindutva in the Indian plains, the number of pilgrims began to increase exponentially. By 2008 more than five hundred thousand pilgrims visited the Amarnath cave, in large groups, their passage often sponsored by Indian business houses. To many people in the valley this dramatic increase in numbers was seen as an aggressive political statement by an increasingly Hindu-fundamentalist Indian state.[4] Rightly or wrongly, the land transfer was viewed as the thin edge of the wedge. It triggered an apprehension that it was the beginning of an elaborate plan to build Israeli-style settlements, and change the demography of the valley. Days of massive protest forced the valley to shut down completely. Within hours the protests spread from the cities to villages. Young stone pelters took to the streets and faced armed police who fired straight at them, killing more than fifty of them. For people as well as the government, it resurrected memories of the uprising in the early nineties. Throughout the weeks of protest, hartal and police firing, while the Hindutva publicity machine in India charged Kashmiris with committing every kind of communal excess, the five hundred thousand Amarnath pilgrims completed their pilgrimage, not just unhurt, but touched by the hospitality they had been shown by local people.[5]

Eventually, taken completely by surprise at the ferocity of the response, the government revoked the land transfer.[6] But by then the land transfer had become a non-issue, and the protests had spiralled out of control.

Massive protests against the revocation erupted in Hindu-dominated Jammu. There too the issue snowballed into something much bigger. People began to raise issues of neglect and discrimination by the Indian state. (For some odd reason they blamed Kashmiris for that neglect.) The protests led to the blockading of the Jammu–Srinagar highway, the only functional road-link between Kashmir and India.[7] The army was called out to clear the highway and allow safe passage of trucks between Jammu and Srinagar. But incidents of violence against Kashmiri truckers were being reported from as far away as Punjab, where there was no protection at all.[8] As a result, Kashmiri truckers fearing for their lives, refused to drive on the highway. Truckloads of perishable fresh fruit and valley produce began to rot. It became very obvious that the blockade had caused the situation to spin out of control. The government announced that the blockade had been cleared and that trucks were going through. Embedded sections of the Indian media, quoting the inevitable 'intelligence' sources, began to refer to it as a 'perceived' blockade, and even suggest that there had never been one.[9]

But it was too late for those games, the damage had been done. It had been demonstrated in no uncertain terms to people in Kashmir that they lived on sufferance, and that if they didn't behave themselves they could be put under siege, starved, deprived of essential commodities and medical supplies. The real blockade became a psychological one. The last fragile link between India and Kashmir was all but snapped.

To expect matters to end there was, of course, absurd. Hadn't anybody noticed that in Kashmir even minor protests about civic issues like water and electricity inevitably turned into demands for Azadi? To threaten them with mass starvation amounted to committing political suicide.

Not surprisingly, the voice that the government of India has tried so hard to silence in Kashmir has massed into a deafening roar. Hundreds of thousands of unarmed people have come out to reclaim their cities, their streets and mohallas. They have simply overwhelmed the heavily armed security forces by their sheer numbers, and with a remarkable display of raw courage.

Raised in a playground of army camps, check-posts and bunkers, with screams from torture chambers for a soundtrack, the young generation has suddenly discovered the power of mass protest, and above all, the dignity of being able to straighten their shoulders and speak for themselves, represent themselves. For them it is nothing short of an epiphany. They're in full flow, not even the fear of death seems to hold them back. And once that fear has gone, of what use is the largest or second largest army in the world? What threat does it hold? Who should know that better than the people of India who won their independence in the way that they did?

The circumstances in Kashmir being what they are, it is hard for the spin doctors to fall back on the same old same old; to claim that it's all the doing of Pakistan's ISI, or that people are being coerced by militants. Since the thirties the question of who can claim the right to represent that elusive thing known as 'Kashmiri sentiment' has been bitterly contested. Was it Sheikh Abdullah? The Muslim Conference? Who is it today? The mainstream political parties? The Hurriyat? The militants? This time around, the people are in charge. There have been mass rallies in the past, but none in recent memory that have been so sustained and wide-spread. The mainstream political parties of Kashmir—National Conference, People's Democratic Party—feted by the deep state and the Indian media despite the pathetic voter turn out in election after election, appear dutifully for debates in New Delhi's TV studios, but can't muster the courage to appear on the streets of Kashmir. The armed militants, who through the worst years of repression were seen as the only ones carrying the torch of Azadi forward, if they are around at all, seem content to take a back seat and let people do the fighting for a change.

The Separatist leaders who do appear and speak at the rallies are not leaders so much as followers, being guided by the phenomenal spontaneous energy of a caged, enraged people that has exploded on Kashmir's streets. The leaders, such as they are, have been presented with a full-blown revolution. The only condition seems to be that they have to do as the people say. If they say things that people do not wish to hear, they are gently persuaded to come out, publicly apologize and correct their course. This applies to all of them, including Syed Ali Shah Geelani who at a public rally recently proclaimed himself the movement's only leader. It was a monumental political blunder that very nearly shattered the fragile new alliance between the various factions of the struggle. Within hours he retracted his statement.[10] Like it or not, this is democracy. No democrat can pretend otherwise.

Day after day hundreds of thousands of people swarm around places that hold terrible memories for them. They demolish bunkers, break through cordons of concertina wire and stare straight down the barrels of soldiers' machine guns, saying what very few in India want to hear. Hum Kya Chahtey? Azaadi! *We Want Freedom*. And, it has to be said, in equal numbers and with equal intensity: Jeevey Jeevey Pakistan. *Long live Pakistan*.

That sound reverberates through the Valley like the drumbeat of steady rain on a tin roof, like the roll of thunder during an electric storm. It's the plebiscite that was never held, the referendum that has been indefinitely postponed.

On 15 August India's Independence day, the city of Srinagar shut down completely. The Bakshi stadium where the Governor hoisted the flag, was empty except for a few officials. Hours later, Lal Chowk, the nerve centre of the city, (where in 1992 Murli Manohar Joshi, BJP leader and mentor of the controversial 'Hinduization' of children's history text books, started a tradition of flag-hoisting by the Border Security Force), was taken over by thousands of people who hoisted the Pakistani Flag and wished each other 'Happy belated Independence day' (Pakistan celebrates Independence on 14 August) and 'Happy Slavery Day'. Humour obviously, has survived India's many prisons and torture centres in Kashmir.

On 16 August hundreds of thousands of people marched to Pampore, to the village of the Hurriyat leader Sheikh Abdul Aziz, who was shot down in cold blood five days earlier.[11] He was part of a massive march to the Line of Control demanding that since the Jammu road had been blocked, it was only logical that the Srinagar–Muzaffarabad highway be opened for goods and people, the way it used to be before Kashmir was partitioned.

On 18 August hundreds of thousands also gathered in Srinagar in the huge TRC grounds (Tourist Reception Centre, not the Truth and Reconciliation Committee) close to the United Nations Military Observer Group in India and Pakistan (UNMOGIP) to submit a memorandum asking for three things: the end to Indian Rule, the deployment of a UN peacekeeping force and an investigation into two decades of war crimes committed with almost complete impunity by the Indian army and police.[12]

The day before the rally the deep state was hard at work. A senior journalist friend called to say that late in the afternoon the home secretary called a high level meeting in New Delhi. Also present were the defence secretary and intelligence chiefs. The purpose of the meeting he said, was to brief the editors of TV news channels that the government had reason to believe that the insurrection was being managed by a small splinter cell of the ISI and to request the channels to keep this piece of exclusive, highly secret intelligence in mind while covering (or preferably not covering?) the news from Kashmir. Unfortunately for the deep state things have gone so far that TV channels, were they to obey those instructions, would run the risk of looking ridiculous. Thankfully, it looks as though this revolution will, after all, be televised.

On the night of 17 August the police sealed the city. Streets were barricaded, thousands of armed police manned the barriers. The roads leading into Srinagar were blocked. For the first time in eighteen years the police had to plead with Hurriyat leaders to address the rally at the TRC grounds instead of marching right up to the UNMOGIP office which is on Gupkar Road, Srinagar's Green Zone, where, for years, the Indian Establishment has barricaded itself in style and splendour.

On the morning of 18 August people began pouring into Srinagar from villages and towns across the valley. In trucks, tempos, jeeps, buses and on foot. Once again, barriers were broken and people reclaimed their city. The police were faced with a choice of either stepping aside or executing a massacre. They stepped aside. Not a single bullet was fired.

The city floated on a sea of smiles. There was ecstasy in the air. Everyone had a banner; houseboat owners, traders, students, lawyers, doctors. One said, 'We are all prisoners, set us free.' Another said, 'Democracy without freedom is Demon-crazy.' Demon Crazy. That was a good one. Perhaps he was referring to the twisted logic of a country that needed to commit communal carnage in order to bolster its secular credentials. Or the insanity that permits the world's largest democracy to administer the world's largest military occupation and continue to call itself a democracy.

There was a green flag on every lamppost, every roof, every bus stop and on the top of chinar trees. A big one fluttered outside the All India Radio building. Road signs to Hazratbal, Batmaloo, Sopore were painted over. Rawalpindi they said. Or simply Pakistan. It would be a mistake to assume that the public expression of affection for

Pakistan automatically translates into a desire to accede to Pakistan. Some of it has to do with gratitude for the support—cynical or otherwise—for what Kashmiris see as their freedom struggle, and the Indian state sees as a terrorist campaign. It also has to do with mischief. With saying and doing what galls India most of all.

It's easy to scoff at the idea of a 'freedom struggle' that wishes to distance itself from a country that is supposed to be a democracy, and align itself with another that has, for the most part been ruled by military dictators. A country whose army has committed genocide in what is now Bangladesh. A country that is even now being torn apart by its own ethnic war. These are important questions, but right now perhaps it's more useful to wonder what this so-called democracy did in Kashmir to make people hate it so?

Everywhere there were Pakistani flags, everywhere the cry: Pakistan se rishta kya? La illaha illallah. *What is our bond with Pakistan? There is no god but Allah.*

Azadi ka matlab kya? La illaha illallah. *What does Freedom mean? There is no god but Allah.*

For somebody like myself, who is not Muslim, that interpretation of freedom is hard—if not impossible—to understand. I asked a young woman whether freedom for Kashmir would not mean less freedom for her, as a woman. She shrugged and said, 'What kind of freedom do we have now? The freedom to be raped by Indian soldiers?' Her reply silenced me.

Standing in the grounds of the TRC, surrounded by a sea of green flags, it was impossible to doubt or ignore the deeply Islamic nature of the uprising taking place around me. It was equally impossible to label it a vicious, terrorist jihad. For Kashmiris it was a catharsis. A historical moment in a long and complicated struggle for freedom with all the imperfections, cruelties and confusions that freedom struggles have. This one cannot by any means call itself pristine, and will always be stigmatized by, and will some day, I hope, have to account for, among other things, the brutal killings of Kashmiri Pandits in the early years of the uprising, culminating in the exodus of almost the entire community from the Kashmir valley.

As the crowd continued to swell I listened carefully to the slogans, because rhetoric often clarifies things and holds the key to all kinds of understanding. I'd heard many of them before a few years ago at a militant's funeral. A new one, obviously coined after the blockade was Kashmir ki mandi! Rawalpindi! (It doesn't lend itself to translation, but it means: Kashmir's marketplace? Rawalpindi!) Another was Khooni lakir tod do, aar paar jod do. (*Break down the blood-soaked Line of Control, let Kashmir be united again.*) There were plenty of insults and humiliation for India: Ay jabiron ay zalimon, Kashmir hamara chhod do (*Oh oppressors, Oh wicked ones, Get out of our Kashmir*). Jis Kashmir ko khoon se seencha, voh Kashmir hamara hai (*The Kashmir we have nurtured with our blood, that Kashmir is ours*)!

The slogan that cut through me like a knife and clean broke my heart was this one: Nanga bhookha Hindustan, jaan se pyaara Pakistan. (*Naked, starving India, More precious than life itself—Pakistan.*) Why was it so galling, so painful to listen to this? I tried to work it out and settled on three reasons. First because we all know that the first part of the slogan is the embarrassing and unadorned truth about India, the emerging superpower. Second because all Indians who are not nanga or bhooka are—and have been—complicit in complex and historical ways with the elaborate cultural and economic systems that make Indian society so cruel, so vulgarly unequal. And third, because it was painful to listen to people who have suffered so much themselves, mock others who suffer, in different ways, but no less intensely, under the same oppressor. In that slogan I saw the seeds of how easily victims can become perpetrators.

It took hours for Mirwaiz Umar Farooq and Syed Ali Shah Geelani to wade through the thronging crowds and make it on to the podium. When they arrived they were born aloft on the shoulders of young men, over the surging crowd to the podium. The roar of greeting was deafening. Mirwaiz Umar spoke first. He repeated the demand that the Armed Forces Special Powers Act, the Disturbed Areas Act and the Public Safety Act—under which thousands have been killed, jailed and tortured—be withdrawn. He called for the release of political prisoners, for the Srinagar–Muzaffarabad road to be opened for the free movement of goods and people, and for the de-militarization of the Kashmir Valley.

Syed Ali Shah Geelani began his address with a recitation from the Koran. He then said what he has said before, on hundreds of occasions. The only way for the struggle to succeed he said, was to turn to the Koran for guidance. He said Islam would guide the struggle and that it was a complete social and moral code that would govern the people of a free Kashmir. He said Pakistan had been created as the home of Islam, and that that goal should never be subverted. He said just as Pakistan belonged to Kashmir, Kashmir belonged to Pakistan. He said minority communities would have full rights and their places of worship would be safe. Each point he made was applauded.

Oddly enough the apparent doctrinal clarity of what he said, made everything a little unclear. I wondered how the somewhat disparate views of the various factions in this Freedom Struggle would resolve themselves—the Jammu and Kashmir Liberation Front's vision of an independent state, Geelani's desire to merge with Pakistan and Mirwaiz Umar balanced precariously between them.

An old man with a red eye standing next to me said, 'Kashmir was one country. Half was taken by India, the other half by Pakistan. Both by force. We want freedom.' I wondered if, in the new dispensation, the old man would get a hearing. I wondered what he would think of the trucks that roared down the highways in the plains of India, owned and driven by men who knew nothing of history, or of Kashmir, but still had slogans on their tail gates that said, 'Doodh maango to kheer denge, Kashmir mango to chir denge.' (*Ask for milk, you'll get cream; Ask for Kashmir, we'll cut you open.*)

Briefly, I had another thought. I imagined myself standing in the heart of an RSS or VHP rally being addressed by L.K. Advani. Replace the word Islam with the word Hindutva, replace the word Pakistan with Hindustan, replace the sea of green flags with saffron ones and we would have the BJP's nightmare vision of an ideal India.

Is that what we should accept as our future? Monolithic religious states handing down a complete social and moral code, 'a complete way of life'? Millions of us in India reject the Hindutva project. Our rejection springs from love, from passion, from a kind of idealism, from having enormous emotional stakes in the society in which we live. What our neighbours do, how they choose to handle their affairs does not affect our argument, it only strengthens it.

Arguments that spring from love are also fraught with danger. It is for the people of Kashmir to agree or disagree with the Islamic project (which is as contested by Muslims, in equally complex ways, all over the world, as Hindutva is contested by Hindus). Perhaps now that the threat of violence has receded and there is some space in which to debate views and air ideas, it is time for those who are part of the struggle to outline a vision for what kind of society they are fighting for. Perhaps it is time to offer people something more than martyrs, slogans and vague generalizations. Those who wish to turn to the Koran for guidance, will, no doubt find guidance there. But what of those who do not wish to do that, or for whom the Koran does not make place? Do the Hindus of Jammu and other minorities also have the right to self-determination? Will the hundreds of thousands of Kashmiri Pandits living in exile, many of them in terrible poverty, have the right to return? Will they be paid reparations for the terrible losses they have suffered? Or will a free Kashmir do to its minorities what India has done to Kashmiris for sixty-one years? What will happen to homosexuals and adulterers and blasphemers? What of thieves and lafangas and writers who do not agree with the 'complete social and moral code'? Will we be put to death as we are in Saudi Arabia? Will the cycle of death, repression and bloodshed continue? History offers many models for Kashmir's thinkers and intellectuals and politicians to study. What will the Kashmir of their dreams look like? Algeria? Iran? South Africa? Switzerland? Pakistan?

At a crucial time like this, few things are more important than dreams. A lazy utopia and a flawed sense of justice will have consequences that do not bear thinking about. This is not the time for intellectual sloth or a reluctance to assess a situation clearly and honestly. It could be argued that the prevarication of Maharaja Hari Singh in 1947 has been its great modern tragedy, one that eventually led to unthinkable bloodshed and the prolonged bondage of people who were very nearly free.

Already the spectre of partition has reared its head. Hindutva networks are alive with rumours about Hindus in the Valley being attacked and forced to flee. In response, phone calls from Jammu reported that an armed Hindu militia was threatening a massacre and that Muslims from the two Hindu majority districts were preparing to flee. (Memories of the bloodbath that ensued and claimed the lives of more than a million people when India and Pakistan were partitioned have come flooding back. That nightmare will haunt all of us forever.)

There is absolutely no reason to believe that history will repeat itself. Not unless it is made to. Not unless people actively work to create such a cataclysm. However, none of these fears of what the future holds can justify the continued military occupation of a nation and a people. No more than the old Colonial argument about how the natives were not ready for freedom justified the Colonial project.

Of course, there are many ways for the Indian state to continue to hold on to Kashmir. It could do what it does best. Wait. And hope the peoples' energy will dissipate in the absence of a concrete plan. It could try and fracture the fragile coalition that is emerging. It could extinguish this nonviolent uprising and re-invite armed militancy. It could increase the number of troops from half a million to a whole million. A few strategic massacres, a couple of targeted assassinations, some disappearances and a massive round of arrests should do the trick for a few more years.

The unimaginable sums of public money that are needed to keep the military occupation of Kashmir going, is money that ought by right to be spent on schools and hospitals and food for an impoverished, malnutritioned population in India. What kind of government can possibly believe that it has the right to spend it on more weapons, more concertina wire and more prisons in Kashmir?

The Indian military occupation of Kashmir makes monsters of us all. It allows Hindu chauvinists to target and victimize Muslims in India by holding them hostage to the freedom struggle being waged by Muslims in Kashmir. It's all being stirred into a poisonous brew and administered intravenously, straight into our bloodstream.

At the heart of it all is a moral question. Does any government have the right to take away peoples' liberty with military force?

India needs Azadi from Kashmir just as much—if not more—than Kashmir needs Azadi from India.

NINE IS NOT ELEVEN (AND NOVEMBER ISN'T SEPTEMBER)

This essay was published first by Outlook *magazine (India) on 22 December 2008,* The Guardian *(London) on 12 December 2008, TomDispatch.com on 12 December 2008, and* International Socialist Review, *Issue 63, January–February 2009.*

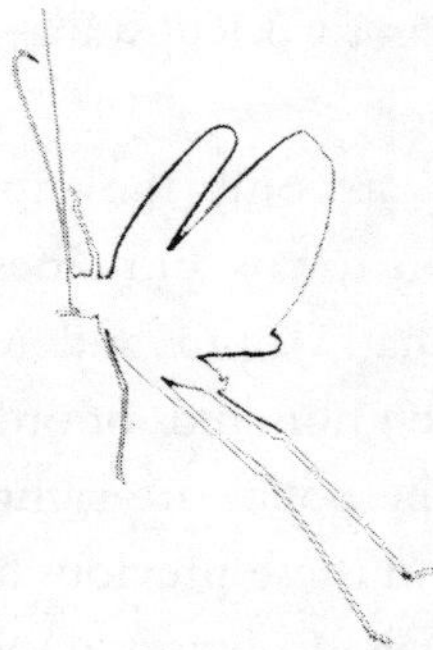

WE'VE FORFEITED the rights to our own tragedies. As the carnage in Mumbai raged on, day after horrible day, our 24-hour news channels informed us that we were watching 'India's 9/11'. And like actors in a Bollywood rip-off of an old Hollywood film, we're expected to play our parts and say our lines, even though we know it's all been said and done before.

As tension in the region builds, US Senator John McCain has warned Pakistan that, if it didn't act fast to arrest the 'bad guys', he had personal information that India would launch air strikes on 'terrorist camps' in Pakistan and that Washington could do nothing because Mumbai was 'India's 9/11'.[1]

But November isn't September, 2008 isn't 2001, Pakistan isn't Afghanistan, and India isn't America. So perhaps we should reclaim our tragedy and pick through the debris with our own brains and our own broken hearts so that we can arrive at our own conclusions.

It's odd how, in the last week of November, thousands of people in Kashmir supervised by thousands of Indian troops lined up to cast their vote, while the richest quarters of India's richest city ended up looking like war-torn Kupwara—one of Kashmir's most ravaged districts.

The Mumbai attacks are only the most recent of a spate of terrorist attacks on Indian towns and cities this year. Ahmedabad, Bangalore, Delhi, Guwahati, Jaipur and Malegaon have all seen serial bomb blasts in which hundreds of ordinary people have been killed and wounded. If the police are right about the people they have arrested as suspects in these previous attacks, both Hindu and Muslim, all Indian nationals, it obviously indicates that something's going very badly wrong in this country.

If you were watching television you might not have heard that ordinary people, too, died in Mumbai. They were mowed down in a busy railway station and a public hospital. The terrorists did not distinguish between poor and rich. They killed both with equal cold-bloodedness. The Indian media, however, was transfixed by the rising tide of horror that breached the glittering barricades of 'India shining' and spread its stench in the marbled lobbies and crystal ballrooms of two incredibly luxurious hotels and a small Jewish centre.[2]

We're told that one of these hotels is an icon of the city of Mumbai. That's absolutely true. It's an icon of the easy, obscene injustice that ordinary Indians endure every day. On a day when the newspapers were full of moving obituaries by beautiful people about the hotel rooms they had stayed in, the gourmet restaurants they loved (ironically one was called Kandahar), and the staff who served them, a small box on the top left-hand corner in the inner pages of a national newspaper (sponsored by a pizza company, I think) said, 'Hungry, kya?' (*'Hungry, eh?'*). It then, with the best of intentions I'm sure, informed its readers that, on the international hunger index, India ranked below Sudan and Somalia. But of course this isn't that war. That one's still being fought in the Dalit bastis (settlements) of our villages; on the banks of the Narmada and the Koel Karo rivers; in the rubber estate in Chengara; in the villages of Nandigram, Singur and Lalgarh in West Bengal, in Chhattisgarh, Jharkhand and Orissa, and the slums and shantytowns of our gigantic cities. That war isn't on TV. Yet. So maybe, like everyone else, we should deal with the one that is.

There is a fierce, unforgiving fault line that runs through the contemporary discourse on terrorism. On one side (let's call it Side A) are those who see terrorism, especially 'Islamist' terrorism, as a hateful, insane scourge that spins on its own axis, in its own orbit, and has nothing to do with the world around it, nothing to do with history, geography or economics. Therefore, Side A says, to try to place it in a political context, or even to try to understand it, amounts to justifying it, and is a crime in itself. Side B believes that though nothing can ever excuse or justify it, terrorism exists in a particular time, place and political context, and to refuse to see that will only aggravate the problem and put more and more people in harm's way. Which is a crime in itself.

The sayings of Hafiz Saeed who founded the Lashkar-e-Toiba (Army of the Pure) in 1990 and who belongs to the hardline Salafi tradition of Islam, certainly bolster the case of Side A. Hafiz Saeed approves of suicide bombing, hates Jews, Shias and Democracy, and believes that jihad should be waged until Islam, his Islam, rules the world. Among the things he said are: 'There can't be any peace while India remains intact. Cut them, cut them—cut them so much that they kneel before you and ask for mercy.'[3] And: 'India has shown us this path for jihad . . . . We would like to give India a tit-for-tat response and reciprocate in the same way by killing the Hindus, just like it is killing the Muslims in Kashmir.'[4]

But where would Side A accommodate the sayings of Babu Bajrangi of Ahmedabad, India, who sees himself as a democrat, not a terrorist? He was one of the major lynchpins of the 2002 Gujarat genocide and has said (on camera):

> We didn't spare a single Muslim shop, we set everything on fire, we set them on fire and killed them . . . . hacked, burnt, set on fire . . . . We believe in setting them on fire because these bastards don't want to be cremated, they're afraid of it . . . . I have just . . . one last wish . . . . Let me be sentenced to death . . . . I don't care if I'm hanged . . . . Give me two days before my hanging and I will go and have a field day in Juhapura [a Muslim dominated area], where seven or eight lakh [seven or eight hundred thousand] of these people stay . . . . I will finish them off . . . . Let a few more of them die . . . . At least twenty-five thousand to fifty thousand should die.[5]

And where in Side A's scheme of things would we place the Rashtriya Swayamsevak Sangh bible, *We, or, Our Nationhood Defined* by M.S. Golwalkar, who became head of the RSS in 1944. It says: 'Ever since that evil day, when Moslems first landed in Hindusthan, right up to the present moment, the Hindu Nation has been gallantly fighting to shake off the despoilers.' Or: 'To keep up the purity of the Race and its culture, Germany shocked the world by her purging of its Semitic Race, the Jews . . . . Race pride at its highest has been manifested there . . . . a good lesson for us in Hindusthan to learn and profit by.'[6]

Of course Muslims are not the only people in the gun sights of the Hindu Right. Dalits have been consistently targeted. Recently, in Kandhamal in Orissa, Christians were the target of two and a half months of violence that left at least sixteen dead.[7] Forty thousand have been driven from their homes, many of whom now live in refugee camps.[8]

All these years Hafiz Saeed has lived the life of a respectable man in Lahore as the head of the Jamaat-ud-Daawa, which many believe is a front organization for the Lashkar-e-Toiba. He continues to recruit young boys for his own bigoted jihad with his twisted, fiery sermons. On 11 December, the United Nations imposed sanctions on the Jamaat-ud-Daawa. The Pakistani government succumbed to international pressure and put Hafiz Saeed under house arrest. Babu Bajrangi, meanwhile, is out on bail and lives the life of a respectable man in Gujarat. A couple of years after the genocide, he left the Vishwa Hindu Parishad (VHP, a militia of the RSS) to join the Shiv Sena (another right-wing nationalist party). Narendra Modi, Bajrangi's former mentor, is still the chief minister of Gujarat. So the man who presided over the Gujarat genocide was re-elected twice, and is deeply respected by India's biggest corporate houses, Reliance and Tata. The policemen who supervised and sometimes even assisted the rampaging Hindu mobs in Gujarat have been rewarded and promoted.

The RSS has sixty thousand branches and more than four million volunteers preaching its doctrine of hate across India. They include Narendra Modi, but also former prime minister A.B. Vajpayee, current leader of the Opposition L.K. Advani and a host of other senior politicians, bureaucrats and police and intelligence officers.

And if that's not enough to complicate our picture of secular democracy, we should place on record that there are plenty of Muslim organizations within India preaching their own narrow bigotry. So, on balance, if I had to choose between Side A and Side B, I'd pick Side B. We need context. Always.

On this nuclear subcontinent, that context is Partition. The Radcliffe Line, which separated India and Pakistan and tore through states, districts, villages, fields, communities, water systems, homes and families, was drawn virtually overnight. It was Britain's final, parting kick to us.

Partition triggered the massacre of more than a million people and the largest migration of a human population in contemporary history. Eight million people, Hindus fleeing the new Pakistan, Muslims fleeing the new kind of India, left their homes with nothing but the clothes on their backs. Each of those people carries, and passes down, a story of unimaginable pain, hate, horror, but yearning too. That wound, those torn but still unsevered muscles, that blood and those splintered bones still lock us together in a close embrace of hatred, terrifying familiarity, but also love. It has left Kashmir trapped in a nightmare from which it can't seem to emerge, a nightmare that has claimed more than sixty thousand lives. Pakistan, the Land of the Pure, became an Islamic Republic, and then very quickly a corrupt, violent military state, openly intolerant of other faiths. India on the other hand declared herself an inclusive, secular democracy.

It was a magnificent undertaking, but Babu Bajrangi's predecessors had been hard at work since the 1920s, dripping poison into India's bloodstream, undermining that idea of India even before it was born. By 1990, they were ready to make a bid for power. In 1992 Hindu mobs exhorted by L.K. Advani stormed the Babri Masjid and demolished it. By 1998, the BJP was in power at the Centre. The US War on Terror put the wind in their sails. It allowed them to do exactly as they pleased, even to commit genocide and then present their fascism as a legitimate form of chaotic democracy. This happened at a time when India had opened its huge market to international finance and it was in the interests of international corporations and the media houses they owned to project it as a country that could do no wrong. That gave Hindu nationalists all the impetus and the impunity they needed.

This, then, is the larger historical context of terrorism on the subcontinent—and of the Mumbai attacks. It shouldn't surprise us that Hafiz Saeed of the Lashkar-e-Toiba is from Shimla (India) and L.K. Advani of the Rashtriya Swayamsevak Sangh is from Sindh (Pakistan).

In much the same way as it did after the 2001 Parliament attack, the 2002 burning of the Sabarmati Express, and the 2007 bombing of the Samjhauta Express, the government of India announced that it has 'clear and incontrovertible proof' that the Lashkar-e-Toiba, backed by Pakistan's Inter-Services Intelligence (ISI), was behind the Mumbai strikes.[9] The Lashkar has denied involvement, but remains the prime accused. According to the police and intelligence agencies, the Lashkar operates in India through an organization called the 'Indian Mujahideen'. Two Indian nationals, Sheikh Mukhtar Ahmed, a special police officer working for the Jammu and Kashmir police, and Tausif Rehman, a resident of Kolkata in West Bengal, have been arrested in connection with the Mumbai attacks.[10] So already the neat accusation against Pakistan is getting a little messy. Almost always, when these stories unspool, they reveal a complicated global network of foot soldiers, trainers, recruiters, middlemen, and undercover intelligence and counter-intelligence operatives working not just on both sides of the India–Pakistan border, but in several countries simultaneously. In today's world, trying to pin down the provenance of a terrorist strike and isolate it within the borders of a single nation state, is very much like trying to pin down the provenance of corporate money. It's almost impossible.

In circumstances like these, air strikes to 'take out' terrorist camps may take out the camps, but certainly will not 'take out' the terrorists. And neither will war. (Also, in our bid for the moral high ground, let's try not to forget that the Liberation Tigers of Tamil Eelam, the LTTE of neighbouring Sri Lanka, one of the world's most deadly militant groups, were first trained by the Indian army.)[11]

Thanks largely to the part it was forced to play as America's ally, first in its war in support of the Afghan Islamists and then in its war against them, Pakistan is reeling under these contradictions, and careening toward civil war. As recruiting agents for America's jihad against the Soviet Union, it was the job of the Pakistani army and the ISI to nurture and channel funds to Islamic fundamentalist organizations. Having wired up these Frankensteins and released them into the world, the US expected it could rein them in like pet mastiffs whenever it wanted to. Certainly it did not expect them to come calling in the heart of the homeland on 11 September. So once again, Afghanistan had to be violently remade. Now the debris of a re-ravaged Afghanistan has washed up on Pakistan's borders.

Nobody, least of all the Pakistani government, denies that it is presiding over a country that is threatening to implode. The terrorist training camps, the fire-breathing mullahs, and the maniacs who believe that Islam will, or should, rule the world are mostly the detritus of two Afghan wars. Their ire rains down on the Pakistani government and Pakistani civilians as much, if not more, than it does on India. If, at this point, India decides to go to war, perhaps the descent of the whole region into chaos will be complete. The debris of a bankrupt, destroyed Pakistan will wash up on India's shores, endangering us as never before. If Pakistan collapses, we can look forward to having millions of 'non-state actors'—with an arsenal of nuclear weapons at their disposal—as neighbours. It's hard to understand why those who steer India's ship are so keen to replicate Pakistan's mistakes and call damnation upon this country by inviting the United States to further meddle clumsily and dangerously in our extremely complicated affairs. A superpower never has allies. It only has agents.

On the plus side, the advantage of going to war is that it's the best way for India to avoid facing up to the serious trouble building on our home front.

The Mumbai attacks were broadcast live (and exclusive!) on all or most of our sixty-seven 24-hour news channels and god knows how many international ones. TV anchors in their studios and journalists at 'ground zero' kept up an endless stream of excited commentary. Over three days and three nights we watched in disbelief as a small group of very young men, armed with guns and gadgets, exposed the powerlessness of the police, the elite National Security Guard and the Marine Commandos of this supposedly mighty, nuclear-powered nation. While they did this, they indiscriminately massacred unarmed people, in railway stations, hospitals and luxury hotels, unmindful of their class, caste, religion or nationality. (Part of the helplessness of the security forces had to do with having to worry about hostages. In other situations, in Kashmir, for example, their tactics are not so sensitive. Whole buildings are blown up. Human shields are used. The US and Israeli armies don't hesitate to send cruise missiles into buildings and drop daisy cutters on wedding parties in Palestine, Iraq and Afghanistan.) This was different. And it was on TV.

The boy-terrorists' nonchalant willingness to kill—and be killed—mesmerized their international audience. They delivered something different from the usual diet of suicide bombings and missile attacks that people have grown inured to on the news. Here was something new. Die Hard 25. The gruesome performance went on and on. TV ratings soared. (Ask any television magnate or corporate advertiser who measures broadcast time in seconds, not minutes, what that's worth.)

Eventually the killers died, and died hard, all but one. (Perhaps, in the chaos, some escaped. We may never know.) Throughout the standoff the terrorists made no demands and expressed no desire to negotiate. Their purpose was to kill people, and inflict as much damage as they could, before they were killed themselves. They left us completely bewildered. When we say, 'Nothing can justify terrorism,' what most of us mean is that nothing can justify the taking of human life. We say this because we respect life, because we think it's precious. So what are we to make of those who care nothing for life, not even their own? The truth is that we have no idea what to make of them, because we can sense that even before they've died, they've journeyed to another world where we cannot reach them.

One TV channel (India TV) broadcast a phone conversation with one of the attackers, who called himself 'Imran Babar'.[12] I cannot vouch for the veracity of the conversation, but the things he talked about were the things contained in the 'terror emails' that were sent out before several other bomb attacks in India. Things we don't want to talk about any more: the demolition of the Babri Masjid in 1992, the genocidal slaughter of Muslims in Gujarat in 2002, the brutal repression in Kashmir.

'You're surrounded,' the anchor told him. 'You're definitely going to die. Why don't you surrender?'

'We die every day,' he replied in a strange, mechanical way. 'It's better to live one day as a lion than die this way.' He didn't seem to want to change the world. He just seemed to want to take it down with him.

If the men were indeed members of the Lashkar-e-Toiba, why didn't it matter to them that a large number of their victims were Muslim, or that their action was likely to result in a severe backlash against the Muslim community in India whose rights they claim to be fighting for? Terrorism is a heartless ideology, and like most ideologies that have their eye on the Big Picture, individuals don't figure in their calculations except as collateral damage. It has always been a part of, and often even the aim of, terrorist strategy to exacerbate a bad situation in order to expose hidden fault lines. The blood of 'martyrs' irrigates terrorism. Hindu terrorists need dead Hindus, Communist terrorists need dead Proletarians, Islamist terrorists need dead Muslims. The dead become the demonstration, the proof of victimhood, which is central to the project. A single act of terrorism is not in itself meant to achieve military victory; at best it is meant to be a catalyst that triggers something else, something much larger than itself, a tectonic shift, a re-alignment. The act itself is theatre, spectacle and symbolism, and today the stage on which it pirouettes and performs its acts of bestiality is Live TV. Even as the Mumbai attacks were being condemned by TV anchors, the effectiveness of the terror strikes was being magnified a thousand-fold by their broadcasts.

Through the endless hours of analysis and the endless op-ed essays, in India at least, there has been very little mention of the elephants in the room: Kashmir, Gujarat and the demolition of the Babri Masjid. Instead, we had retired diplomats and strategic experts debate the pros and cons of a war against Pakistan. We had the rich threatening not to pay their taxes unless their security was guaranteed. (Is it alright for the poor to remain unprotected?) We had people suggest that the government step down and each state in India be handed over to a separate corporation. We had the death of former prime minister V.P. Singh, the hero of Dalits and lower castes, and the villain of upper caste Hindus, pass without a mention. We had Suketu Mehta, author of *Maximum City* and co-writer of the Bollywood film *Mission Kashmir* give us his analysis of why religious bigots, both Hindu and Muslim, hate Mumbai: 'Perhaps because Mumbai stands for lucre, profane dreams and an indiscriminate openness.' His prescription: 'The best answer to the terrorists is to dream bigger, make even more money, and visit Mumbai more than ever.'[13] Didn't George Bush ask Americans to go out and shop after 9/11? Ah yes. 9/11, the day we can't seem to get away from.

Though one chapter of horror in Mumbai has ended, another might have just begun. Day after day, a powerful, vociferous section of the Indian elite, goaded by marauding TV anchors who make Fox News look almost radical and left-wing, have taken to mindlessly attacking politicians, all politicians, glorifying the police and the army, and virtually asking for a police state. It isn't surprising that those who have grown plump on the pickings of democracy (such as it is) should now be calling for a police state. The era of 'pickings' is long gone. We're now in the era of Grabbing by Force, and democracy has a terrible habit of getting in the way.

Dangerous, stupid oversimplifications like the Police are Good/Politicians are Bad, Chief Executives are Good/Chief Ministers are Bad, Army is Good/Government is Bad, India is Good/Pakistan is Bad are being bandied about by TV channels that have already whipped their viewers into a state of almost uncontrollable hysteria.

Tragically this regression into intellectual infancy comes at a time when people in India were beginning to see that, in the business of terrorism, victims and perpetrators sometimes exchange roles. It's an understanding that the people of Kashmir, given their dreadful experiences of the last twenty years, have honed to an exquisite art. On the mainland we're still learning. (If Kashmir won't willingly integrate into India, it's beginning to look as though India will integrate/disintegrate into Kashmir.)

It was after the 2001 Parliament attack that the first serious questions began to be raised. A campaign by a group of lawyers and activists exposed how innocent people had been framed by the police and the press, how evidence was fabricated, how witnesses lied, how due process had been criminally violated at every stage of the investigation. Eventually, the courts acquitted two out of the four accused, including S.A.R. Geelani, the man whom the police claimed was the mastermind of the operation. A third, Shaukat Guru, was acquitted of all the charges brought against him, but was then convicted for a fresh, comparatively minor offence. The Supreme Court upheld the death sentence of another of the accused, Mohammad Afzal. In its judgment the court acknowledged that there was no proof that Mohammed Afzal belonged to any terrorist group, but went on to say, 'The collective conscience of the society will only be satisfied if capital punishment is awarded to the offender.' Even today we don't really know who the terrorists that attacked the Indian Parliament were, and who they worked for.

More recently, on 19 September 2008, we had the controversial 'encounter' at Batla House in Jamia Nagar, Delhi, where the Special Cell of the Delhi police gunned down two Muslim students in their rented flat under seriously questionable circumstances, claiming that they were responsible for serial bombings in Delhi, Jaipur and Ahmedabad in 2008.[14] An assistant commissioner of police, Mohan Chand Sharma, who played a key role in the Parliament attack investigation, lost his life as well. He was one of India's many 'encounter specialists', known and rewarded for having summarily executed several 'terrorists'. There was an outcry against the Special Cell from a spectrum of people, ranging from eyewitnesses in the local community to senior Congress Party leaders, students, journalists, lawyers, academics and activists, all of whom demanded a judicial inquiry into the incident. In response, the BJP and L.K. Advani lauded Mohan Chand Sharma as a 'Braveheart' and launched a concerted campaign in which they targeted those who had dared to question the 'integrity' of the police, saying to do so was 'suicidal' and calling them 'anti-national'.[15] Of course there has been no inquiry.

Only days after the Batla House event, another story about 'terrorists' surfaced in the news. In a report submitted to a Sessions Court, the Central Bureau of Investigation (CBI) said that a team from Delhi's Special Cell (the same team that led the Batla House encounter, including Mohan Chand Sharma) had abducted two innocent men, Irshad Ali and Moarif Qamar, in December 2005, planted two kilograms of RDX (explosives) and two pistols on them, and then arrested them as 'terrorists' who belonged to Al Badr (which operates out of Kashmir).[16] Ali and Qamar, who have spent years in jail, are only two examples out of hundreds of Muslims who have been similarly jailed, tortured and even killed on false charges.

This pattern changed in October 2008 when Maharashtra's Anti-Terrorism Squad (ATS), which was investigating the September 2008 Malegaon blasts, arrested a Hindu preacher Sadhvi Pragya, a self-styled godman, Swami Dayanand Pande, and Lt Col Prasad Purohit, a serving officer of the Indian army. All the arrested belong to Hindu nationalist organizations, including a Hindu supremacist group called Abhinav Bharat.[17] The Shiv Sena, the BJP and the RSS condemned the Maharashtra ATS, and vilified its chief, Hemant Karkare, claiming he was part of a political conspiracy and declaring that, 'Hindus could not be terrorists.'[18] L.K. Advani changed his mind about his policy on the police and made rabble rousing speeches to huge gatherings in which he denounced the ATS for daring to cast aspersions on holy men and women.

On 24 November 2008, newspapers reported that the ATS was considering an investigation into the high profile VHP chief Pravin Togadia's possible role in the blasts in Malegaon (a predominantly Muslim town).[19] Two days later, in an extraordinary twist of fate, the chief of the ATS, Hemant Karkare was killed in the Mumbai attacks. The chances are that the new chief, whoever he is, will find it hard to withstand the political pressure that is bound to be brought on him over the Malegaon investigation. While the Sangh Parivar does not seem to have come to a final decision over whether or not it is anti-national and suicidal to question the police, Arnab Goswami, anchorperson of *Times Now* television, has stepped up to the plate. He has taken to naming, demonizing and openly heckling people who have dared to question the integrity of the police and armed forces. My name and the name of the well-known lawyer Prashant Bhushan have come up several times. At one point, while interviewing a former police officer, Arnab Goswami turned to the camera: 'I hope Arundhati Roy and Prashant Bhushan are listening,' he said. 'We haven't invited them to our show because we think they are disgusting.'[20] For a TV anchor to do this in an atmosphere as charged and as frenzied as the one that prevails today amounts to incitement, as well as threat, and would probably in different circumstances have cost a journalist his or her job.

So, according to a man aspiring to be the next prime minister of India, and another who is the public face of a mainstream TV channel, citizens have no right to raise questions about the police. This in a country with a shadowy history of suspicious terror attacks, murky investigations and fake 'encounters'. This in a country that boasts of the highest number of custodial deaths in the world, and yet refuses to ratify the United Nations Convention Against Torture.[21] A country where the ones who make it to torture chambers are the lucky ones because at least they've escaped being 'encountered' by our Encounter Specialists. A country where the line between the underworld and the Encounter Specialists virtually does not exist.

How should those of us whose hearts have been sickened by the knowledge of all of this view the Mumbai attacks, and what are we to do about them? There are those who point out that US strategy has been successful inasmuch as the United States has not suffered a major attack on its home ground since 9/11. However, some would say that what America is suffering now is far worse. If the idea behind the 9/11 terror attacks was to goad America into showing its true colours, what greater success could the terrorists have asked for? The US military is bogged down in two unwinnable wars, which have made the United States the most hated country in the world. Those wars have contributed greatly to the unravelling of the American economy and who knows, perhaps eventually the American empire. (Could it be that battered, bombed Afghanistan, the graveyard of the Soviet Union, will be the undoing of this one too?) Hundreds of thousands of people, including thousands of American soldiers, have lost their lives in Iraq and Afghanistan. The frequency of terrorist strikes on US allies/agents (including India) and US interests in the rest of the world has increased dramatically since 9/11. George W. Bush, the man who led the US response to 9/11, is a despised figure not just internationally, but also by his own people. Who can possibly claim that the United States is winning the War on Terror?

Homeland Security has cost the US government billions of dollars. Few countries, certainly not India, can afford that sort of price tag. But even if we could, the fact is that this vast homeland of ours cannot be secured or policed in the way the United States has been. It's not that kind of homeland. We have a hostile nuclear-weapons state that is slowly spinning out of control as a neighbour; we have a military occupation in Kashmir and a shamefully persecuted, impoverished minority of more than 150 million Muslims who are being targeted as a community and pushed to the wall, whose young see no justice on the horizon, and who, were they to totally lose hope and radicalize, will end up as a threat not just to India, but to the whole world.

If ten men can hold off the NSG commandos and the police for three days, and if it takes half a million soldiers to hold down the Kashmir valley, do the math. What kind of Homeland Security can secure India?

Nor for that matter will any other quick fix. Anti-terrorism laws are not meant for terrorists; they're for people that governments don't like. That's why they have a conviction rate of less than 2 per cent. They're just a means of putting inconvenient people away without bail for a long time and eventually letting them go. Terrorists like those who attacked Mumbai are hardly likely to be deterred by the prospect of being refused bail or being sentenced to death. It's what they want.

What we're experiencing now is blowback, the cumulative result of decades of quick fixes and dirty deeds. The carpet's squelching under our feet.

The only way to contain—it would be naïve to say end—terrorism is to look at the monster in the mirror. We're standing at a fork in the road. One sign points in the direction of 'Justice', the other says 'Civil War'. There's no third sign, and there's no going back. Choose.

APPENDIX
THE BRIEFING

'The Briefing' was first published in Adam Budak, Anselm Franke/Hila Peleg, Raqs Media Collective (Eds.): Manifesta 7. *Scenarios, Milan (Silvana Editoriale), 2008.*

'The Briefing' is a fictional text that was written for Manifesta 7, *the seventh edition of Manifesta, one of Europe's bienniales of contemporary art.* Manifesta 7 *(curated by Adam Budak, Anselm Franke/Hila Peleg and Raqs Media Collective) took place in Trentino/Alto Adige/Sud Tyrol in Northern Italy from July to November 2008.*

'The Briefing' was written for the section of Manifesta 7 *called 'Projected Scenarios' located in Fortezza/Franzensfeste, a fort built in the Alps by the Hapsburgs in 1833. Though it was designed to withstand every kind of military assault and was used as a military base for more than a hundred years, including by the Nazis, Fortezza has never actually been attacked. For 165 years it remained closed to the public, surrounded by enigma. When Manifesta 7 opened on 19 July it was the first time (since the structure was built) that the grounds of Fortezza/Franzensfeste were thrown open to the public.*

For 'Projected Scenarios' the curators invited ten writers to respond with texts to the enigma of the fortress, to meditate on the idea of a fort that has never been attacked. The texts were directed as an acoustic performance by Ant Hampton, a theatre director, spoken by actors and acoustically situated within listening stations designed by a sound artist creating a sort of soundscape in and around the fort.

'The Briefing' is an allegory, a story about missing gold and the Snow Wars raging in the Alps. A phantom narrator, a militant commander of indeterminate provenance and gender, briefs his/her comrades, preparing them for a mysterious mission.

THE BRIEFING

My greetings. I'm sorry I'm not here with you today but perhaps it's just as well. In times such as these, it's best not to reveal ourselves completely, not even to each other.

If you step over the line and into the circle, you may be able to hear better. Mind the chalk on your shoes.

I know many of you have travelled great distances to be here. Have you seen all there is to see? The pillbox batteries, the ovens, the ammunition depots with cavity-floors? Did you visit the workers' mass grave? Have you studied the plans carefully? Would you say that it's beautiful, this Fort? They say it sits astride the mountains like a defiant lion. I confess I've never seen it. The guidebook says it wasn't built for beauty. But beauty can arrive uninvited, can it not? It can fall upon things unexpectedly, like sunlight stealing through a chink in the curtains. Ah, but then this is the Fort with no chinks in its curtains, the Fort that has never been attacked. Does this mean its forbidding walls have thwarted even Beauty and sent it on its way?

Beauty. We could go on about it all day and all night long. What is it? What is it not? Who has the right to decide? Who are the world's real curators, or should we say the real world's curators? What is the real world? Are things we cannot imagine, measure, analyze, represent and reproduce real? Do they exist? Do they live in the recesses of our minds in a Fort that has never been attacked? When our imaginations fail, will the world fail too? How will we ever know?

How big is it, this Fort that may or may not be beautiful? They say it is the biggest fort ever built in the high mountains. Gigantic, you say? Gigantic makes things a little difficult for us. Shall we begin by mapping its vulnerabilities? Even though it has never been attacked (or so they say) think of how its creators must have lived and re-lived the *idea* of being attacked. They must have *waited* to be attacked. They must have dreamt of being attacked. They must have placed themselves in the minds and hearts of their enemies until they could barely tell themselves apart from those they feared so deeply. Until they no longer knew the difference between terror and desire. And then, from that knothole of tormented love, they must have imagined attacks from every conceivable direction with such precision and cunning as to render them almost real. How else could they have built a fortification like this? Fear must have shaped it; dread must be embedded in its very grain. Is that what this Fort really is? A fragile testament to trepidation, to apprehension, to an imagination under siege?

It was built—and I quote its chief chronicler—to store everything that ought to be defended at all costs. Unquote. That's saying something. What did they store here, comrades? What did they defend?

Weapons. Gold. Civilization itself. Or so the guide book says.

And now, in Europe's time of peace and plenty, it is being used to showcase the transcendent purpose, or, if you wish, the sublime purposelessness, of civilization's highest aspiration: Art. These days, I'm told, Art is Gold.

I hope you have bought the catalogue. You must. For appearances' sake at least.

As you know, the chances are that there's gold in this Fort. Real gold. Hidden gold. Most of it has been removed, some of it stolen, but a good amount is said to still remain. Everyone's looking for it, knocking on walls, digging up graves. Their urgency must be palpable to you.

They know there's gold in the Fort. They also know there's no snow on the mountains. They want the gold to buy some snow.

Those of you who are from here—you must know about the Snow Wars. Those of you who aren't, listen carefully. It is vital that you understand the texture and fabric of the place you have chosen for your mission.

Since the winters have grown warmer here, there are fewer 'snowmaking' days and as a result there's not enough snow to cover the ski-slopes. Most ski-slopes can no longer be classified as 'snow-reliable'. At a recent press conference—perhaps you've read the reports—Werner Voltron, president of the Association of Ski-instructors said, 'The future, I think is black. Completely black.' [Scattered applause that sounds as though its coming from the back of the audience. Barely discernable murmurs of *Bravo! Viva! Wah! Wah! Yeah Brother!*] No no no . . . comrades, comrades . . . you misunderstand. Mr Voltron was not referring to the Rise of the Black Nation. By black he meant ominous, ruinous, hopeless, catastrophic and bleak. He said that every one degree Celsius increase in winter temperatures spells doom for almost one hundred ski-resorts. That, as you can imagine, is a lot of jobs and money.

Not everybody is as pessimistic as Mr Voltron. Take the example of Guenther Holzhausen, CEO of MountainWhite, a new branded snow product, popularly known as Hot Snow (because it can be manufactured at two to three degrees Celsius above the normal temperature). Mr Holzhausen said—and I'll read this out to you—'The changing climate is a great opportunity for the Alps. The extremely high temperatures and rising sea levels brought about by global warming will be bad for seaside tourism. Ten years from now people usually headed for the Mediterranean will be coming to the comparatively cooler Alps for skiing holidays. It is our responsibility, indeed our *duty*, to guarantee snow of the highest quality. MountainWhite guarantees dense, evenly spread snow which skiers will find is far superior to natural snow.' Unquote.

MountainWhite snow, comrades, like most artificial snows, is made from a protein located in the membrane of a bacterium called *Pseudomonas syringae*. What sets it apart from other snows is that in order to prevent the spread of disease and other pathogenic hazards, MountainWhite guarantees that the water it uses to generate snow for skiing is of the highest quality, sourced directly from drinking water networks. 'You can bottle our ski slopes and drink them!' Guenther Holzhausen is known to have once boasted. [Some restless angry murmuring on the soundtrack.] I understand . . . But calm your anger. It will only blur your vision and blunt your purpose.

To generate artificial snow, nucleated, treated water is shot out of high-pressure power-intensive snow cannons at high speed. When the snow is ready it is stacked in mounds called whales. The snow whales are groomed, tilled and fluffed before the snow is evenly spread on slopes that have been shaved of imperfections and natural rock formations. The soil is covered with a thick layer of fertilizer to keep the soil cool and insulate it from the warmth generated by Hot Snow. Most ski resorts use artificial snow now. Almost every resort has a cannon. Every cannon has a brand. Every brand is at war. Every war is an opportunity.

If you want to ski on—or at least *see*—natural snow, you'll have to go further, up to the glaciers that are wrapped in giant sheets of plastic foil to protect them from the summer heat and prevent them from shrinking. I don't know how natural that is, though—a glacier wrapped in foil. You might feel as though you're skiing on an old sandwich. Worth a try, I suppose. I wouldn't know, I don't ski. The Foil Wars are a form of high-altitude combat—not the kind that some of you are trained for [chuckles]. They are separate, though not entirely unconnected to the Snow Wars.

In the Snow Wars, MountainWhite's only serious adversary is Scent n' Sparkle, a new product introduced by Peter Holzhausen, who, if you will pardon me for gossiping, is Guenther Holzhausen's brother. Real brother. Their wives are sisters. [A murmur.] What's that? Yes . . . real brothers married to real sisters. The families are both from Salzburg.

In addition to all the advantages of MountainWhite, Scent n' Sparkle promises whiter, brighter snow with a fragrance. At a price, of course. Scent n' Sparkle comes in three aromas, Vanilla, Pine and Evergreen. It promises to satisfy tourists' nostalgic yearning for old-fashioned holidays. Scent n' Sparkle is a boutique product poised to storm the mass market, or so the pundits say, because it is a product with vision, and an eye to the future. Scented snow anticipates the effects that the global migration of trees and forests will have on the tourism industry. [Murmur] Yes. I did say tree migration.

Did any of you read *Macbeth* in school? Do you remember what the witches on the heath said to him? *'Macbeth shall never vanquished be, until Great Burnam Wood to high Dunsinane Hill shall come against him*'?

Do you remember what *he* said to them?

[A voice from the audience somewhere at the back says, *'That will never be. Who can impress the forest, bid the tree unfix his earthbound root?'*]

Ha! Excellent. But Macbeth was dead wrong. Trees *have* unfixed their earthbound roots and are on the move. They're migrating from their devastated homes in the hope of a better life. Like people. Tropical palms are moving up into the lower Alps. Evergreens are climbing to higher altitudes in search of a colder climate. On the ski slopes, under the damp carpets of Hot Snow, in the warm, fertilizer-coated soil, stowaway seeds of new hothouse plants are germinating. Perhaps soon there'll be fruit trees and vineyards and olive groves in the high mountains.

When the trees migrate, birds and insects, wasps, bees, butterflies, bats and other pollinators will have to move with them. Will they be able to adapt to their new surroundings? Robins have already arrived in Alaska. Alaskan caribou plagued by mosquitoes are moving to higher altitudes where they don't have enough food to eat. Mosquitoes carrying malaria are sweeping through the Lower Alps.

I wonder how this Fort that was built to withstand heavy artillery fire will mount a defence against an army of mosquitoes.

The Snow Wars have spread to the plains. MountainWhite now dominates the snow market in Dubai and Saudi Arabia. It is lobbying in India and China, with some success, for dam construction projects dedicated entirely to snow cannons for all-season ski resorts. It has entered the Dutch market for dyke reinforcement and for sea homes built on floating raft foundations, so that when the sea levels rise and the dykes are finally breached and Holland drifts into the ocean, MountainWhite can harness the rising tide and turn it into gold. *Never fear, MountainWhite is here!* works just as well in the flatlands. Scent n' Sparkle has diversified too. It owns a popular TV channel and controlling shares in a company that makes—as well as defuses—landmines. Perhaps their new batch will be scented—strawberry, cranberry, jojoba—in order to attract animals and birds as well as children. Other than snow and landmines, Scent n' Sparkle also retails mass-market, battery-operated prosthetic limbs in standard sizes for Central Asia and Africa. It is at the forefront of the campaign for Corporate Social Responsibility and is funding a chain of excellently appointed corporate orphanages and NGOs in Afghanistan which some of you are familiar with. Recently it has put in a tender for the dredging and cleaning of lakes and rivers in Austria and Italy that have once again grown toxic from the residue of fertilizer and artificial snowmelt.

Even here, at the top of the world, residue is no longer the past. It is the future. At least some of us have learned over the years to live like rats in the ruins of other peoples' greed. We have learned to fashion weapons from nothing at all. We know how to use them. These are our combat skills.

Comrades, the stone lion in the mountains has begun to weaken. The Fort that has never been attacked has laid siege to itself. It is time for us to make our move. Time to replace the noisy, undirected spray of machine-gun fire with the cold precision of an assassin's bullet. Choose your targets carefully.

When the stone lion's stone bones have been interred in this, our wounded, poisoned earth, when the Fort That Has Never Been

Attacked has been reduced to rubble and when the dust from the rubble has settled, who knows, perhaps it will snow again.

That is all I have to say. You may disperse now. Commit your instructions to memory. Go well, comrades, leave no footprints. Until we meet again, godspeed, *khuda hafiz* and keep your powder dry.

[Shuffle of footsteps leaving. Fading away.]

Arundhati Roy

ENDNOTES

INTRODUCTION: DEMOCRACY'S FAILING LIGHT

1. See P. Chidambaram's interview to Shoma Chaudhury and Shantanu Guha Ray, *Tehelka*, Vol. 5, Issue 21, 31 May 2008.

2. P. Sainath, 'Neo-Liberal Terrorism in India: The Largest Wave of Suicides in History', *CounterPunch*, 12 February 2009.

3. See United Nations Children's Fund (UNICEF), *The State of Asia-Pacific's Children 2008* (May 2008). Report available online at: http://www.unicef.org/publications/index_45086.html (accessed 29 March 2009).

4. For a detailed account of the Mumbai riots of 1993, see the Report of the Justice B.N. Srikrishna Commission of Enquiry. Available online at http://www.sabrang.com/srikrish/sri%20main.htm (accessed 29 March 2009).

5. Sachar Committee Report, November 2006. Available online at http://minorityaffairs.gov.in/newsite/sachar/sachar.asp

6. Arundhati Roy, 'The End of Imagination', in *The Cost of Living* (New York: Modern Library, 1999), pp. 106–08.

7. See the Rejoinder Affidavit of the Citizens For Justice & Peace through its president Vs The Dist. Collector, Ahmedabad & Ors . . . Respondents in Writ Petition Civil 3770/2003. Rejoinder filed in October 2006 http://www.cjponline.org/compensation/note.pdf.

8. See Celia W. Dugger, 'India Orders Inquiry Into Missionary's Killing', *New York Times*, 29 January 1999, p. A9.

9. See Angana Chatterji, 'Hindutva's Violent History', *Tehelka*, 13 September 2008. See also Angana P. Chatterji, *Violent Gods: Hindu Nationalism in India's Present; Narratives from Orissa* (Gurgaon: Three Essays Collective, 2009).

10. See Somini Sengupta, 'Attack on Women at an Indian Bar Intensifies a Clash of Cultures', *New York Times*, 8 February 2009, p. A5.

11. 'Lok Sabha Polls to Cost More Than US Presidential Poll', *Times of India*, 1 March 2009.

12. See Shantanu Guha Ray, 'Offer Valid Till Votes Last', *Tehelka*, 27 May 2009.

13. Election Commission of India. http://www.eci.nic.in

14. Of India's population of 1000 million, the registered voter base is 672 million. In 2009, only 356 million Indians voted, a turnout of 53 per cent. Of this the UPA vote share was approximately 33 per cent, i.e., less than 120 million voted for the UPA. http://eciresults.nic.in/frmPercentVotesPartyWiseChart.aspx

15. See 'BJP, Congress should join hands, says Govindacharya', Press Trust of India, Indore, 15 May 2009.

16. See 'India, Pak Unite to Block Anti-Lanka Move at UN', *Indian Express*, 28 May 2009.

17. See 'Journalism on Wheels', photo by Rajeev Bhatt of BBC's India Election Special Train, *The Hindu*, 26 April 2009.

18. See 'Vote for reforms, says India Inc', *Sunday Hindustan Times*, 17 May 2009.

19. See 'Corporate Captains feel easy without Left', *Sunday Hindustan Times*, 17 May 2009.

20. The theme song from the hit film *Slumdog Millionaire*, which was bought by the Congress Party for its election campaign for a sum of Rs 1 crore ($200,000).

21. See Uday Khandeparkar, 'Behind the Nano Hype', *Wall Street Journal*, 19 March 2009.

22. D.K. Singh, '"In logon ko pakad pakad ke nasbandi karana padega"' ('These People Must Be Caught and Sterilized'), *Indian Express*, 22 March 2009.

23. See Pratap Bhanu Mehta, 'A Country in 40 Acres', *Indian Express*, 6 August 2008. See also Vir Sanghvi, 'Think the Unthinkable', *Hindustan Times*, 16 August 2008, and Swaminathan Iyer, 'Pushing Kashmir towards Pakistan', *Economic Times*, 13 August 2008.

24. For an appraisal of the recently concluded elections in Jammu and Kashmir, see Gautam Navlakha, 'Jammu and Kashmir Elections: A Shift in Equations', and Rekha Chowdhary, 'Separatist Sentiments and Deepening of Democracy', *Economic and Political Weekly*, 17–23 January 2009.

25. For a detailed report, see Rajeev Upadhyay, 'The Melting of the Siachen Glacier', *Current Science*, 10 March 2009, pp. 646–48.

DEMOCRACY: WHO'S SHE WHEN SHE'S AT HOME?

1. 'Sayeeda' is a pseudonym. ॐ ('Om') is a sacred symbol of the Hindus. The violence in Gujarat was directed especially at women. See, for example, the following: 'A doctor in rural Vadodara said that the wounded who started pouring in from February 28 had injuries of a kind he had never witnessed before even in earlier situations of communal violence. In a grave challenge to the Hippocratic oath, doctors have been threatened for treating Muslim patients, and pressured to use the blood donated by RSS volunteers only to treat Hindu patients. Sword injuries, mutilated breasts and burns of varying intensity characterized the early days of the massacre. Doctors conducted post-mortems on a number of women who had been gang-raped, many of whom had been burnt subsequently. A woman from Kheda district who was gang-raped had her head shaved and "Om" cut into her head with a knife by the rapists. She died after a few days in the hospital. There were other instances of "Om" engraved with a knife on women's backs and buttocks.' From Laxmi Murthy, 'In the Name of Honour', CorpWatch India, 23 April 2002. Available online at: http://www.indiaresource.org/issues/globalization/2003/inthenameofhonor.html (accessed 29 March 2009).

2. 'Stray Incidents Take Gujarat Toll to 544', *Times of India*, 5 March 2002. For a comprehensive account of the events in Gujarat in 2002, see Siddharth Varadarajan, ed., *Gujarat: The Making of a Tragedy* (New Delhi: Penguin Books India, 2002), Dionne Bunsha, *Scarred: Experiments with Violence in Gujarat* (New Delhi: Penguin Books India, 2006), and the special March–April 2002 issue of *Communalism Combat* (available online at: http://www.sabrang.com/cc/archive/2002/marapril/index.html (accessed 29 March 2009), and Rakesh Sharma's documentary *Final Solution* (Mumbai, 2004). Information on the film is available online at: http://rakeshfilm.com/.

3. Edna Fernandes, 'India Pushes Through Anti-Terror Law', *Financial Times* (London), 27 March 2002, p. 11; 'Terror Law Gets President's Nod', *Times of India*, 3 April 2002; Scott Baldauf, 'As Spring Arrives, Kashmir Braces for Fresh Fighting', *Christian Science Monitor*, 9 April 2002, p. 7; Howard W. French and Raymond Bonner, 'At Tense Time, Pakistan Starts to Test Missiles', *New York Times*, 25 May 2002, p. A1; Edward Luce, 'The Saffron Revolution', *Financial Times* (London), 4 May 2002, p. 1; Martin Regg Cohn, 'India's "Saffron" Curriculum', *Toronto Star*, 14 April 2002, p. B4; Pankaj Mishra, 'Holy Lies', *The Guardian* (London), 6 April 2002, p. 24. Edward Luce, 'Battle Over Ayodhya Temple Looms', *Financial Times* (London), 2 February 2002, p. 7.

4. 'Gujarat's Tale of Sorrow: 846 Dead', *Economic Times of India*, 18 April 2002. The figure was recently updated to 1,180. See Press Trust of India, '2002 Gujarat Riots: Missing Persons to Be Declared Dead', *Indian Express*, 1 March 2009. See also Celia W. Dugger, 'Religious Riots Loom Over Indian Politics', *New York Times*, 27 July 2002, p. A1; Edna Fernandes, 'Gujarat Violence Backed by State, Says EU Report', *Financial Times* (London), 30 April 2002, p. 12. See also Human Rights Watch, '"We Have No Orders to Save You": State Participation and Complicity in Communal Violence in Gujarat', volume 14, number 3 (C), April 2002 [hereafter: 'HRW Report']. Available online at: http://www.hrw.org/legacy/reports/2002/india/ and at: http://www.hrw.org/legacy/reports/2002/india/gujarat.pdf (accessed 29 March 2009). See also Human Rights Watch, Press Release, 'India: Gujarat Officials Took Part in Anti-Muslim Violence', New York, 30 April 2002.

5. See 'A Tainted Election', *Indian Express*, 17 April 2002; Meena Menon, 'A Divided Gujarat Not Ready for Snap Poll', Inter Press Service, 21 July 2002; HRW Report, pp. 7, 15–16, 27–31, 45; Dugger, 'Religious Riots Loom Over Indian Politics', p. A1; 'Women Relive the Horrors of Gujarat', *The Hindu*, 18 May 2002; Harbaksh Singh Nanda, 'Muslim Survivors Speak in India', United Press International, 27 April 2002; 'Gujarat Carnage: The Aftermath: Impact of Violence on Women', OnlineVolunteers.org, 2002. Available online at: http://www.onlinevolunteers.org/gujarat/women/index.htm (accessed 29 March 2009); Justice A.P. Ravani, Submission to the National Human Rights Commission, New Delhi, 21 March 2002, Appendix 4. Available online at: http://el.doccentre.info/eldoc/l53a/GujCarnage.htm (accessed 29 March 2009). See also 'Artists Protest Destruction of Cultural Landmarks', Press Trust of India, 13 April 2002, and Rama Lakshmi, 'Sectarian Violence Haunts Indian City: Hindu Militants Bar Muslims from Work', *Washington Post*, 8 April 2002, p. A12.

6. *Communalism Combat* (March–April 2002) recounted Jaffri's final moments:

> Ehsan Jaffri is pulled out of his house, brutally treated for 45 minutes, stripped, paraded naked, and asked to say, 'Vande Maataram!' and 'Jai Shri Ram!' He refuses. His fingers are chopped off, he is paraded around in the locality, badly injured. Next, his hands and feet are chopped off. He is then dragged, a fork-like instrument clutching his neck, down the road before being thrown into the fire.

See also '50 Killed in Communal Violence in Gujarat, 30 of Them Burnt', The Press Trust of India, 28 February 2002.

7. HRW Report, p. 5. See also Dugger, 'Religious Riots Loom Over Indian Politics', p. A1.

8. 'Gujarat Carnage', OnlineVolunteers.org, 2002. See also 'Verdict on Gujarat Deaths: It's Premeditated Murder', *Straits Times* (Singapore), 7 June 2002.

9. 'ML Launches Frontal Attack on Sangh Parivar', *Times of India*, 8 May 2002.

10. HRW Report, pp. 21–27. See also the remarks of Kamal Mitra Chenoy of Jawaharlal Nehru University who led an independent fact-finding mission to Gujarat, 'Can India End Religious Revenge?' *CNN International*, 'Q&A with Zain Verjee', 4 April 2002.

11. Tavleen Singh, 'Out of Tune', *India Today*, 15 April 2002, p. 21. See also Sharad Gupta, 'BJP: His Excellency', *India Today*, 28 January 2002, p. 18.

12. Khozem Merchant, 'Vajpayee Visits Scene of Communal Clashes', *Financial Times* (London), 5 April 2002, p. 10. Pushpesh Pant, 'Atal at the Helm, or Running on Auto?' *Times of India*, 8 April 2002.

13. Bharat Desai, 'Will Vajpayee See through All the Window Dressing?' *Economic Times,* 5 April 2002.

14. Agence France-Press, 'Singapore, India to Explore Closer Economic Ties', 8 April 2002.

15. 'Medha [Patkar] Files Charges against BJP Leaders', *The Economic Times*, 13 April 2002.

16. HRW Report, p. 30. See also Burhan Wazir, 'Militants Seek Muslim-Free India', *The Observer* (London), 21 July 2002, p. 20.

17. Mishra, 'Holy Lies', p. 24.

18. On the attacks on women, see 'Seven More Held for Assaulting Women', *Express Buzz* (Chennai), 25 January 2009. On the attacks on Christians, see Angana Chatterji, 'Hindutva's Violent History', *Tehelka*, 13 September 2008, and Harsh Mander, 'Cry, the Beloved Country: Reflections on the Gujarat Massacre', 13 March 2002. Available online at: http://www.sacw.net/Gujarat2002/Harshmandar2002.html (accessed 29 March 2009). See also Chatterji, *Violent Gods*.

19. See *Communalism Combat*, 'Godhra' (November–December 2002). Available online at: http://www.sabrang.com/cc/archive/2002/novdec02/godhra.html (accessed 29 March 2009). See also Jyoti Punwani, 'The Carnage at Godhra', in Varadarajan, ed., *Gujarat*.

20. HRW Report, pp. 13–14. Siddharth Srivastava, 'No Proof Yet on ISI Link with Sabarmati Attack: Officials', *Times of India*, 6 March 2002,

'ISI behind Godhra Killings, Says BJP', *Times of India*, 18 March 2002. Uday Mahurkar, 'Gujarat: Fuelling The Fire', *India Today*, 22 July 2002, p. 38. 'Bloodstained Memories', *Indian Express*, 12 April 2002. Celia W. Dugger, 'After Deadly Firestorm, Indian Officials Ask Why', *New York Times*, 6 March 2002, p. A3.

21. 'Blame it on Newton's Law: Modi', *Times of India*, 3 March 2002. See also Fernandes, 'Gujarat Violence Backed by State', p. 12.

22. 'RSS Cautions Muslims', Press Trust of India, 17 March 2002. Sanghamitra Chakraborty, 'Minority Guide to Good Behaviour', *Times of India*, 25 March 2002.

23. 'Modi Offers to Quit as Gujarat CM', *The Economic Times*, 13 April 2002. 'Modi Asked to Seek Mandate', *The Statesman* (India), 13 April 2002.

24. M.S. Golwalkar, *We, or, Our Nationhood Defined* (Nagpur: Bharat Publications, 1939) and Vinayak Damodar Savarkar, *Hindutva* (New Delhi: Bharti Sadan, 1989). See also Editorial, 'Saffron Is Thicker Than ...', *The Hindu*, 22 October 2000. David Gardner, 'Hindu Revivalists Raise the Question of Who Governs India', *Financial Times* (London), 13 July 2000, p. 12.

25. See Arundhati Roy, 'Power Politics', in *Power Politics,* second edition (Cambridge: South End Press, 2002), p. 57.

26. Manoj Mitta and H.S. Phoolka, *When a Tree Shook Delhi: The 1984 Carnage* (New Delhi: Lotus Books, 2008).

27. HRW Report, 39–44.

28. John Pilger, 'Pakistan and India on Brink', *The Mirror* (London), 27 May 2002, p. 4.

29. Alison Leigh Cowan, Kurt Eichenwald and Michael Moss, 'Bin Laden Family, with Deep Western Ties, Strives to Re-establish a Name', *New York Times*, 28 October 2001, p. 1: 9.

30. See Steven Mufson, 'Pentagon Changing Color of Airdropped Meals: Yellow Food Packs, Cluster Bomblets on Ground May Confuse Afghans', *Washington Post*, 2 November 2001, p. A21.

31. Sanjeev Miglani, 'Opposition Keeps up Heat on Government over Riots', Reuters, 16 April 2002.

32. Sucheta Dalal, 'Either Govern or Just Go', *Indian Express*, 1 April 2001.

33. 'It's War in Drawing Rooms', *Indian Express*, 19 May 2002.

34. Ranjit Devraj, 'Pro-Hindu Ruling Party Back to Hardline Politics', Inter Press Service, 1 July 2002. 'An Unholy Alliance', *Indian Express*, 6 May 2002.

35. Nilanjana Bhaduri Jha, 'Congress [Party] Begins Oust-Modi Campaign', *The Economic Times*, 12 April 2002.

36. On 8 June 2006, Zakiya Jaffri, widow of the late member of parliament Ehsan Jaffri, sought to register a First Information Report against Chief Minister Narendra Modi and sixty-two others, including cabinet ministers, senior bureaucrats and policemen, under section 154 of the Code of Criminal Procedure. See *Communalism Combat*, 'The Charge Sheet' (June 2007). Available online at: http://www.sabrang.com/cc/archive/2007/june07/crime.html (accessed 29 March 2009).

37. See Richard Benedetto, 'Confidence in War on Terror Wanes', *USA Today*, 25 June 2002, p. 19A, and David Lamb, 'Israel's Invasions, 20 Years Apart, Look Eerily Alike', *Los Angeles Times*, 20 April 2002, p. A5.

38. Roy, 'The End of Imagination', in *The Cost of Living*.

39. 'I would say it is a weapon of peace guarantee, a peace guarantor', said Abdul Qadeer Khan of Pakistan's nuclear bomb. Imtiaz Gul, 'Father of Pakistani Bomb Says Nuclear Weapons Guarantee Peace', Deutsche Presse-Agentur, 29 May 1998. Raj Chengappa, *Weapons of Peace: The Secret Story of India's Quest to Be a Nuclear Power* (New Delhi: HarperCollins, 2000).

40. Edward Luce, 'Fernandes Hit by India's Coffin Scandal', *Financial Times* (London), 13 December 2001, p. 12.

41. 'Arrested Growth', *Times of India*, 2 February 2000.

42. Edna Fernandes, 'EU Tells India of Concern over Violence in Gujarat', *Financial Times* (London), 3 May 2002, p. 12; Alex Spillius, '"Please Don't Say This Was a Riot. It Was Genocide, Pure and Simple"', *Daily Telegraph* (London), 18 June 2002, p. 13.

43. 'Gujarat is an internal matter and the situation is under control,' said Jaswant Singh, India's foreign affairs minister. See Shishir Gupta, 'The Foreign Hand', *India Today*, 6 May 2002, p. 42, and sidebar.

44. Hina Kausar Alam and P. Balu, 'J&K [Jammu and Kashmir] Fudges DNA Samples to Cover up Killings', *Times of India*, 7 March 2002.

45. 'Laloo Wants Use of POTA [Prevention of Terrorism Act] Against VHP, RSS', *Times of India*, 7 March 2002.

HOW DEEP SHALL WE DIG?

1. On the 14 February 2003, murder of I.G. Khan, see Parvathi Menon, 'A Man of Compassion', *Frontline* (India), 29 March–11 April, 2003. Available online at: http://www.frontlineonnet.com/fl2007/stories/20030411004511400.htm (accessed 29 March 2009).

2. Hina Kausar Alam and P. Balu, 'J&K [Jammu and Kashmir] Fudges DNA Samples to Cover up Killings', *Times of India*, 7 March 2002.

3. See Comunalism Combat, 'Godhra', and Jyoti Punwani, 'The Carnage at Godhra', in Varadarajan, ed., *Gujarat*.

4. Somit Sen, 'Shooting Turns Spotlight on Encounter Cops', *Times of India*, 23 August 2003.

5. W. Chandrakanth, 'Crackdown on Civil Liberties Activists in the Offing?' *The Hindu*, 4 October 2003, which notes:

> Several activists have gone underground fearing police reprisals. Their fears are not unfounded, as the State police have been staging encounters at will. While the police frequently release the statistics on naxalite violence, they avoid mentioning the victims of their own violence. The Andhra Pradesh Civil Liberties Committee (APCLC), which is keeping track of the police killings, has listed more than 4,000 deaths, 2,000 of them in the last eight years alone.

See also K.T. Sangameswaran, 'Rights Activists Allege Ganglord-Cop Nexus', *The Hindu*, 22 October 2003.

6. A study by the Jammu Kashmir Coalition for Civil Society, *State of Human Rights in Jammu and Kashmir 1990–2006* (Srinagar, 2006), estimates that the real death toll in Jammu and Kashmir between 1990 and 2004 was more than seventy thousand, while the Indian State reported a death toll of

only forty-seven thousand from 1990 to 2005. See also Aijaz Hussain, 'Muslim, Hindu Protests in Indian Kashmir', Associated Press, 1 July 2008; David Rohde, 'India and Kashmir Separatists Begin Talks on Ending Strife', *New York Times*, 23 January 2004, p. A8; and Deutsche Presse-Agentur, 'Thousands Missing, Unmarked Graves Tell Kashmir Story', 7 October 2003.

7. Unpublished reports from the Association of Parents of Disappeared People (APDP), Srinagar.

8. See Edward Luce, 'Kashmir's New Leader Promises "Healing Touch"', *Financial Times* (London), 28 October 2002, p. 12.

9. Ray Marcelo, 'Anti-Terrorism Law Backed by India's Supreme Court', *Financial Times* (London), 17 December 2003, p. 2.

10. People's Union for Civil Liberties (PUCL), 'A Preliminary Fact Finding on POTA Cases in Jharkhand', Delhi, India, 2 May 2003. Available online at: http://www.pucl.org/Topics/Law/2003/poto-jharkhand.htm (accessed 29 March 2009).

11. 'People's Tribunal Highlights Misuse of POTA', *The Hindu*, 18 March 2004.

12. 'People's Tribunal.' See also 'Human Rights Watch Ask Centre to Repeal POTA', The Press Trust of India, 8 September 2002.

13. See Leena Misra, '240 POTA Cases, All against Minorities', *Times of India*, 15 September 2003, and 'People's Tribunal Highlights Misuse of POTA', 18 March 2004. The *Times of India* misreported the testimony presented. As the Press Trust of India article notes, in Gujarat, 'The only non-Muslim in the list is a Sikh, Liversingh Tej Singh Sikligar, who figured in it for an attempt on the life of Surat lawyer Hasmukh Lalwala, and allegedly hung himself in a police lock-up in Surat in April [2003].' On Gujarat, see Roy, 'Democracy: Who Is She When She Is at Home?' (chapter 1 of this book).

14. See The People's Tribunal on POTA (Prevention of Terrorism Act) and Other Security Legislations, *The Terror of POTA* (New Delhi, India, 13–14 March 2004). Available online at: http://www.sabrang.com/pota.pdf (accessed 29 March 2009).

15. 'A Pro-Police Report', *The Hindu*, 20 March 2004. See also Amnesty International, 'India: Report of the Malimath Committee on Reforms of

the Criminal Justice System: Some Comments', 19 September 2003 (ASA 20/025/2003).

16. 'J&K [Jammu and Kashmir] Panel Wants Draconian Laws Withdrawn', *The Hindu*, 23 March 2003. See also South Asian Human Rights Documentation Centre (SAHRDC),'Armed Forces Special Powers Act: A Study in National Security Tyranny', November 1995, http://www.hrdc.net/sahrdc/resources/armed_forces.htm (accessed 29 March 2009).

17. 'Growth of a Demon: Genesis of the Armed Forces (Special Powers) Act, 1958' and related documents, in *Manipur Update* (December 1999). Available online at: http://www.geocities.com/manipurupdate/december_feature_1.htm (accessed 29 March 2009).

18. On the lack of any convictions for the massacres in Gujarat, see Edward Luce, 'Master of Ambiguity', *Financial Times* (London), 3–4 April 2004, p. 16. On the 31 March 1997 murder of Chandrashekhar Prasad, see Andrew Nash, 'An Election at JNU', *Himal*, December 2003.

19. P. Sainath, 'Neo-Liberal Terrorism in India: The Largest Wave of Suicides in History', *Counterpunch*, February 2009. Available online at: http://www.counterpunch.org/sainath02122009.html.

20. N.A. Mujumdar, 'Eliminate Hunger Now, Poverty Later', *Business Line*, 8 January 2003.

21. 'Foodgrain Exports May Slow Down This Fiscal [Year]', *India Business Insight*, 2 June 2003; 'India: Agriculture Sector: Paradox of Plenty', *Business Line*, 26 June 2001; Ranjit Devraj, 'Farmers Protest against Globalization', Inter Press Service, 25 January 2001.

22. Utsa Patnaik, 'Falling Per Capita Availability of Foodgrains for Human Consumption in the Reform Period in India', *Akhbar 2* (October 2001). Available online at: http://indowindow.virtualstack.com/akhbar/article.php?article=44&category=3&issue=12 (accessed 29 March 2009). P. Sainath, 'Have Tornado, Will Travel', *The Hindu Magazine*, 18 August 2002. Sylvia Nasar, 'Profile: The Conscience of the Dismal Science', *New York Times*, 9 January 1994, p. 3: 8. Maria Misra, 'Heart of Smugness: Unlike Belgium, Britain Is Still Complacently Ignoring the Gory Cruelties of Its Empire', *The Guardian* (London), 23 July 2002, p. 15. See also Utsa Patnaik, 'On Measuring "Famine"

Deaths: Different Criteria for Socialism and Capitalism?' *Akhbar 6* (November–December 1999). Available online at: http://www.indowindow.com/akhbar/article.php?article=74&category=8&issue=9 (accessed 29 March 2009).

23. Amartya Sen, *Development as Freedom* (New York: Alfred A. Knopf, 1999).

24. 'The Wasted India', *The Statesman* (India), 17 February 2001. 'Child-Blain', *The Statesman* (India), 24 November 2001.

25. Utsa Patnaik, *The Republic of Hunger and Other Essays* (Gurgaon: Three Essays Collective, 2007).

26. Praful Bidwai, 'India Amidst Serious Agrarian Crisis', *Central Chronicle* (Bhopal), 9 April 2004.

27. Roy, *Power Politics*, second edition, p. 13.

28. See, for example, Randeep Ramesh, 'Bangladeshi Writer Goes into Hiding', *The Guardian* (London), 27 November 2007, p. 25, about the case of exiled Bangladeshi writer Taslima Nasrin, who had been living in Kolkata since 2004; Randeep Ramesh, 'Banned Artist Misses Delhi's First Art Show', *The Guardian* (London), 23 August 2008, p. 22, about the exiled artist Maqbool Fida Husain; and Somini Sengupta, 'At a University in India, New Attacks on an Old Style: Erotic Art', *New York Times*, 19 May 2007, p. B7, about an attack on a student art show at Maharaja Sayajirao University. See also Arundhati Roy, 'Taslima Nasrin and "Free Speech"', New Delhi, India, 13 February 2008. Available online at: http://www.zmag.org/znet/viewArticle/16646 (accessed 29 March 2009).

29. Shiv Sena chief Bal Thackeray 'called for the burning of all copies of' a book by James W. Laine, *Shivaji: Hindu King in Islamic India* (Oxford: Oxford University Press, 2003). See 'Mockery of the Law', *The Hindu*, 3 May 2007. See also Praful Bidwai, '"McCarthy, Where Are You?"' *Frontline* (India), 10–23 May 2003, writing about the campaign against historian Romila Thapar, and Anupama Katakam, 'Politics of Vandalism', *Frontline* (India), 17–30 January 2004, on the attack on the Bhandarkar Institute in Pune.

30. See Mike Davis, *Late Victorian Holocausts: El Niño Famines and the Making of the Third World* (New York: Verso, 2002), 'Table P1: Estimated Famine Mortality', p. 7.

31. Among other sources, see Edwin Black, *IBM and the Holocaust: The Strategic Alliance between Nazi Germany and America's Most Powerful Corporation* (New York: Three Rivers Press, 2003).

32. 'For India Inc., Silence Protects the Bottom Line', *Times of India*, 17 February 2003. 'CII Apologises to Modi', *The Hindu*, 7 March 2003.

33. Advani made the journey starting in Somnath on 25 September 1990. In 2005, he said 'his "historic" Ram rath yatra 15 years ago would be considered "complete" only when the temple was constructed in Ayodhya.' See Special Correspondent, 'Yatra Complete Only After Temple Is Built, Says Advani', *The Hindu,* 26 September 2005.

34. See Roy, *Power Politics*, second edition, pp. 35–86.

35. See, among other accounts, Nirmalangshu Mukherji, 'Trail of the Terror Cops', ZNet, 17 November 2008. Available online at: http://www.zmag.org/zspace/nirmalangshumukherji (accessed 29 March 2009).

36. India was the only country to abstain on 22 December 2003, from UN General Assembly Resolution, 'Protection of Human Rights and Fundamental Freedoms While Countering Terrorism', A/RES/58/187 (April 2004).

37. See Press Trust of India, 'India's Naxalites Making Efforts to Spread to New Areas', BBC Worldwide Monitoring, 4 May 2003, and 'Maoist Call Freezes Jharkhand, Neighbours', *The Statesman* (India), 15 June 2006.

38. The United Progressive Alliance government, led by the Congress Party, repealed the Prevention of Terrorism Act (POTA) in 2004 because it was found to be draconian, and said it had been misused and was counterproductive, but then enacted a tougher terror law in the form of amendments to the already draconian Unlawful Activities Prevention Act. The amendments were introduced in Parliament on 15 December 2008, and adopted the next day. There was virtually no debate. See Prashant Bhushan, 'Terrorism: Are Stronger Laws the Answer?' *The Hindu*, 1 January 2009.

39. See Arundhati Roy, 'Public Power in the Age of Empire', in *An Ordinary Person's Guide to Empire* (New Delhi: Penguin Books India, 2005). Also published as Arundhati Roy, *Public Power in the Age of Empire* (New York: Seven Stories Press, 2004).

'AND HIS LIFE SHOULD BECOME EXTINCT'

1. The high court claimed that 'The fire power was awesome enough to engage a battalion and had the attack succeeded, the entire building with all inside would have perished.' See the court's verdict of 29 October 2003. For details of the Parliament Attack and the subsequent trial, see Nandita Haksar, *Framing Geelani, Hanging Afzal: Patriotism in the Time of Terror* (New Delhi: Promilla, 2007); Praful Bidwai et al., *13 December—A Reader: The Strange Case of the Attack on the Indian* Parliament (New Delhi: Penguin Books India, 2006); Syed Bismillah Geelani, *Manufacturing Terrorism: Kashmiri Encounters With Media and the Law* (New Delhi: Promilla, 2006); Nirmalangshu Mukherji, *December 13: Terror Over Democracy* (New Delhi: Promilla, 2005); Peoples Union for Democratic Rights, *Balancing Act: High Court Judgment on the 13th December 2001 Case* (New Delhi, 19 December 2003); Peoples Union for Democratic Rights, *Trial of Errors: A Critique of the POTA Court Judgment on the 13 December Case* (New Delhi, 15 February 2003).

2. Judge S.N. Dhingra, Judgment of the Special Prevention of Terrorism Act Court, Mohammed Afzal vs the State (NCT of Delhi), 16 December 2002.

3. Statement by Home Minister L.K. Advani, 18 December 2001. Text available online at the Embassy of India (Washington): http://www.indianembassy.org/new/parliament_dec_13_01.htm (accessed 29 March 2009).

4. See Susan Milligan, 'Despite Diplomacy, Kashmir Troops Brace', *Boston Globe*, 20 January 2002, p. A1; Farah Stockman and Anthony Shadid, 'Sanctions Fueling Ire Between India, Pakistan', *Boston Globe*, 28 December 2001, p. A3; Zahid Hussai, 'Tit-for-Tat Bans Raise Tension on Kashmir', *The Times* (London), 28 December 2001; and Ghulam Hasnain and Nicholas Rufford, 'Pakistan Raises Kashmir Nuclear Stakes', *Sunday Times* (London), 30 December 2001.

5. Dhingra, Judgment of the Special Prevention of Terrorism Act Court.

6. See Somini Sengupta, 'Indian Opinion Splits on Call for Execution', *International Herald Tribune,* 9 October 2006, and Somini Sengupta and

Hari Kumar, 'Death Sentence in Terror Attack Puts India on Trial', *New York Times*, 10 October 2006, p. A3.

7. 'Advani Criticizes Delay in Afzal Execution', *The Hindu*, 13 November 2006.

8. Maqbool Butt, a founder of the Jammu and Kashmir Liberation Front, was hanged in New Delhi on 11 February 1984. See 'India Hangs Kashmiri for Slaying Banker', *New York Times,* 12 February 1984, sec. 1, p. 7. Details about Maqbool Butt are available online at: http://www.maqboolbutt.com and at: http://www.geocities.com/jklf-kashmir/maqboolstory.html (accessed 29 March 2009).

9. Lakshmi Balakrishnan, 'Reliving a Nightmare', *The Hindu*, 12 December 2002, p. 2. See also Shuddhabrata Sengupta, 'Media Trials and Courtroom Tribulations', in Bidwai et al., *13 December—A Reader*, p. 46.

10. Press Trust of India, 'S[upreme]C[ourt] Allows Zee [TV] to Air Film on Parliament Attack', IndiaInfo.com, 13 December 2002.

11. 'Five Bullets Hit Geelani, Says Forensic Report', *Hindustan Times,* 25 February 2005.

12. See 'Police Force', *Indian Express*, 15 July 2002; 'Editor's Guild Seeks Fair Trial for Iftikhar', *Indian Express,* 20 June 2002; and 'Kashmir Time Staffer's Detention Issue Raised in Lok Sabha', *Business Recorder,* 4 August 2002.

13. Iftikhar Gilani, *My Days in Prison* (New Delhi: Penguin Books India, 2005). In 2008 the Urdu translation of this book received one of India's highest literary awards from the Sahitya Akademi. http://www.indianexpress.com/news/iftikhar-gilani-wins-sahitya-akademi-award/424871/

14. Doordarshan Television (New Delhi), 'Court Releases Kashmir Times Journalist from Detention', BBC Monitoring South Asia, 13 January 2003.

15. Statement of Sayed Abdul Rahman Geelani, New Delhi, 4 August 2005. Available online at: http://www.revolutionarydemocracy.org/parl/geelanistate.htm (accessed 29 March 2009). See also Basharat Peer, 'Victims of December 13', *The Guardian* (London), 5 July 2003, p. 29.

16. 'Special Cell ACP Faces Charges of Excesses, Torture', *Hindustan Times*, 31 July 2005. Singh was later murdered, in March 2008, in what is widely believed to be an underworld property dispute. See Press Trust of India, 'Encounter Specialist Rajbir Singh Shot Dead', *Hindustan Times*, 25 March 2008.

17. See the articles '"Terrorists Were Close-Knit Religious Fanatics"', and 'Police Impress with Speed But Show Little Evidence', *Times of India*, 21 December 2001. Available online at: http://timesofindia.indiatimes.com/articleshow/1600576183.cms and at: http://timesofindia.indiatimes.com/articleshow/1295243790.cms (accessed 29 March 2009).

18. Emily Wax and Rama Lakshmi, 'Indian Official Points to Pakistan', *Washington Post*, 6 December 2008, p. A8.

19. Mukherji, *13 December*, p. 43.

20. Statement of Mohammad Afzal to the Court under Section 313 of the Criminal Procedure Code in the Court of Shri S.N. Dhingra, ASJ, New Delhi S/V Afzal Guru and Others, FIR 417/01, September 2002. Available online at: http://www.outlookindia.com/fullprint.asp?choice=1&fodname=20061019&fname=nirmalangshu&sid=2 (accessed 29 March 2009).

21. Aijaz Hussain, 'Killers in Khaki', *India Today*, 11 June 2007. See also 'PUDR Picks Several Holes in Police Version on Pragati Maidan Encounter', *The Hindu*, 3 May 2005, and the Peoples Union for Democratic Rights, *An Unfair Verdict: A Critique of the Red Fort Judgment* (New Delhi, 22 December 2006) and *Close Encounter: A Report on Police Shoot-Outs in Delhi* (New Delhi, 21 October 2004).

22. See 'A New Kind of War', *Asia Week,* 7 April 2000, and Ranjit Dev Raj, 'Tough Talk Continues Despite Peace Demands', Inter Press Service, 19 April 2000.

23. See '"Five Killed after Chattisinghpora Massacre Were Civilians"', Press Trust of India, 16 July 2002, and 'Judicial Probe Ordered into Chattisinghpora Sikh Massacre', Press Trust of India, 31 October 2000.

24. Public Commission on Human Rights, Srinagar 2006, 'State of Human Rights in Jammu and Kashmir 1990–2005', p. 21.

25. 'Probe into Alleged Fake Killings Ordered', *Daily Excelsior* (Janipura), 30 August 2005.

26. M.L. Kak, 'Army Quiet on Fake Surrender by Ultras', *The Tribune* (Chandigarh), 14 December 2006.

27. 'Storm over a Sentence', *The Statesman* (India), 12 February 2003.

28. The analysis that follows is based on the judgments of the Supreme Court of India, the Delhi High Court, and the POTA Trial Court cited earlier.

29. Mukherji, *December 13*. Peoples Union for Democratic Rights, *Trial of Errors* and *Balancing Act*.

30. 'As Mercy Petition Lies with Kalam, Tihar Buys Rope for Afzal Hanging', *Indian Express*, 16 October 2006.

BREAKING THE NEWS

1. Statement of Mohammad Afzal to the Court under Section 313 Criminal Procedure Code, September 2002.

2. '"Terrorists Were Close-Knit Religious Fanatics"', and 'Police Impress with Speed but Show Little Evidence', 21 December 2001.

3. Judgment of the Supreme Court of India on Mohammad Afzal vs the State (NCT of Delhi), 4 August 2005.

4. Press Trust of India, 'Book on December 13 Parliament Attack', 13 December 2006.

5. Petitions asking for clemency and retrial as well as an inquiry into the case are available online at: http://www.petitiononline.com/ekta1/petition.html and at: http://www.petitiononline.com/CMAG/petition.html (accessed 29 March 2009).

6. Speech made by Manmohan Singh on 18 December 2001—then leader of the opposition, and later prime minister—in the Rajya Sabha. See the full text in Rajya Sabha, Official Day's Proceedings, 18 December 2001, paragraph 4, p. 430.

7. Davinder Kumar, 'The Ham Burger—Did Delhi Police Sleuths Jump the Gun with the Wrong One?' *Outlook* (India), 21 January 2002.

8. Priya Ranjan Dasmunshi, '"Advaniji Too Was Confused"', *Outlook*, 24 December 2001.

9. For the full text of the Parliament Attack charge sheet, see Mukherji, *December 13*, Annexure 1.

10. See 'Scandal', *The Economist*, 28 August 1999, and Sarah Delaney and Michael Evans, 'Britain Joined Plot to Overthrow a Communist Italian Government', *The Times* (London), 14 January 2008, p. 31. On the political context, see Noam Chomsky, *Turning the Tide: U.S. Intervention in Central America and the Struggle for Peace,* 2nd ed. (Cambridge: South End Press, 1987), pp. 67, 195.

11. 'Show No Mercy, Hang Afzal: BJP', *Indian Express*, 23 November 2006.

12. Chandan Mitra, 'Celebrating Treason', *The Pioneer*, 7 October 2006.

13. Swapan Dasgupta, 'You Can't Be Good to Evil', *The Pioneer*, 1 October 2006.

14. Siddhartha Gautam, 'The Other Side of Afzal's Surrender', CNN-IBN, 27 November 2006. Text available online at: http://ibnlive.in.com/news/the-other-side-of-afzals-surrender/27157-3.html (accessed 29 March 2009). Video available online at: http://www.ibnlive.com/videos/27157/the-other-side-of-afzals-surrender.html (accessed 29 March 2009). See also Narendra Nag, 'Afzal Gets Mixed Bag from Politcos', CNN-IBN, 28 November 2006. Text available online at: http://ibnlive.in.com/news/afzal-gets-mixed-bag-from-politcos/27182-3.html (accessed 29 March 2009). Video available online at: http://www.ibnlive.com/videos/27182/afzal-gets-mixed-bag-from-politcos.html (accessed 29 March 2009).

15. Siddhartha Gautam, 'Tortured, but Kept Alive for a Deal', CNN-IBN, 27 November 2006. Text available online at: http://ibnlive.in.com/news/tortured-but-kept-alive-for-a-deal/27164-3.html (accessed 29 March 2009). Video available online at: http://www.ibnlive.com/videos/27164/tortured-but-kept-alive-for-a-deal.html (accessed 29 March 2009).

16. Dravinder Singh, interview with Parvaiz Bukhari, October 2006,

in Srinagar, unpublished MS, provided in personal corespondence to the author 7 March 2009.

17. 'Advani Criticizes Delay in Afzal Execution', *The Hindu*, 13 November 2006.

18. See Judgment of the Supreme Court of India on Mohammad Afzal vs the State (NCT of Delhi), 4 August 2005.

CUSTODIAL CONFESSIONS, THE MEDIA AND THE LAW

1. Sengupta, 'Indian Opinion Splits on Call for Execution', 9 October 2006.

2. See the letter of N.D. Pancholi to NDTV, 26 December 2006. Full text of the letter available online at: http://www.sacw.net/free/pancholitoNDTV.html (accessed 29 March 2009).

3. Despite the court judgments, the media continues to publish custodial confessions. See Mihir Srivastava, 'Inside the Mind of the Bombers', *India Today*, 2 October 2008.

4. Barkha Dutt, 'Death of the Middle Ground', *Hindustan Times*, 16 December 2006.

5. In November 2002, undercover Delhi police 'encounter specialists' killed two alleged Lashkar-e-Toiba terrorists. A doctor who witnessed the attack said the victims were unarmed and a number of holes quickly emerged in the official account of the incident.

6. See pp. 56 and 57 ('And His Life Should Become Extinct') for details on the Iftikhar Gilani case and how it was reported in the media.

7. Maloy Krishna Dhar, *Open Secrets: India's Intelligence Unveiled* (New Delhi: Manas Publications, 2005), p. 20.

BABY BUSH, GO HOME

1. See United Press International, 'Bush to Address Indians from Ancient Fort', 24 February 2006, and 'Veil of Secrecy over Bush Visit', *Hindustan Times*, 22 February 2006.

2. 'US President Arrives on Maiden India Visit', *Hindustan Times*, 1 March 2006.

3. See Mukul Sharma, 'Myanmar: Rhetoric and Reality of Indian Democracy', *The Hindu*, 9 August 2007, commenting on Than Shwe's 25 October 2004, visit to Rajghat.

ANIMAL FARM II

1. George W. Bush, 'President Bush Delivers Remarks to the Asia Society', Washington DC, 22 February 2006.

SCANDAL IN THE PALACE

1. See Hans Dembowski, *Taking the State to Court: Public Interest Litigation and the Public Sphere in Metropolitan India* (Oxford: Oxford University Press, 2001) and Videh Upadhyaya, *Public Interest Litigation in India: Concepts, Cases, Concerns* (New Delhi: LexisNexis Butterworths India, 2007).

2. Howard Zinn, *The Zinn Reader: Writings on Disobedience and Democracy* (New York: Seven Stories Press, 2003), p. 373.

3. Committee for Judicial Accountability. http://www.judicialreforms.org

4. See Prashant Bhushan, 'Judges in Their Own Cause: Contempt of Court', no date. Available online at: http://www.judicialreforms.org/files/contempt_article_pb.pdf (accessed 29 March 2009). See also Prashant Bhushan, 'The Judiciary: Cutting Edge of a Predator State', CounterCurrents.org, 7 December 2006. See also Arundhati Roy, 'Defence of Dissent', Outlookindia.com, 30 April 2001, and 'Contempt Of Court?' Outlookindia.com, 21 January 2002.

5. See Sam Rajappa, 'Crime and Punishment', *The Statesman* (India), 25 August 2002.

6. 'Shops Down Shutters Against Sealing', Press Trust of India, 11 May 2006. Bhadra Sinha, 'MCD [Municipal Corporation of Delhi] Gets Another SC Rap on Sealing', *Hindustan Times*, 10 March 2008.

7. See Shveta Sarda, 'Nangla Maachi: Court Proceedings. Note. 9th

May 2006', as well as other reports available online at: http://nangla.freeflux.net/ (accessed 29 March 2009).

8. Quoted in *Forest Case Update*, Issue 29 (October 2006). Available online at: http://www.forestcaseindia.org. See also 'Decide on Vasant Kunj malls in 2 months, SC tells Forest Ministry', *Hindustan Times*, 17 October 2006.

9. Two years later one of the biggest accounting scams in corporate India broke. See 'Ramalinga Raju Quits Satyam: Admits to Fraud', *Indian Express*, 7 January 2009, and Press Trust of India, 'Satyam Collapse Likely to Affect Investor Confidence: Experts', *Economic Times*, 7 January 2009.

10. See Committee for Judicial Accountability, *Whither Judicial Accountability? The Case of Justice Sabharwal: Disquieting Facts, Disturbing Implications* (New Delhi: 3 August 2007). Available online at: http://www.judicialreforms.org/justice_yk_sabharwal.htm (accessed 29 March 2009), along with other reports and compilations of the *Mid Day* reports. See also the web site for *Mid Day* at: http://www.mid-day.com.

11. J.S. Verma, interview with Karan Thapar, *India Tonight*, CNBC India, 16 August 2007.

12. Y.K. Sabharwal, 'A Former Chief Justice of India Defends His Honour', *Times of India*, 2 September 2007, p. 10.

13. High Court of Delhi at New Delhi, *suo motu* case vs. M.K. Tayal et al., 11 September 2007. See also 'Court Holds Mid-Day Editor Guilty of Contempt of Court', *The Hindu*, 12 September 2007.

LISTENING TO GRASSHOPPERS: GENOCIDE, DENIAL AND CELEBRATION

1. Figures given by Peter Balakian, talk at the World Affairs Forum, San Francisco, California, 2 November 2003. Audio and transcript available from Alternative Radio at: http://www.alternativeradio.org/programs/BALP002.shtml.

2. Araxie Barsamian, speaking at the University of Colorado at Denver,

Colorado, 26 September 1986. Audio and transcript available from Alternative Radio at: http://www.alternativeradio.org/programs/BAAR-FISR001.shtml.

3. See Susanne Fowler, 'Turkey, a Touchy Critic, Plans to Put a Novel on Trial', *New York Times*, 15 September 2006, p. A4, and Nicholas Birch, 'Speaking Out in the Shadow of Death', *The Guardian* (London), 7 April 2007, p. 30.

4. See Bunsha, *Scarred*.

5. 'Tata, Ambani Bag Gujarat Garima Awards', *Business Standard* (India), 13 January 2004.

6. Mishra, 'A Mediocre Goddess', *New Statesman*, 9 April 2001.

7. United Nations Convention on the Prevention and Punishment of the Crime of Genocide, approved and proposed for signature and ratification or accession by General Assembly resolution 260 A (III) of 9 December 1948, and entered into force on 12 January 1951.

8. Frank Chalk and Kurt Jonassohn, *The History and Sociology of Genocide: Analyses and Case Studies* (New Haven: Yale University Press, 1990), p. 23.

9. Quoted in Howard Zinn, *A People's History of the United States: 1492–Present* (New York: Harper Perennial Classics, 2001), p. 15.

10. Babu Bajrangi, '"After Killing Them, I Felt Like Maharana Pratap"', *Tehelka*, 1 September 2007.

11. Talk by Robert J. Lifton, Center for the Study of Violence and Human Survival, John Jay College, City University of New York, 29 January 1996. Transcript available from Alternative Radio at: http://www.alternativeradio.org/programs/LIFR-SMIR001.shtml. See also Robert J. Lifton and Greg Mitchell, *Hiroshima in America: A Half Century of Denial* (New York: Harper Perennial, 1996).

12. See Mahmood Mamdani, 'The Politics of Naming: Genocide, Civil War, Insurgency', *London Review of Books*, 8 March 2007.

13. See Anthony Arnove, ed., *Iraq Under Siege: The Deadly Impact of Sanctions and War* (Cambridge: South End Press, 2002), pp. 63 and 145.

14. See Rachel L. Swarns, 'Overshadowed, Slavery Debate Boils in Durban', *New York Times*, 6 September 2001, p. A1, and Chris McGreal

Durban, 'Africans Back Down at the UN Race Talks', *Observer* (London), 9 September 2001, p. 16.

15. See Sven Linqvist, *A History of Bombing* (New York: The New Press, 2003), Marilyn B. Young and Yuki Tanaka, ed., *Bombing Civilians: A Twentieth-Century History* (New York: The New Press, 2009), and Gabriel Kolko, *Century of War: Politics, Conflict, and Society Since 1914* (New York: The New Press, 1995).

16. See Marilyn B. Young, *The Vietnam Wars: 1945–1990* (New York: Harper Perennial, 1991), Stephen Kinzer, *Overthrow: America's Century of Regime Change from Hawaii to Iraq* (New York: Times Books, 2007), and Chalmers Johnson's trilogy, *Blowback: The Costs and Consequences of American Empire*, second edition, *The Sorrows of Empire: Militarism, Secrecy, and the End of the Republic*, and *Nemesis: The Last Days of the American Republic* (New York: Metropolitan Books, 2004, 2004, and 2008).

17. Robert McNamara, interviewed by Errol Morris, in *The Fog of War: Eleven Lessons from the Life of Robert S. McNamara* (Sony Pictures, 2004), 95 minutes. Transcript available online at: http://www.errolmorris.com/film/fow_transcript.html (accessed 29 March 2009).

18. See Carl Hulse, 'U.S. and Turkey Thwart Armenian Genocide Bill', *New York Times,* 26 October 2007, p. A12. Similar resolutions have also been consistently defeated in the Knesset in Israel. See, for example, Gideon Alon, 'Knesset Opts Not to Discuss Armenian Genocide at P[rime] M[inister]'s Request', *Ha'aretz*, 15 March 2007.

19. See Heinz Heger, *The Men with the Pink Triangle: The True Life-and-Death Story of Homosexuals in the Nazi Death Camps,* second edition (New York: Alyson Books, 1994), Daniel Guérin, *The Brown Plague: Travels in Late Weimar and Early Nazi Germany* (Durham, North Carolina: Duke University Press, 1994), *The Nazi Persecution of the Gypsies* (New York: Oxford University Press, 2000), and Catherine Merridale, *Ivan's War: Life and Death in the Red Army, 1939–1945* (New York: Picador, 2007).

20. Balakian, World Affairs Forum, 2 November 2003. See also Peter Balakian, *The Burning Tigris: The Armenian Genocide and America's Response* (New York: Harper Perennial, 2004).

21. Sven Lindqvist, *'Exterminate All the Brutes': One Man's Odyssey into the Heart of Darkness and the Origins of European Genocide* (New York: The New Press, 1997).

22. See Adam Hochschild, *King Leopold's Ghost: A Story of Greed, Terror, and Heroism in Colonial Africa* (New York: Mariner Books, 1999). Leonard Courtney, president of the Royal Statistical Society in London, gave a lecture titled 'An Experiment in Commercial Expansion', on 13 December 1898, at the Society's annual meeting. See 'Colonial Lessons from the Congo Free State', *Public Opinion* (New York), 5 January 1899, p. 11.

23. Lindqvist, '*Exterminate All the Brutes*'.

24. See 'RSS Aims for a Hindu Nation', BBC News, 10 March 2003, and Press Trust of India, 'RSS Might Get Trendy Uniform Next Year', Rediff.com, 23 July 2004.

25. Leena Misra, '240 POTA Cases, All Against Minorities', *Times of India*, 15 September 2003; 'People's Tribunal Highlights Misuse of POTA', 18 March 2004. *The Times of India* misreported the testimony presented. As the Press Trust of India article notes, in Gujarat, 'The only non-Muslim in the list is a Sikh, Liversingh Tej Singh Sikligar, who figured in it for an attempt on the life of Surat lawyer Hasmukh Lalwala, and allegedly hung himself in a police lock-up in Surat in April [2003].'

26. On the violence in Nandigram, West Bengal, see http://sanhati.com/november-2007-violence-in-nandigram-archive-of-events/

27. Quoted in Lindqvist, '*Exterminate All the Brutes*', p. 154. See also Woodruff D. Smith, 'Friedrich Ratzel and the Origins of Lebensraum', *German Studies Review*, Vol. 3, No. 1 (February 1980), pp. 1–68.

28. Davis, *Late Victorian Holocausts*, p. 7.

29. Neeta Lal, 'Malnutrition Rampant, May Trigger Crisis', *India Together*, 2 April 2007.

30. See Arundhati Roy, 'The Greater Common Good', in *The Algebra of Infinite Justice*. Also published in Roy, *The Cost of Living*. See also R. Rangachari, et al., *Large Dams: India's Experience* (World Commission

on Dams, November 2002). Available online at: http://www.dams.org/kbase/studies/in/ (accessed 29 March 2009).

31. See 'Chhattisgarh Govt. Risking Civilian Lives Through Anti-Naxal Camps: ACHR', *Hindustan Times,* 17 March 2006.

32. See Aman Sethi, 'New Battle Zones', *Frontline* (India), 8–21 September 2007.

33. Lifton, City University of New York, 29 January 1996.

34. Shahrukh Khan, interview with Namrata Joshi, '"Films Are For Entertainment, Messages Are For The Post Office"', *Outlook* (India), 22 October 2007.

35. Ramachandra Guha, *India After Gandhi: The History of the World's Largest Democracy* (London: Macmillan, 2007), pp. 755–56. See also the review by Sanjay Kak, 'A Chronicle of "India Shining"', *Biblio: A Review of Books*, July–August 2007, pp. 1–3.

36. 'The Denial of an American Visa Is a Political Boon for Narendra Modi', *The Economist*, 26 March 2005, quoting Vir Sanghvi.

37. Amitabh Bachchan, '"India Poised" Anthem', India Poised web site. Video available online at: http://www.indiapoised.com/video2.htm (accessed 29 March 2009).

38. Lifton, City University of New York, 29 January 1996.

39. Sudeep Chakravarti, *Red Sun: Travels in Naxalite Country* (New Delhi: Penguin Books India, 2007).

40. 'Naxal March: Timebomb Ticks at Home', *Hindustan Times*, 8 August 2006.

41. Hartosh Singh Bal, 'Stamp Out Naxals', *Mail Today*, 10 January 2008.

AZADI

1. See Yaroslav Trofimov, 'A New Tack in Kashmir', *Wall Street Journal*, 15 December 2008, p. A1.

2. Human Rights Watch, *India's Secret Army in Kashmir: New Patterns of*

Abuse Emerge in the Conflict (Washington DC, May 1996). See also reports by the International Crisis Group at: http://www.crisisgroup.org/ and Amnesty International (http://www.amnesty.org).

3. See Sonia Jabbar, 'Politics of Pilgrimage', *Hindustan Times*, 29 June 2008.

4. Gautam Navlakha, 'State Cultivation of the Amarnath Yatra', *Economic and Political Weekly* (Mumbai), 26 July 2008. See also Navlakha, 'Jammu and Kashmir: Pilgrim's Progress Causes Regression', *Economic and Political Weekly* (Mumbai), 8 July 2006.

5. See Indo-Asian News Service, 'Amid Amarnath Land Row, Pilgrimage Keeps its Peace', *Hindustan Times*, 14 August 2008, and Indo-Asian News Service, 'Muslims Holding Makeshift Kitchens for Stranded Amarnath Pilgrims', *Hindustan Times*, 1 July 2008.

6. Andrew Buncombe, 'Kashmir Tries to Defuse Shrine Riots by Revoking Deal', *The Independent* (London), 2 July 2008, p. 26.

7. Indo-Asian News Service, 'Amarnath Land Row', *Hindustan Times*, 4 August 2008.

8. 'On Punjab–J&K [Jammu and Kashmir] Border, Parivar Pitches Tent, Calls the Shots', *Indian Express*, 6 August 2008. See also Indo-Asian News Service, 'Land Row Makes Kashmir Economy Bleed', *Hindustan Times*, 7 August 2008.

9. '"No Highway Blockade, It's Only Propaganda"', *Times of India*, 17 August 2008; 'Gov[ernmen]t Counters Blockade Propaganda with Bulletins', *Economic Times* (India), 14 August 2008; and Karan Thapar, 'Jammu Discriminated and Kashmir Favoured: Jaitley', CNN-IBN, 24 August 2008.

10. 'Hawk Geelani Says He's "Sole" Azadi Leader, Then Apologises', *Indian Express*, 19 August 2008. See also interview with Rediff, '"I Do Not Want to Be Compared with Osama [bin Laden]"', Rediff News, 25 August 2008.

11. Aijaz Hussain, 'Kashmiri Muslims March in Call for Freedom', Associated Press, 17 August 2008. 'Indian Kashmir Separatists Announce Protests to Continue Till Demands Met', BBC Monitoring South Asia, 17 August 2008.

12. 'Protestors March to UN Office in Kashmir Capital Srinagar', Deutsche Presse-Agentur, 18 August 2008.

NINE IS NOT ELEVEN (AND NOVEMBER ISN'T SEPTEMBER)

1. Rezaul H. Laskar, 'India May Carry Out Surgical Strikes on Pak[istan], Warns McCain', Press Trust of India, 7 December 2008.

2. Yossi Melman, 'Mumbai Terrorists Badly Tortured Chabad House Victims', *Ha'aretz*, 26 December 2008.

3. Patrick French, 'They Hate Us—and India Is Us', *New York Times*, 8 December 2008, p. A29.

4. Mohammad Shah, '"Killing Hindus" Better than Dialogue with India: Lashkar-e-Toiba Chief', Agence France-Presse, 3 April 2003.

5. Bajrangi, '"After Killing Them, I Felt Like Maharana Pratap"', *Tehelka*, 1 September 2007.

6. M.S. Golwalkar, *We, or, Our Nationhood Defined* (Nagpur: Bharat Publications, 1939), pp. 35, 37 and 62. Quoted in William Dalrymple, 'India: The War Over History', *New York Review of Books*, 7 April 2005.

7. Chatterji, 'Hindutva's Violent History'. See also Hari Kumar and Heather Timmons, 'Violence in India Is Fueled by Religious and Economic Divide', *New York Times*, 4 September 2008, p. A6.

8. 'Situation in Kandhamal Out of Control: Archbishop', *The Hindu*, 29 September 2008.

9. Emily Wax and Rama Lakshmi, 'Indian Official Points to Pakistan', *Washington Post*, 6 December 2008, p. A8.

10. Damien McElroy, 'At Least Two More Terrorists Are on the Run, Police Admit', *The Sunday Telegraph* (London), 7 December 2008, p. 30.

11. V.K. Shashikumar, 'Recruited by RAW, Trained by Army: LTTE', CNN-IBN, 2 July 2006. Available online at: http://ibnlive.in.com/news/recruited-by-raw-trained-by-army-ltte/14462-3-1.html (accessed 29 March 2009).

12. Emily Wax, 'Calls Shed Light on Gunmen's Motives', *Washington Post*, 16 December 2008, p. A14.

13. Suketu Mehta, 'What They Hate About Mumbai', *New York Times*, 28 November 2008.

14. See 'Batla House Residents Speak Out', *Hindustan Times*, 27 September 2008, and Hamari Jamatia, 'Jamia Teachers' Group Points Finger at Batla House Encounter', IndianExpress.com, 21 February 2009. See also Jamia Teachers' Solidarity Group, '"Encounter" at Batla House: Unanswered Questions', 24 February 2009. Available online at: http://www.sacw.net/article691.html (accessed 29 March 2009).

15. L.K. Advani, Inauguration of National Seminar on Terrorism, New Delhi, 4 October 2008. See also 'Advani Cautions Against President's Rule', *The Hindu*, 6 October 2008, and 'Braveheart Delhi Cop Sharma Laid to Rest', *Times of India*, 20 September 2008.

16. Parul Abrol, 'CBI Wants Action Against Delhi Police Special Officer', Indo-Asian News Service, 18 November 2008.

17. United News of India, 'Malegon Bomb Blast', 14 November 2008.

18. F. Ahmed, 'ATS Is Lying, Hindus Can't Be Terrorists: V.K. Malhotra', Indo-Asian News Service, 17 November 2008.

19. Press Trust of India, 'Togadia Denies Links with Malegaon Blast Case: CBI Too Distances Itself', *Financial Express*, 25 November 2008.

20. See Shoma Chaudhury, 'Is Kali a Wimp?' *Tehelka*, 13 December 2008.

21. See Asian Centre for Human Rights, 'Torture in India 2008: A State of Denial', New Delhi, India, June 2008. Available online at: http://www.achrweb.org/reports/india/torture2008.pdf (accessed 29 March 2009). 'Is Torture Ever Justified?' *The Economist*, 22 September 2007. The United Nations Convention Against Torture and Other Cruel, Inhuman or Degrading Treatment or Punishment was opened for discussion on 4 February 1985.

ACKNOWLEDGEMENTS

Aijaz Hussain and Parvez Bukhari for being my friends and my family and for revealing another world. Prashant Bhushan and Shuddha Sengupta whose friendship and conversation are like food and drink. Anthony Arnove, editor, comrade and friend, I'd be in a mess without you. Koray Caliskan, Betul Tanbay, Ayse Berktay and Ayca Cubukcu for leading me to Istanbul. David Godwin for his support and patience. David Barsamian for his work and our conversations and for Araxie's grasshoppers. S. Anand, Jiten Y. Kumar, Himanshu Thakker, Shripad Dharmadhikary, Nandini Oza, Chittaroopa Palit, Nikhil Dey, Pankaj Mishra, Tarun Bharatiya, Jawed Naqvi, Shohini Ghosh, for everything that we have shared. Sudhir Patnaik, Samarendra Das, Himanshu Kumar, Shubhranshu Chaudhary for unforgettable journeys through Orissa and Chhattisgarh. Khurram Parvez and Parvez Imroze for their insight and their warehouse full of stories. Nirmalangshu Mukherjee for his courageous work on the 13 December case. S.A.R. Geelani, G.N. Saibaba, Radhika Menon, Kavita Krishnan, Amit Sengupta for the work they do. Ranjan Palit for his way of seeing. Noam Chomsky, Howard Zinn, Eduardo Galeano and John Berger (phew!!!!) for their companionship, wisdom, generosity, grace and utter brilliance. Ravi Singh and Bena Sareen (design partner from heaven) for the pleasure we've had working together. Vinod Mehta, Tarun Tejpal and Shoma Chaudhury for their trust and support. Bindia Thapar whose love, laughter and beautiful, barefaced courage mean the world to me. Ashwin Desai for proving that you can have a PhD and still be a street-fighting thug. Golak Khandual, Joanna Van Gruisen, Raghu Chundawat, Suprabha Seshan, Veena and Philip Oldenburg, for their love and support. Pia and Mithva, for being stubbornly incorrigible, and still mine. LKC, Mary, Maria and Mary Roy, my refuge. Pradip Krishen for his love, and for teaching me how important it is to look for wild flowers in a war zone. And Sanjay Kak for everything, and without whom.

INDEX